W9-AGU-053

WEST GERMAN POLITICS

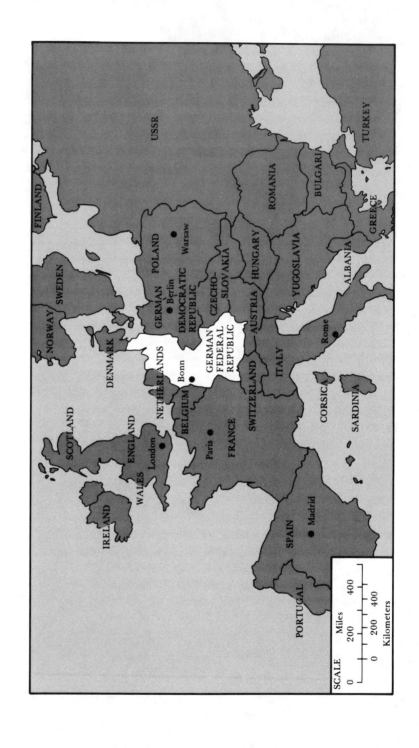

WEST GERMAN POLITICS

Lewis J. Edinger

COLUMBIA UNIVERSITY PRESS
NEW YORK 1986

Library of Congress Cataloging in Publication Data

Edinger, Lewis Joachim, 1922—
  West German politics,

  Bibliography: p.
  Includes index.
  1. German (West)—Politics and government.
I. Title.
DD258.75.E34   1986   320.943   85-11703
ISBN 0-231-06090-4
ISBN 0-231-06091-2 (pbk.)

Columbia University Press
New York   Guildford, Surrey
Copyright © 1986 Columbia University Press
All rights reserved
Printed in the United States of America

This book is Smyth-sewn and printed
on permanent and durable acid-free paper.

Designed by Ken Venezio

For Hanni

Contents

Figures and Tables

Preface

This book represents my fourth major effort in about three decades to interpret ongoing political developments in the German Federal Republic. Over this time the constitutional framework for West German politics has remained the same, but the conditions have changed a good deal. This has compelled me to take my bearings anew each time I returned to the task of description and analysis.

Germany Rejoins the Powers, written together with Karl W. Deutsch in the early years of the Federal Republic, reflected the then prevailing uncertainties about the fate of the new state and, especially, its liberal democratic form of government. *Politics in Germany,* written in the mid-1960's, dealt with what turned out to be a transitional period from political reconstruction to regime institutionalization. *Politics in West Germany,* my next effort, was a work of the 1970s and pictured the Federal Republic as a prosperous country with a well-established and exceptionally stable political system. The present volume is a thoroughly revised version of this last study and reflects new uncertainties that exist in the 1980s about the future course of West German politics.

My approach to West German politics remains eclectic. It adopts a comparative perspective for focusing on public policy processes in one of several complex modern societies with representative forms of government and advanced capitalist economic systems.

I have omitted extensive footnote references because most of the pertinent literature is in German and I assume that most readers are not familiar with that language. Moreover, many of my published and unpublished sources are not likely to be easily available to my intended audience of interested nonspecialists in English-speaking countries. For readers wanting more information I have listed suggestions for further reading at the end of the book.

I continue to be keenly conscious of the expertise of my professional colleagues standing ready to roast me over the fires of their critical disdain for errors of omission and commission. As I have sought to simplify complex matters, I realized only too well that my generalizations slighted details that others might feel should have been included, that current affairs might be interpreted from a different theoretical stance, and that new information and future developments might not support my analysis.

I have attempted to resolve the attendant dilemmas by choosing a middle road, sacrificing on the one hand some of the educative advantages of simplification and on the other some of the illuminating advantages of specificity in matters of detail. Thus, I have endeavored to be as factually accurate as the available evidence would permit while keeping description and analysis from becoming mired in details.

Directly or indirectly I am deeply indebted to the work of far too many persons to be named here. I feel however obligated to single out a few individuals and organizations to whom I owe a very special debt of gratitude. Friedrich Kratochwill and Ioanni Sinanoglou offered most useful comments on the completed manuscript. I learned a great deal about the less visible aspects of West German politics in recent years from my conversations with Wolfgang Bergsdorf, Karl Dietrich Bracher, Warnfried Dettling, John Herz, Hans-Adolf Jacobsen, Hanne and Peter Pollmann, Dieter Piel, and John Tagliabue. Ursula Hoffmann-Lange generously supplied unpublished material from her recent study of West German leaders and Shinsaku Kohei material from opinion surveys conducted by NHK, the Japanese Broadscasting Corporation. Jay Helvey, Lauren Kelly, Elizabeth Kier and, above all, Aurelia Enache, deserve much thanks for assisting in the composition of this book. Marianne Strenger of Inter Nationes in Bonn, the German Information Service in New York, and the New York Press and Information Office of the Commission of the European Communities provided published and unpublished materials that would otherwise not have been available to me. Finally I want to express my appreciation for assistance from the Institute on Western Europe of Columbia University and its director Elliot Zupnick.

APRIL 1985

1

Introduction

This book is about politics in a state that is not a nation-state, about West German politics but not politics in Germany, and about politics in some respects similar to those in other countries and in other respects dissimilar. It will not tell you everything there is to know about anything that might be called political in the German Federal Republic. Its purpose is rather to identify general features that will help you to understand political processes there and allow you to make informed comparisons. What sort of comparisons? That depends on what you are looking for, what you see, and what you make of it. Proceeding from a conception of what seems important, you may observe and describe and, perhaps, analyze similarities and differences in the manifestation of particular phenomena in various political systems.

Governmental stability, for example, has seemed to many scholars a significant measure of the extent and intensity of partisan conflict in political systems. They have noted that the Federal Republic has been fairly stable, and have contrasted this stability with past political turmoil in Germany, or with contemporary instability in other parts of the world. Both are descriptive comparisons.

Analytical comparisons take us a step further in search of explanations for the observed variance. Why has the Federal Republic had only six chiefs of government in almost four decades, whereas other governments in Germany and elsewhere have followed each other in rapid succession? Here some scholars have attributed such differences primarily to specific constitutional arrangements, others to existing circumstances, and still others to leadership factors. The lack of governmental stability in previous periods and in other countries is said to be due to the absence of one or another of these determinants.

How one approaches politics in the Federal Republic thus depends on one's point of view and consequent comparative points of reference. What therefore seems particularly important to some observers is for others quite unimportant. One scholar may not consider economic or sociocultural phenomena that another scholar feels are crucial. An "insider" involved in West German politics may see matters quite differently than an outsider. The way indisputable facts are selected for emphasis and interpretation may vary with different theoretical perspectives, political value preferences, or both.

Take, for instance, differences in the treatment of past events. Some observers hold that these events have little bearing on contemporary politics and that it is quite enough to know about more immediate developments to understand what is going on. Others maintain that German politics in our own day can be comprehended only in terms of a causal chain or changing or unchanging configurations that go back as much as a century or more. Communist writers in the (East) German Democratic Republic, for example, embrace historical determinism. They conclude that whereas in their Germany the oppressed working people have after a long struggle assumed control of their own destiny, the traditional ruling class continues to dominate in "capitalist" West Germany. Quite to the contrary, assert historians there. From their view of German history, the politics of the "liberal" Federal Republic reflect the realization of previously frustrated demands for liberty and social justice. "Over there," on the other hand, the autocratic patterns of the past are seen as preserved in a new form.

Both the writers and the readers of books such as this one need therefore to be aware of the variety of comparative perspectives and personal values that are brought to the study of its subject. Do we see political conflict as a pathological or healthy character- istic of a political system? Do we consider a democratic regime better than an autocratic one, and, if so, what standards are we using to make the distinction and how do we apply those criteria to evaluating political conditions in the Federal Republic? Do we assume that the political life of a people is rooted in distinctive cultural traits? Or do we think that their politics are more or less typical of those found in other advanced industrial societies with representative forms of government?

If you keep questions such as these constantly in mind, they will help you discern the perspectives of the author and assess your own reaction to what is presented and how. For in learning about the points of view of others and about politics in another country, one may arrive at a clearer awareness of one's own political outlook and come to see politics in one's own country somewhat differently than before.

POLITICS AND PUBLIC POLICY

To put it briefly, our subject is politics with a German accent. In the broadest sense of the term, politics deal with matters of public concern, and political issues focus on what these matters are, what should be done about them, and who should do it. A somewhat narrower and specific definition will, however, be more useful for our purposes. Politics, in this sense, revolve around governmental activities that affect relations between and within independent states. Within such states, they center on the choice and execution of public policies that may, to a greater or lesser extent, involve the entire population and, perhaps, its descendants.

But though there are politics everywhere, they are obviously not everywhere the same. They vary in time and place with differences in the organization of political life and the environment for public policies. They vary, too, due to differences in the outlook, relationships, and style of behavior of the involved actors. And they vary with public policy issues that may lead to or result from governmental actions in different contexts and settings.

To begin with, then, the Federal Republic is defined by the boundaries and qualities of an independent West German state. That is, it is a formal organization of people living in a particular territory who are bound together by exclusive and inclusive rules of public law and government. Ultimate responsibility for the formulation and enforcement of those rules is vested in public officials, such as government leaders and civil servants, whose formal authority extends throughout, but not beyond the confines of the sovereign state.

In this state, as in others, the scope and natures of public authority are formally defined by the rules of the regime, its form of government. Basic constitutional norms and derivative principles of public law set standards for the proper relationship between governors and governed and delineate the realm of public policy. In the Federal Republic these norms and principles call for popular participation and control through elections and representative bodies as well as for compliance with the decisions of officials charged with the formulation and execution of public policies. They also provide for the distribution of public authority among various branches and levels of government and between elected and appointed officials of the state. These formal arrangements will be described in the next chapter.

Public policies are the products and sources of political developments within and beyond the boundaries of independent states. They vary however not only with differences in the nature of the political systems, but with differences in the economic, social, and cultural setting. Trade relations as well as diplomatic relations with other states may give rise to political issues and demands for government action, and foreign and domestic affairs may be influenced by what the government does or fails to do. We shall consider the external and domestic socioeconomic environment for public policy in the Federal Republic in chapter 3. In some respects, as we will see, this setting closely resembles that in other advanced industrial societies, and resulting political issues are therefore only variations on common themes. At the same time, particular circumstances have led to politically relevant attitude and behavioral patterns that distinguish politics in West Germany from those in otherwise kindred societies.

Beginning with chapter 4 we will focus on explicitly political processes that shape and are shaped by public policies in the Federal Republic. In chapter 4 we shall first examine the current relevance of German experiences with earlier political systems and then consider how contemporary West Germans relate to the present regime. In chapter 5 we will look at learning processes that shape ongoing political attitudes and behavior patterns and then analyze the prevailing structure of political participation and influence. Chapter 6 deals with partisan organizations that serve primarily to recruit political leaders and to mobilize support for or opposition to their policies. In chapter 7 we will examine the nature of pressure group politics and the particularly important role of a few key interest associations.

In the last three chapters we will bring all of these elements together to study the interaction between politics and public policies in the Federal Republic. In chapter 8 the emphasis will be on policymaking, whereas in chapter 9 it will be primarily on the consequences of policy decisions. We will conclude our analysis of West German politics in chapter 10 with a brief look at future problems and prospects.

2

Organization of the State

Throughout this book we will be concerned with the interaction between state and society and between the constitutional regime and the political system in the Federal Republic. A state, like other organizations, encompass more or less enduring membership positions which are occupied by different individuals over the course of time. And in every sovereign state there are formal regime rules defining the nature and relationship of such positions, the qualifications needed to occupy them, and the "lawful" conduct of citizens, public officials, and aliens. These rules vary with the organizational structure of different states and with the dynamics of their political processes.

Formal arrangements are often observed more in theory than in practice, and constitutional and other legally mandated procedures may be honored more in the breach than in the observance because political actors do not respect them. However, in the contemporary political life of the Federal Republic, attitudes and behavior are widely patterned by the formal framework for selecting and processing public policies. It is therefore particularly appropriate that we begin by seeing how the present state and regime came to be constituted and how they are structured.

THE BASIC LAW

The Federal Republic and its constituent "Basic Law" of 1949 are the products of the defeat of a united Germany in World War II and the inability of the conquerors to agree on the form of its political reconstruction. Although the leaders of the four powers that in 1945 assumed control over its territory in separate American, British, French, and Russian zones of military occupation pledged themselves initially to collaborate in establishing a democratic regime for all of Germany, their ideas of what this meant and how it might be attained proved irreconcilable. Within two years the American and British zones were merged into an embryonic West German state which, with the addition of the French zone, became in 1949 the German Federal Republic. The Soviet Union responded by sponsoring the establishment of the German Democratic Republic as a second successor state to the former German Reich. The old capital city of Berlin, in the middle of that state, continued to be nominally under the control of all four powers. However, one section became in fact the capital of the Democratic Republic while the rest was associated with but not formally incorporated into the Federal Republic. West Berlin remains to this day under joint American, British, and French jurisdiction and protection and is therefore outside the sovereignty of the Federal Republic. Former German territories east of the Democratic Republic became part of Poland and the Soviet Union (see figure 2.1).

The Basic Law of 1949, according to its preamble, was supposed to provide a temporary organization for a temporary state, pending the reunification of Germany and the ultimate incorporation of the entire country in a European union. It was drafted by the representatives of the three occupation powers—the United States, Britain, and France—and those of West German leaders acceptable to them in the name of the entire "German people," including "those Germans to whom participation was denied" because they lived in the area controlled by the Soviet Union. According to Article 146, it was to "cease to be in force on the day

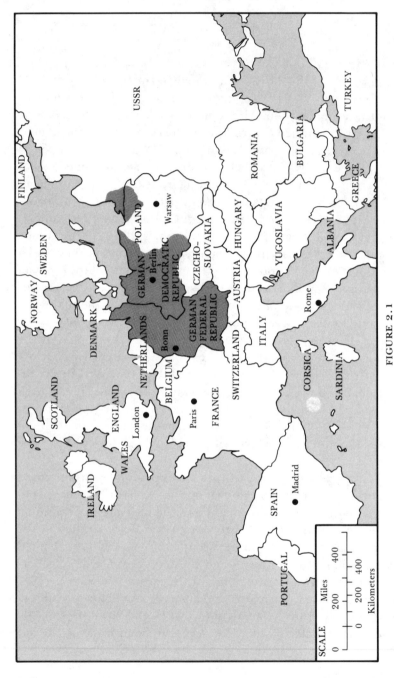

FIGURE 2.1
German Frontiers, 1937

on which a constitution adopted by a free decision of the German people comes into force."

The declared object of the framers of the Basic Law of 1949 was thus "to give a new order to political life for a transitional period," as the preamble puts it. The lengthy document they drew up was not an expression of prevailing political norms in Western Germany but a compromise between the various views of the members of the constituent assembly and of the American, British, and French military governors and their advisers. Based on constitutional theories derived from German and non-German political philosophies and experiences, it was never put to a direct popular test in a referendum and remained to be "bought" by the affected population.

By specifying in considerable detail how the new political system was to work in a "democratic and social federal state," the founding fathers sought to structure future relationships between political actors, among component parts of the state, and between state and society. Their design was intended to ensure long-range political stability and to provide ironclad legal safeguards against the recurrence of developments which they believed had led to the failure of previous German experiments with democracy. To guide Germans along what was expected to be a difficult road of transition from an authoritarian past to a firmly established democratic order in a pluralist society, they therefore laid down rather precise norms of political conduct under the new regime.

The roles assigned to the governed reflected the belief of the authors of the Basic Law that too much "direct" democracy was likely to lead to political instability and, possibly, to the destruction of their design. Accordingly they carefully sought to regulate popular participation in politics through organizational arrangements that for the most part assigned to the average citizen only intermittent and indirect roles in the policymaking processes of a "representative" democracy. Implied in the governmental structures that were established was the expectation that strong governmental leadership would need to ensure the smooth operation of the new system and to create political orientations that would give the regime legitimacy among the mass of the population. An educative function was thus linked to a stabilizing function of the constitution by the assumption that the efficient operation of the organization of the state would in time induce its citizens to embrace the role assignments and norms set forth in the Basic Law, and thus institutionalize the new political order.

The roles assigned to the governors were designed to provide for a democratic state ruled by law and under law by responsible public officials (a Rechtstaat). Toward this end, the framers of the Basic Law first anchored a bill of fundamental human and civil rights and provisions for representative government in constitutional doctrine. Second, to prevent the concentration of governmental powers, they provided for the dispersion of public authority through a complex system of checks and balances among various organs of government. Here their design called for the fusion of a federal with a parliamentary form of government and a balance between executive, legislative, and judicial powers at various levels of government.

Under the constitutional principles of 1949 governors as well as governed were obliged not only to respect but, if need be, to defend the established regime. The rules of responsible citizenship imposed on the governed the obligation to obey the legitimate decisions of public officials and actively to oppose illegitimate acts of governmental authority. In turn, principles of responsible government inposed on the agents of the state an obligation to observe and uphold the formal rules for their selection, their conduct, and the scope of their authority. And although the Basic Law subordinated individual and group interests to the "public interest," the state and its officials were to serve rather than dominate the people. Majority rule was to prevail, but it was not to give representative governments a mandate to ignore the constitutional rights of minorities in the name of the popular will or "interests of state."

Amendments to the Basic Law require a two-thirds majority in each of the two houses of the federal parliament. The constitution has been altered more often in less than forty years than the American in two hundred. However, political leaders have on the whole avoided tampering with the constitutional essence of the regime. The original provisions remain essentially the formal foundations of the political system of the Federal Republic, and both past and contemplated alterations have generally been directed to adapting the Basic Law to changing conditions and policies without affecting its fundamental principles.[1]

SOURCES AND SCOPE OF PUBLIC AUTHORITY

"All state authority emanates from the people," according to Article 20 of the Basic Law. "It shall be exercised by the people by means of elections and voting and by specific legislative, executive, and judicial organs." This key provision introduces four basic distinctions in the constitutional order of the Federal Republic. One is between citizens and noncitizens, the second between citizens who are entitled to vote and those who are not, a third between the enfranchised population and public officials who exercise state authority in the name of "the people," and a fourth among different governmental agents of that authority.

Every "domestic juristic person" is considered subject to the authority of the state under the Basic Law. That term applies not only to individuals, but to organizations such as political parties, interest associations, religious associations, and business enterprises. All of these "persons" are expected to pay taxes levied on them by public authorities, to respect the laws of the Federal Republic, and to follow the instructions of duly authorized public officials.

Anyone living within the Federal Republic and any organization subject to its jurisdiction is thus supposed to obey its laws or suffer the penalties set for the infraction of those laws. But not everyone who has these legal obligations is entitled to claim all the basic rights set forth in the constitution. Some rights are for "everyone," but others apply only to the "Germans." Everyone is for instance declared to be entitled to the human rights of liberty, legal equality and redress, and freedom of religion and expression. But only

1. Updated texts of the Basic Law are regularly published in English by the Press and Information Office of the Government of the Federal Republic.

Germans are granted the civic rights of assembly, association, and travel within the territory of the Federal Republic.

Who then is a citizen? The most obvious answer, anyone born or naturalized in the Federal Republic, would at present exclude about half of the people, all those who were born before the establishment of the state. Article 116 of the Basic Law therefore bestows automatic citizenship on all who were citizens of Germany before its division, or who were admitted to its 1937 territory as refugees of "German stock," or who are the wives or descendants of such persons. Strictly interpreted, this article might mean that citizenship extends not only to anyone in the German Federal Republic who meets these criteria, but to all those who are thus defined as Germans but live in former German territories now parts of Poland and the Soviet Union.

Here the language of the Basic Law reflects the unwillingness of its authors to recognize the legality of a second successor state to the old German Reich and the legality of annexation by conquest. However, as with other articles, this one applies only "unless otherwise provided by law." In the course of regularizing "intra-German" relations with the East German Democratic Republic and "foreign" relations with Poland and the Soviet Union, ordinary legislation and treaty arrangements have actually limited the claim to citizenship in the Federal Republic to Germans on its territory.

Any citizen, male or female, who is eighteen years or older may not only vote but run for public office. However, the basic law provides that a candidate must possess the necessary "aptitude, qualifications, and professional achievements" which, in effect as we shall see, restrict entry into elective positions.

No constitution, however detailed its provisions, can specify exactly how it is to be applied in every instance. The Basic Law of the Federal Republic allows key public officials considerable flexibility in the choice and implementation of public policies by qualifying constitutional principles or leaving their interpretation in the hands of the legislative, executive, and judicial organs of the state. Accordingly, parliamentary acts, governmental regulations, and court decisions have over the years defined and redefined the scope of public authority more explicitly.

Article 6 of the Basic Law, for example, provides that "marriage and the family shall enjoy the special protection of the state." It calls the upbringing of children "a natural right. . . and duty" of parents, but it also stipulates that "the national community shall watch over their endeavors." This provision has been interpreted by public authorities as giving them the license to set and enforce standards for the "proper" care and treatment of children at home, as well as the responsibility for seeing to their education in schools under the supervision of the state. Article 2 provides that the inviolability of personal freedoms may be curbed by law in the public interest, and here the provisions of the Criminal Code have been used to impose authoritative restraints on the exercise of such freedoms. Article 18 bars the "misuse" of the freedom of expression. This provision has permitted governmental agencies to confiscate "seditious" literature and to censor publications on the grounds that they corrupted "public morals" or threatened the sanctity of marriage and the family. Under articles 9 and 21, public authorities have the power to curb freedom of association and ban organizations found to be directed against the constitutional order. Accordingly, groups and individuals accused of supporting "subversive" causes have been prosecuted in the courts, and barred from public service employment and in the 1950s both the Communist and a radical right-wing party were outlawed.

Agents of Public Authority

Public officeholders are defined by the positions that constitutional and derivative public law assigns to them among the organizational components of the machinery of the state. When a person is elected or appointed to a public office, he is invested with some elements of the authority which by the Basic Law is delegated by the people to legislative, executive, and judicial instruments of public policy. Correspondingly, when a parliamentary deputy, policeman, or judge is not acting in his proper official capacity, or ceases to exercise his public function, he is divested of that authority and the legal responsibilities and privileges that go with his position.

In terms of the formal organization of the state, what matters here is thus the office and its relationships to other positions, such as those of citizen, voter, and resident alien. It is the office that distinguishes the officeholder from other members of the organization and involves him more directly in the making or implementation of public policies. And it is the office that identifies the extent of his legal authority over others and others over him.

In the Federal Republic one individual may hold several offices in various areas and at different levels of authority. For example, a person can at the same time be an elected federal legislator, an appointed federal minister, and a member of the nonfederal civil service as a university professor. Each position carries a title, and rights and duties, which under law go with being a member of the legislature, the cabinet, or the public administration. These rights and duties do not overlap, but they may be accumulative. Thus, parliamentary immunity does not permit the professor to libel his professional colleagues and students in the academic community; however, a minister may accumulate pension rights above and beyond those due to him as a member of parliament and the civil service.

Division and Fusion of Public Authority

Federalism and the Federal Council. Among the major states of Europe, the Federal Republic is the only one with a federal rather than a centralized organization of government. As in the United States, legislative, executive, and judicial authority is dispersed among various geographic units. The essential jurisdictional division is between the organs of the Federation (the Bund), the national parliament, government, and judiciary, and those of its ten constituent states (the Länder) (see figure 2.2).

As in every other federation, the component regions are subject to national regulations. The Basic Law thus gives the central government the responsibility to enforce its provisions in the constituent states of the Federal Republic. Federal law has preeminence over state law, the human and civil rights set forth in the Basic Law must be respected by authorities in the states, and the consti-

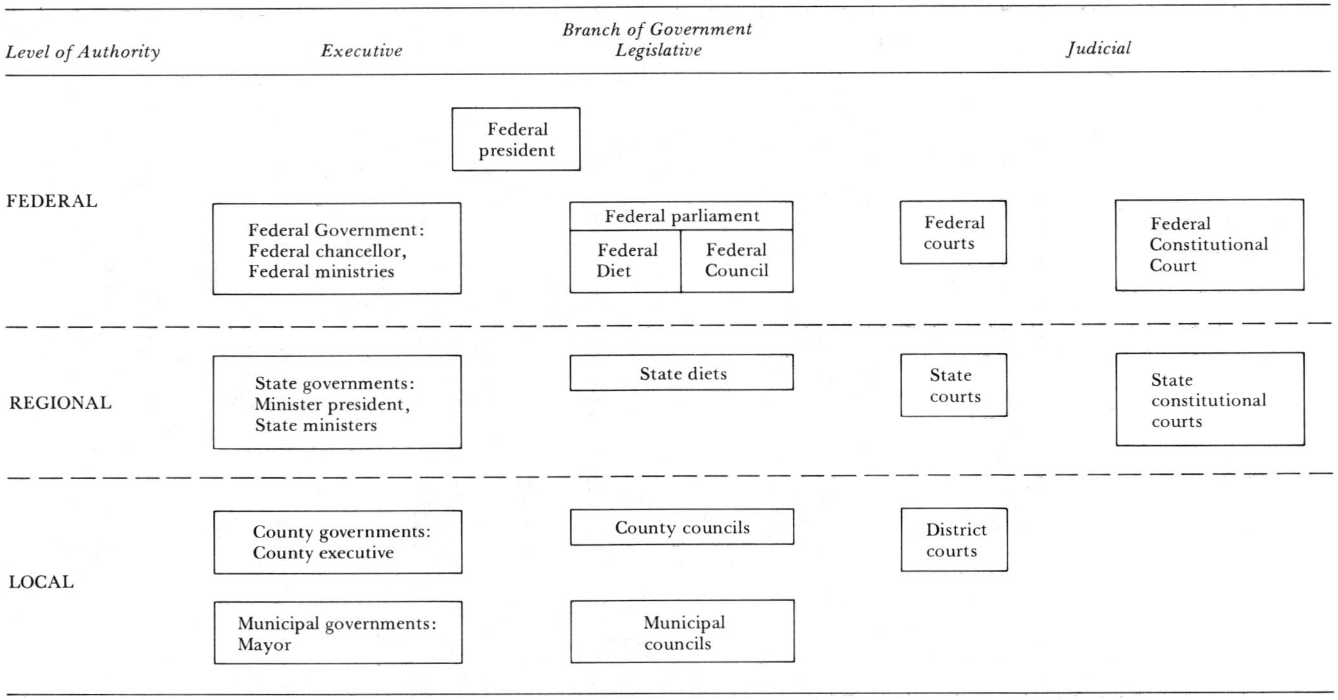

FIGURE 2.2

Organization of the Federal Republic

| Level of Authority | Branch of Government | | |
	Executive	*Legislative*	*Judicial*
FEDERAL	Federal president		
	Federal Government: Federal chancellor, Federal ministries	Federal parliament — Federal Diet / Federal Council	Federal courts — Federal Constitutional Court
REGIONAL	State governments: Minister president, State ministers	State diets	State courts — State constitutional courts
LOCAL	County governments: County executive	County councils	District courts
	Municipal governments: Mayor	Municipal councils	

tutional order of the states must conform to the principles of "republican, democratic, and social government based on the rule of law" laid down in the federal constitution. For example, since the death penalty is outlawed by the Basic Law it may not be imposed in any of the states and their local governments must include legislative bodies "chosen in general, direct, free, equal, and secret elections" by the enfranchised population.

Legislatures, governments, and courts in the constituent states are constitutionally responsible for the uniform application of federal laws and regulations. Powers that are not specifically assigned to the states under the Basic Law—for the most part affecting educational and cultural matters—are either the exclusive preserve of the Federation, like defense and foreign policy, or shared in the form of concurrent legislative authority. Subject to these provisions, public officials of the states control most of the public administration, the police, radio and television stations, and the disbursement and use of public funds by county and municipal authorities.

To balance the obligations of the states and the limitations on their autonomy, the Basic Law assigns to their elected representatives key positions in federal politics. They participate in selecting the Federal president and the justices of the principal Federal courts and, more importantly, they have a very significant voice in the making and implementation of federal policies through the Federal Council (Bundesrat).

The Federal Council—which is actually a council of the constituent, nonsovereign states—is the upper house of the Federal parliament and formally one of the strongest second chambers in the world. Unlike the lower house, it cannot be dissolved; and its constitutional powers are far greater than, for instance, those of the French Senate and the British House of Lords, and, in some respects at least, equal to those of the American Senate. However, in contrast to that body, membership in the Federal Council is not by direct election and the constituent states are not equally represented. The forty-one seats are allocated to the various states roughly on the basis of their population, and vary from five for the most populous of the ten states to three for the smallest. The corresponding votes are cast in a unit on the instructions of state governments chosen by and responsible to popularly elected state Diets.

The Federal Council is a vital link in the constitutional relationship between national and regional authorities, between the federal executive and the lower house of the Federal parliament, and between the central government and local governments. For example, federal officials may not bypass or overrule state authorities without the express approval of a majority vote in the Federal Council. The Federal Government must submit all of its legislative drafts to the upper house before they go to the lower, and most bills passed by the latter need the consent of the former.[2] All Federal executive ordinances must be approved by a majority in the Federal Council, and emergency executive government without the participation of the lower house must have the support of the upper chamber.

The Federal Presidency. Whereas under American principles of division of powers national executive authority rests in a single office, the Basic Law provides for a dual executive. Like the American president, the president of the Federal Republic (Bundespräsident) is not a member of the legislature, but unlike him he is not the head of the Federal Government as well as of the state. As in all countries with a parliamentary form of government, the chief of state has no significant policymaking responsibilities—at least under normal conditions—and in no respect does the federal president have the more far-reaching constitutional authority of the French president. He is enjoined from engaging in "partisan" activities, bound to accept the decisions of the Federal Government, Federal parliament, and courts, and largely restricted to the exercise of ceremonial functions.

In contrast to the hereditary chiefs of state in parliamentary monarchies, the federal president holds an elective office for a fixed period; but unlike the French president he is not directly

2. Either by a simple plurality or, in the case of constitutional amendments and certain key legislation, by a two-thirds majority.

chosen by the people. Instead he is selected for a five-year term by the Federal Convention (Bundesversammlung)—an electoral college composed of the deputies of the lower house of the Federal parliament and an equal number of delegates elected by the state diets on the basis of proportional representation. Actually, the choice lies in the hands of the leaders of the political parties who control the Federal Convention. An incumbent may be reelected for a second, but not a third term.

All of the president's "public acts"—including his official letters, speeches, and publications—formally require the approval of the politically responsible executive, the Federal chancellor (Bundeskanzler). He cannot veto actions of the Federal Government or Federal parliament and must sign all legislation, decrees, and letters of appointment and dismissal submitted to him by the chancellor or ministers. At the same time he does not enjoy the political immunity of the British monarch; impeachment proceedings before the Federal Constitutional Court may be initiated by a two-thirds majority in either house of the Federal parliament against a president believed to have violated his constitutional responsibilities.

The occupant of the office must therefore be extremely circumspect in observing the formal limits of his authority. He may try to warn and admonish policymakers in statements designed to express or mobilize public opinion and he may attempt to exploit his constitutional right to be informed and consulted by the chancellor to influence governmental policy. Experience has shown, however, that governmental leaders supported by solid parliamentary majorities will not and need not accept presidential interference and advice.

In the opinion of some German constitutional lawyers the president may possess some reserve powers to block or, at least, delay policy decisions and exercise greater influence under exceptional circumstances. As yet untested provisions of the Basic Law might allow a president so inclined to play a more independent and decisive role in a conflict between government and legislature by using his rather limited power to dissolve the lower house or support a minority government.

The Federal Government. Constitutional provisions for a system of checks and balances between the Federal Government (Bundes-regierung) and Federal parliament call for the fusion as well as separation of executive and legislative authority. Here the framers of the Basic Law sought to legitimate as well as restrict majority rule in a representative democracy by formal arrangements regulating the interplay between government and opposition parties and elected and appointed public officials. The politically responsible governing leaders were made less dependent on the constant support of a legislative majority than in a pure parliamentary system but more so than in an American-type presidential system. In this way indirect popular control of the executive branch through the legislative representatives of the electorate was to be ensured and arbitrary government to be avoided. At the same time, these arrangements were to provide for strong and stable governmental leadership under emergency conditions and in situations when irreconcilable conflicts among the popularly elected representatives produced a deadlock in the legislature.

Government actions and statements are usually announced in the name of the Federal Government as a whole, but constitutional responsibility rests with its chief. The Basic Law provides neither for executive leadership by a committee chosen by the legislature, as in Switzerland, nor for a collegial cabinet government whose members are collectively responsible to parliament, as in England. Executive authority and majoritarian government are primarily linked through the position of federal chancellor. He alone is chosen by the popularly elected Federal Diet (Bundestag), and he alone is accountable to it for the conduct of all members of the Federal Government.

Unless a chancellor resigns or dies in office, a candidate for the position is normally nominated by the federal president immediately after the election of a new Diet. The nominee, who need not be a member of either house of the Federal parliament, must obtain more than half of the votes in the lower house to obtain the office. If its deputies reject him they can, by a similar absolute majority, nominate their own candidate, and then the president must appoint him. Should no one manage to gain such support, a simple plurality will suffice to elect a candidate of the Federal Diet, but in this case the president need not appoint him and can, if he wishes, dissolve the chamber on his own authority.

Once in office, a chancellor cannot be impeached, nor can he be forced to resign unless an absolute majority of the Federal Diet elects a successor under a unique constitutional provision requiring a "positive vote of no confidence." Should a majority refuse to give him a vote of confidence, but at the same time be unable to agree on a replacement, he may either ask the federal president to order new Diet elections, or continue to govern up to six months if he has the support of the Federal Council and president.[3] However, these rights lapse as soon as the lower chamber elects a new chancellor.

The exclusive constitutional responsibility of the chief of the Federal Government is formally matched by exclusive powers that give him primary authority over the formulation of governmental policies and over the activities of his associates in the Federal Government. Neither the president nor parliament can legally compel the chancellor to include anyone in his cabinet or to dismiss any of his ministers or advisers; the decision is officially his own. He may appoint them or remove them as he sees fit. The chancellor also controls the federal bureaucracy subject to civil service regulations, and he exercises considerable discretion in the distribution of public funds and the implementation of legislation. And although the chancellor ordinarily needs the approval of one or both houses of the Federal parliament for his policy proposals and budgetary requests, he may legally withhold information requested by the legislature, ignore its wishes and expression of disapproval, and veto budgetary appropriations that exceed his requests.

Like the American president and other chief executives, the chancellor is aided in the conduct of his office by a staff of trusted advisers. Most are public officials attached to the Federal Chan-

---

3. In the states, which have no dual executives and only unicameral legislatures, the failure of a positive vote of no confidence in the chief of government in some instances permits him to order new elections and in others requires the state Diet to dissolve itself.

cellery (Bundeskanzleramt), headed at various times either by a federal minister or senior civil servant. Its members assist the chancellor in planning and coordinating government policies and supervising the activities of the entire Federal Government. They may also serve as emissaries to other agencies of government and foreign leaders, and to non-governmental associations and political parties.

The federal ministers are formally not the chancellor's peers but his subordinates, and are responsible to him rather than to the Federal parliament. They are appointed and dismissed by the president on the chancellor's recommendation; their terms of office end automatically with the death, resignation, or replacement of the chancellor, and they can neither be censured nor singled out for special vote of confidence by the legislature. The number of ministers and their specific field of responsibility is left to the chancellor's discretion by the Basic Law. There have been as many as twenty and as few as twelve; there have been ministers with and without specific portfolios. One of them is usually appointed deputy chancellor; other key posts correspond to the major constitutional responsibilities of the Federal Government for foreign, defense, and economic policies.

Under the constitution and the standing rules of the Federal Government, its ministers have four primary policymaking responsibilities. First, as members of the cabinet, they may participate in formulating decisions which the chancellor has the formal right to accept or reject. Second, they may individually advise the chancellor on policy matters, but he is entitled to ignore or overrule their recommendations. Third, they are charged with supervising and planning policy within their departments if they are not ministers without specific portfolios. Such responsibilities may include not only preparing bills for consideration by the cabinet and parliament but, more directly, formulating administrative and legal ordinances (Rechtsverordnungen) that spell out in detail the application of federal laws. Fourth, ministers have the formal authority to supervise the implementation of federal policies by subordinate officials, including state officials responsible for administering federal laws and derivative ministerial regulations.

Serving under the chancellor and the members of his cabinet are parliamentary secretaries, who are members of the Federal Diet, and state secretaries who are senior career officials of the Federal civil service. These officials may represent their chiefs in the Federal parliament and its committees and serve as their delegates in various other capacities. All of them are formally political appointees—like most deputy and assistant secretaries in the United States government—and may be removed from their positions at the discretion of their superiors. The parliamentary secretaries are in effect junior members of the Federal Government without cabinet rank, and their term of service ends with that of the chancellor. The state secretaries, on the other hand, remain members of the public administration beyond the tenure of any particular government. However, they may be moved to another position or temporarily pensioned if a federal chancellor or cabinet member wants someone else to advise and assist him.

The Federal Diet. The parliamentary elements in the constitutional order make the Federal Diet (Bundestag) formally the more important of the two chambers in the national legislature. According to the design of the Basic Law, it is to be the primary lawmaking organ for the entire country and the principal representative body for popular control over the Federal Government. The deputies of the Diet are elected directly by enfranchised West German voters, normally every four years, whereas the Federal president, chancellor, and the members of the Federal Council representing the state governments are elected indirectly.

Under the West German system of checks and balances the official authority of the Diet is greater than that of the French National Assembly, but in some ways not as great as that of the British House of Commons or the United States House of Representatives. Unlike the legislative powers of the House of Commons, those of the West German Diet are curbed by the federalist features of the Basic Law, by judicial review, and by the right of the executive branch to exercise a veto when the Diet goes beyond its budgetary proposals. And in contrast to the House of Representatives, the chamber may be dissolved by the president when it is deadlocked with the executive branch and unable to elect a new chief of government.

Collectively the deputies of the countrywide electorate have an equal voice with the representatives of the states in the selection of the federal president and chief justices of the federal judiciary, but have sole control over the selection of the federal chancellor. Constitutional amendments and bills that fall under the joint legislative authority of the Federation and its member states require the consent of the Federal Council, but legislation on policy matters within the exclusive jurisdiction of federal organs does not. International treaties, for instance, must only be ratified in the Diet. Under the Basic Law a conference committee of the two chambers is to resolve differences over legislation requiring the approval of both of them. All told, the approval of a majority of the Diet is needed to give constitutional legitimacy to federal policy under all but exceptional emergency conditions.

The Basic Law charges the federal deputies with supervising the federal executive on behalf of the people through debates, questions, and investigations as well as by binding legislation. They have the right to summon members of the Federal Government to appear before the Diet and its committees, but cannot compel them to disclose information, reply to questions, or debate an issue. On the other hand, the chancellor, ministers, or their representatives may attend plenary and committee sessions—even if they are not deputies—and present their views any time they wish. The same applies to members of the Federal Council.

Like the Federal Council and Federal Government, the Federal Diet operates under formal rules of organizational procedure which have changed little over the years. By these rules the business of the lower house is conducted under the direction of a Council of Elders. It includes the Diet's president, its vice-presidents, and about fifteen other deputies and sets the agenda for the chamber and supervises its proceedings.

Most of the legislative work of the deputies is conducted in committee sessions. Except for the Committee on Defense, none of the nineteen or so regular or standing committees has the formal investigatory powers of congressional committees in the

United States. Under Article 44 of the Basic Law special commit-tees of inquiry, empowered to conduct open or secret hearings, must be established on the motion of one-fourth of the deputies. This provision has repeatedly enabled opposition deputies to in-itiate legislative investigations into the conduct of the executive branch.

Public Policy Administration

Formal responsibility for the application of governmental policies is shared by central, regional, and local authorities. Federal min-istries exercise direct constitutional control primarily over policy implementation in foreign relations and defense and over interre-gional services, such as the countrywide public transportation and communications networks. Federal monetary policies are admin-istered by the central Federal Bank and social service policies by independent federal administrative agencies similar to the Social Security and Veterans Administration in the United States. Most other administrative tasks are assigned to state and local author-ities (see figure 2.3).

In the implementation of most routine domestic policies that directly affect the average citizens of the Federal Republic, the state governments exercise primary administrative authority. In addition to seeing to the enforcement of laws and regulations within their exclusive jurisdiction, the state ministries and their respective bureaucratic infrastructures occupy strategic interven-ing positions between central and local authorities in the appli-cation of federal legislation and ministerial ordinances.

Whereas the countrywide system of public administration for the Federation is thus for the most part regionally dispersed among the ten constituent states, the administrative organization within the states is highly centralized. Here the lines of author-ity run from the state governments, especially their ministries for interior and educational affairs, through state district ad-ministrations to county and local government agencies. In the last analysis, most laws and administrative regulations are exe-cuted by local officials directly or indirecctly accountable to

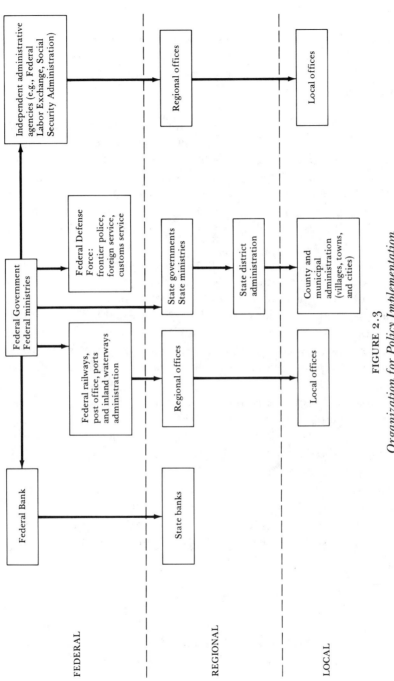

FEDERAL

REGIONAL

LOCAL

Federal Bank

Federal Government
Federal ministries

Independent administrative
agencies (e.g., Federal
Labor Exchange, Social
Security Administration)

Federal railways,
post office, ports
and inland waterways
administration

Federal Defense
Force:
frontier police,
foreign service,
customs service

State banks

State governments
State ministries

Regional offices

Regional offices

State district
administration

Local offices

County and
municipal
administration
(villages, towns
and cities)

Local offices

FIGURE 2.3
Organization for Policy Implementation

appropriate state authorities and not by the comparatively few local agents of the Federal Government. The collection of all income taxes, for example, rests with the state governments who stricly supervise the policy implementing functions of local authorities.

The Basic Law grants self-governing communities far less autonomy than enjoyed by their counterparts in the United States. Although it allows them to regulate their own affairs "within the limits set by law," this provision gives local governments little policymaking authority. Under the federal and state constitutions, schools, police departments, social services, in fact almost all but local public transportation and utility services, are controlled by state authorities.

Corresponding to the distribution of administrative responsibilities, the public administration is composed of several distinct but interlocking structures and interdependent but not overlapping bureaucratic hierarchies. In 1985, these took in about one out of ten employed West Germans. Most public employees are however not government officials, whereas the civil servants *(Beamten)* represent governmental authority by virtue of their executive position.

Most civil servants, including university professors, are career officials employed by the state governments and, directly or indirectly, subject to their control. As teachers, policemen, tax collectors, and the like, they provide the general population with most of its immediate contacts with public authorities. The small federal ministerial bureaucracy is on the whole not involved in such relationships. Apart from exercising those domestic tasks falling under their immediate jurisdiction, its members primarily plan and supervise the uniform implementation of federal policies throughout the country (see table 2.1).

The Judiciary

Under the constitutional system of checks and balances judicial authority is vested in an independent judiciary. Ordinary courts are divided horizontally into a number of functional hierarchies,

TABLE 2.1

Government Employees in the German Federal Republic, 1982
(N = 2,869,903)

	CIVIL SERVANTS AND JUDGES	SALARIED EMPLOYEES	WAGE EARNERS	TOTAL
Federal[a]	4%	3%	4%	11%
State[b]	34%	16%	6%	56%
Local	5%	18%	10%	33%
Total	43%	37%	20%	100%

Source: Calculated from data in Statistisches Jahrbuch für die Bundesrepublik Deutschland, 1983, p. 430.
[a] Not including about 1 million employed by public enterprises, such as Federal railways; Federal postal, telegraph, and telephone service, and members of the armed forces.
[b] Including teachers and university professors who constituted 43.1 percent of state personnel and 24.1 percent of all public administration personnel in West Germany

each of which is closely integrated vertically through a network of local, regional, and supreme federal courts (see figure 2.4). The constitutional courts in the Federation and states are coequal with the executive and legislative branches of government and have the authority to overrule them and other courts within their jurisdiction.

German jurisprudence distinguishes among universal, general, and absolute principles of justice (Recht) and relativist, particular, and finite principles of law (Gesetz). By the prevailing rules of a democratic Rechtstaat the courts are supposed to combine both sets of principles and render equal justice under law. Constitutional provisions stipulate that judges shall base their verdicts on what the law provides as well as on their interpretation of desirable or established social values. Trial by jury is rare. Most courts are collegial bodies, and the verdict of a majority of their members is handed down in the name of the entire bench. Individual opinions supporting or dissenting from the majority decision are usually not made public or recorded, as in the American judicial system.[4] Anonymity is supposed to protect the courts against outside in-

4. The single exception is the Federal Constitutional Court whose individual concurring and dissenting opinions have been published since December 1970.

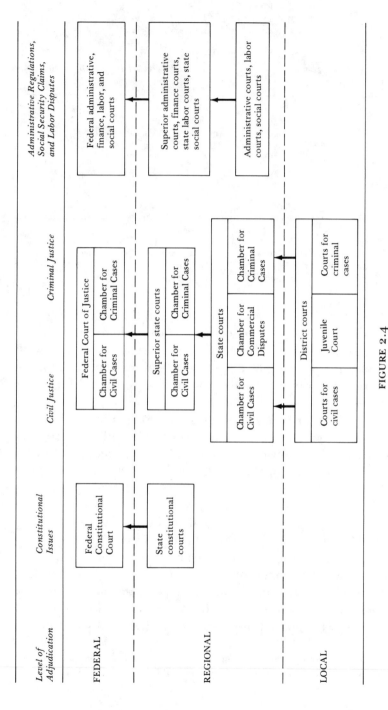

FIGURE 2.4
Organization of the Courts

terference and reinforce the prestige of the judicial organ of public authority.

The judicial pyramid of the regular court system is topped by the Federal Court of Justice (Bundesgerichtshof), an appellate court. As in other continental European countries, civil and criminal procedures and penalties are governed by codes of law, and review proceedings before higher courts concern only the application of uniform rules to specific cases. For instance, penalties for the infraction of traffic regulations are the same throughout the Federal Republic, whereas they vary from state to state and city to city in the United States.

As in the United States, an individual or organization indicted for violating the legal order is assumed to be innocent until proven guilty in court. In other respects, however, legal procedures are rather different and do not rest on common law traditions. A person arrested for violating the criminal code and bound over for trial by an examining magistrate may be incarcerated for months if the official believes that the accused might interfere with the pretrial investigation by the state's prosecuting attorney. Both judges and prosecutors are legally bound by their offices to ascertain the facts in the case objectively in pretrial as well as trial proceedings. In court they jointly examine witnesses and exhibits to ascertain whether the criminal code has indeed been violated as charged. The counsel for the defense is not, however, a public official but a private attorney. It is his task to show that the evidence does not warrant a conviction, or that the specific section of the criminal code under which the accused is tried does not apply in this case.

The pyramid of the administrative court system consists of chambers staffed jointly by professional and lay judges and is capped by the Federal Administrative Court (Bundesverwaltungsgericht). As elsewhere in continental Europe, these courts allow an individual to seek redress from the state for alleged injuries caused by the administrative actions of its official representatives. Their justices are supposed to decide whether a government agency or one of its officials conformed with proper administrative procedures in the performance of their legal responsibilities in such cases. The issue to be adjudicated may be whether a policeman had the formal right to make an arrest, or whether a teacher followed correct procedures in meting out punishment to an unruly pupil. A businessman may claim that he suffered damages through the error of a postal clerk and a worker that an injury sustained on his job was caused by the inadequate enforcement of governmental safety regulations.

The administrative court system also allows government agencies and officials to appeal the decisions of superior authorities on the grounds that these violated administrative regulations. And in cases that do not involve constitutional issues, the Federal Administrative Court may rule on disputes between state governments, between Federal and state executive organs, and among various administrative agencies.

Other segments of the judiciary deal with specialized issues of public and private law. Industrial disputes, for instance, are dealt with by federal labor courts, usually composed of an equal number of employer and employee representatives plus a professional specialist. Or, to take another example, disputes over unemployment benefits, social security payments, and workmen's compensation claims fall under the jurisdiction of the system of Federal social courts.

The Federal Constitutional Court (Bundesverfassungsgericht) is modeled after the American Supreme Court but deals exclusively with constitutional issues. The sixteen judges of its two chambers are bound only by the Basic Law and may, on appeal, set aside the verdict of any other court—including the constitutional courts of the states—if they find it to conflict with the spirit or the letter of the Basic Law. The court has original jurisdiction in the constitutional disputes between the Federal Government and state governments, between the Federal executive and parliament, between different states, and between other courts. It may also consider—and reject—complaints by individuals and organizations who claim that their constitutional rights have been violated by public authorities and that they have no other recourse for redress. And, it may outlaw organizations and practices deemed to be inconsistent with the constitutional order and the duties of responsible citizenship.

The formal patterns of positions and relationships we have surveyed provide the general organizational setting for public policy processes in the Federal Republic. Particular actors, issues, and events provide the more dynamic ingredients of political life. As we noted at the beginning of this chapter, and as we shall observe more closely in later chapters, contemporary political attitudes and actions need to be seen in terms of the profound influence of the formal arrangements and rules of the regime. For the participating actors, constitutional principles structure as well as legitimate the interplay between shifting electoral, interest group, and leadership alignments. Above all, party government, the outstanding feature of present-day politics in the Federal Republic, is both sanctioned and restricted by the principles of the Basic Law.

3

The Policy Environment

The constitutional principles of the Basic Law differentiate between state and society, public and private matters, and domestic
and foreign affairs. Such formal distinctions are of basic importance for the legal regulation of West German politics, but they
also tend to obscure the dynamic interaction between policy processes and policy context. Some observers consider them merely
traditional vestiges of earlier versions of the Rechtstaat that have
little or no real significance today. According to a prominent West
German political scientist, everything now touches on or is touched
by government and practically all aspects of life but the weather
are therefore politically relevant.[1] If we tried to carry analysis too
far, it would be easy to obliterate any meaningful distinction between the organization and operation of the political system and
its policy environment. Therefore, to obtain a clear understanding
of contextual conditions and relationships a more differentiated
approach is advisable.

1. Christian Graf von Krakow, "Mehr Demokratie—weniger Freiheit?" *Die Zeit*,
March 2, 1973. If everybody talks about the weather but nobody does anything
about it, as Mark Twain observed, it is because the weather is as yet uncontrollable.
Should it become controllable, as it may in the not too distant future, weather
regulations will no doubt become another issue in domestic and international
politics.

A POLYCENTRIC URBAN SETTING

The Federal Republic is one of the most densely settled and urban among the larger world powers.[2] In area it is only the size of Oregon—about the same as Britain but smaller than France—but the country ranks tenth in the world and first in Europe in population (see table 3.1). Unlike Britain, France, and Japan, the Federal Republic has no single center for its political, socio-economic, and cultural affairs. These activities are dispersed among the major metropolitan clusters. About twenty-four clusters extend from the Hamburg area on the North Sea to the

TABLE 3.1

Major Countries: Areas and Population

COUNTRY	AREA (IN 1,000 SQ. KM.)	1981 POPULATION (IN MILLIONS)	POPULATION DENSITY (PER SQ. KM.)	1990 PROJECTED POPULATION (IN MILLIONS)
G.F.R.[a]	248	61.7	248	60.6
France	544	53.9	99	56.1
U.K.	244	56.0	230	57.0
Italy	301	57.2	190	57.3
Japan	377	117.6	312	123.2
U.S.	9,369	229.8	25	245.2
USSR	22,402	267.7	12	290.2

Source: Statistical Office of the European Community, *Basic Statistics of the Community, 1982–1983*, p. 97.
[a] Includes West Berlin.

2. The data in this chapter are derived and calculated from too many sources to be cited in extensive footnotes. Principal sources include the following: *Statistisches Jahrbuch für die Bundesrepublik Deutschland* 1983; *Datenreport: Zahlen und Fakten über die Bundesrepublik Deutschland* (Bonn: Schriftenreihe der Bundeszentrale für politische Bildung, 1983); Statistical Office of the European Communities, *Basic Statistics of the Community*, 23 ed. (1983); Manfred Dloczik et al., *Der Fischer Informationsatlas: Bundesrepublik Deutschland* (Frankfurt, 1982); Horst Poller, *Politik im Querschnitt: Zahlenspiegel '81/'82* (Bonn, 1981); Bernhard Schäfers, *Sozialstruktur und Wandel in der Bundesrepublik Deutschland* (Stuttgart, 1979); reports by Inter Nationes; *Die Zeit, The German Tribune, Der Spiegel*, and various other newspapers, periodicals, and books in German. For additional references see the section on Contemporary Society, Economy and Culture in the Suggestions for Further Reading at the end of this book.

Munich area near the foothills of the Alps (see figure 3.1). Bonn, the federal capital, is the seat of the central government and parliament and focus of foreign relations. However, other key federal agencies—such as the central bank and the top federal courts—are located in other cities. Most of the public administration and, to a considerable extent, domestic policymaking are regionally dispersed among the capital cities of the ten states of the Federal Republic. Nongovernmental activities are also directed from centers scattered throughout the country. For instance, the headquarters for the great industrial and commercial empires, and for the principal media of mass communication, are not in Bonn but in Frankfurt, Hamburg, Munich, Cologne, and other cities.

These polycentric and regional patterns support the geographic division of formal governmental authority, particularly in domestic politics. At the same time, however, the relative smallness of the Federal Republic and the excellence of its communications facilitate the operation of countrywide networks of formal and informal relationships, especially among leaders in various sectors of public life.

The geographic distribution and mobility of the population accentuates the political significance of interregional and intra-regional distinctions in the Federal Republic. Two-thirds of the people live in just three of its component states (see table 3.2) and about half are concentrated in the twenty-four urban clusters. In recent decades the population of urban concentrations in the two southern states has increased disproportionately, lending increased weight to geographic political alignments identified with policy concerns of central cities and peripheral suburbs in the south.

Regional attachments and corresponding political orientations have apparently not been changed significantly by a good deal of geographic mobility. People who move tend to remain in the same general area—usually going from inner cities to adjoining suburbs—rather than settling in another part of the country. And whereas it seemed for a time that traditional local and provincial loyalties were rapidly waning among West Germans, such parti-

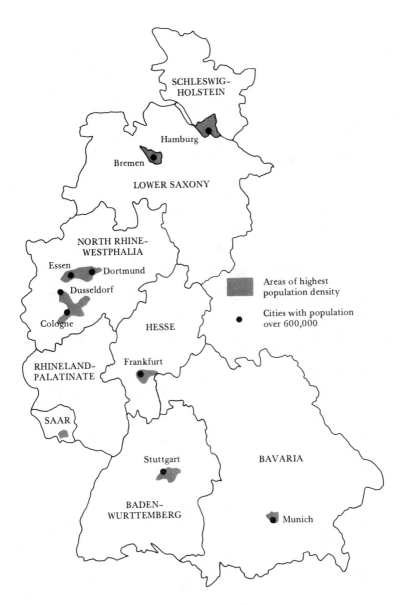

FIGURE 3.1

States and Major Urban Centers

TABLE 3.2

States of the Federal Republic: Area and Population, 1982

	PERCENT- AGE OF TOTAL AREA	POPULA- TION DENSITY (PER SQ. KM.)	PERCENT- AGE OF TOTAL POPULA- TION	PERCENTAGE CHANGE IN POPU- LATION SIZE, 1970–1982
Federal Republic	100[a]	248	100[b]	+0.9
Northern states				
Schleswig-Holstein	6.3	167	4.3	+4.3
Hamburg	0.3	2,152	2.6	−9.5
Bremen	0.2	1,696	1.1	−6.8
Lower Saxony	19.0	153	11.8	+1.9
Central states				
North Rhine-				
Westphalia	13.6	498	27.6	−0.3
Hesse	8.5	265	9.1	+3.2
Saarland	1.0	411	1.7	−5.6
Rhineland-Palatinate	7.9	183	5.9	−0.6
Southern states				
Baden-Württemberg	14.4	269	15.1	+3.5
Bavaria	28.4	155	17.8	+3.8
West Berlin	0.2	3,984	3.0	−11.6

Source: Calculated from data in *Statistisches Jahrbuch für die Bundesrepublik Deutschland, 1983,* pp. 40–41, 52.
[a] 248,630 km².
[b] 61,546,000.

cularistic sentiments appear to have become more common again in recent times.

Generational differences in geographic mobility have been of some importance in contemporary German politics. The older and generally more conservative generations are likely to stay put, whereas the younger generations tend to be on the move. According to one survey, young adults without children have been going to the big cities to further their educational or occupational objectives, or to join a spouse. Young families with children, on the other hand, are leaving inner-city apartments for larger suburban homes. Older people, it seems, prefer to remain or settle in more rural settings.

Geographic mobility has thus widened the gap not only between the sizes of urban and rural population, but has caused a greater imbalance in their age structure. In the villages and provincial towns of the more sparsely settled areas—such as the northeast corner of Bavaria—one sees comparatively few young persons and a disproportionate number close to, or past the age of retirement. The style of life there is on the whole more tranquil and unchanging than in the urban clusters, social relationships are more intimate, and traditional cultural and political values are more deeply entrenched. Foreign tourists may be enchanted by the gabled houses and crooked streets of the "old" Germany, and pensioners find such communities restful havens from the hectic pace of city life; but the younger generations consider them rather dull. They prefer to live in a less parochial urban environment.

In the urban centers one may pass from one municipality to another, even across state boundaries, without ever leaving built-up areas. Here pastoral scenes exist only in pictures on museum walls. And here, too, one encounters the conditions that have pushed urban problems to the forefront in domestic politics.

These problems are to a considerable extent the fruits of a vast, but poorly coordinated reconstruction process after World War II. Practically every city and factory town had suffered immense damage, and a severe housing shortage was further aggravated by an influx of some 12 million refugees from Eastern Germany and Eastern Europe. Industrial and home construction could not wait for the development of comprehensive urban and regional planning programs; buildings were erected in a hurry wherever there was space. Zoning laws were either weak or nonexistent and generous governmental tax incentives and subsidies encouraged speculators to take advantage of the availability of cheap real estate. Thousands of profitable new office and factory buildings went up in and around the cities and some 12 million new homes were built under public and private auspices within 25 years—one for every five inhabitants of the Federal Republic.

The result was a radical transformation of the urban landscape over a fairly brief period. In the inner cities luxury apartments, parking garages, and department stores now occupy the sites of former parks and residential buildings. Further out, huge industrial and housing developments have replaced peripheral green-belts and farm lands, and once remote towns and villages have become sprawling suburban bedroom communities. Streets and highways are choked with the cars of commuting office and factory workers and trucks thundering through by day and night. Industrial waste pollutes the air and waters, and noisy factories add to the roar of the cities.

Urban migration and expansion have proven to be a mixed blessing. On the one hand, persons who did not even have homes after World War II or lived in dank city tenements and antiquated farmhouses are now a lot more comfortable. By and large, urban homes are neat and modern and equipped with all sorts of conveniences; the sordid city slums one still finds in many other industrial societies do not exist in the Federal Republic. On the other hand, urban renewal has evidently aggravated rather than alleviated some of the familiar ecological problems of cities and suburbs in technologically advanced societies. The public concern with such problems has increased enormously in recent times. As long as urban noise, congestion, pollution, and the like seemed to be unavoidable by-products of a *quantitative* increase in homes, jobs, and private cars for them, people apparently felt they had to be tolerated. Lately, however, proposals for governmental measures that will improve the *quality* of urban life have gained wide support—in part, no doubt, just because reconstruction was so successful.

POLITICAL ECONOMY

The Federal Republic is one of the world's leading economic powers (see table 3.3). Its industrial exports and extensive foreign investments have given the country a key position in international economic relations, and the Deutsche Mark has been a favorite currency in international financial transactions. These circum-

TABLE 3.3

Economic Profile of Major Non-Communist Industrial Countries

	G.F.R.	U.K.	FRANCE	JAPAN	U.S.
G.D.P. 1981 (in billions)	$685.7	$500.0	$574.2	$1133.3	$2906.3
Per capita income, 1981 (in purchasing power parities at market prices)	9,590	7,627	9,268	8,862	11,706
Output by economic sector, 1981[a]					
Agriculture[b]	2.1	2.0	4.0	3.6	2.8
Industry[c]	44.7	39.3	36.5	41.2	38.8
Services[d]	53.2	58.6	59.5	55.2	63.5

Source: Calculated from data in Statistical Office of the European Communities, *Basic Statistics of the Community, 1983,* pp. 39–40, 43.

[a] Data in rounded off percentages.

[b] Includes forestry, hunting, and fishing.

[c] Includes mining, manufacturing, and construction.

[d] Includes trade, finance, transport, and utilities.

stances have conditioned foreign policy in the Federal Republic as well as the policies of other states toward that country.

Since the establishment of the Federal Republic, technological developments and changes in the patterns of production and consumption have resulted in politically significant shifts in its economy. Although agricultural production increased by more than 350 percent between 1959 and 1981, its contribution to total economic output dropped in the same time from 10 to 2 percent. Private and public services, on the other hand, have contributed an ever larger share. In the course of the 1970s they replaced industrial production as the dominant sector of economic output. As we shall see, these shifts are reflected in corresponding changes in sociocultural factors that enter into West German politics, and in the scope and nature of governmental policies and foreign relations.

As in other non-Communist industrial countries, the economy is a mixed one dominated by big private and public enterprises. The private sector takes in a larger proportion of key economic enterprises than in Britain, France, and Italy, but a smaller one than in the United States and Japan. Most farms, banks, industrial firms, and commercial concerns are owned by private individuals and corporations. Practically all public utilities, employment agencies, and other key economic services are government operated.

This combination is in line with patterns going back a century or more that were formally reaffirmed by the Basic Law. The present mix is, however, not immutable under the constitution. The right to private wealth and its uses for personal gain in a competitive market economy are safeguarded only as they do not conflict with the general welfare. In fact, the constitution provides for the expropriation of private property in the public interest.[3] In the last analysis overall coordinative and regulatory control of the economy is the constitutional responsibility of the agencies of the West German state and its officials.

How the balance between private enterprise and public control has been struck, and to what effect, has been due to economic as much as political factors. On the whole the trend has been toward tightening the interdependent relationship between the private and public sectors. These developments have posed new issues about the role of big business on the one hand and big government on the other in the formulation and implementation of domestic and foreign economic policies.

German big business has adapted to and survived several drastic changes in the political order—including the rise and fall of the Nazi regime—and it played a major role in the economic reconstruction after World War II. Rapid recovery was the order of the day and was associated by dominant policymakers with free enterprise capitalism rather than with state ownership of the means of production and government planning. Under the leadership of Chancellor Konrad Adenauer (1949–1963), and with the active support of various American governments, political means were employed for economic ends in the belief that the new state and regime had to rest on solid material foundations. Large concerns

3. Article 14 guarantees the right to private property, but Article 15 permits land, natural resources, and the means of production to be transferred to public ownership.

were not expropriated, as in the German Democratic Republic, nor were key economic enterprises transferred to public ownership, as in Britain, France, and Italy. They were, on the contrary, encouraged to expand by governmental policies that promised large profits to venturesome businessmen and committed the resources of the state to the support of private trade and industry. Mass unemployment, swollen by the influx of millions of refugees, provided an abundant supply of cheap labor, and vast American financial assistance provided investment capital. What had been an impoverished, war-devastated country staged a very rapid recovery in what came to be known as the spectacular "German Economic Miracle" of the 1950s.[4] Most significantly, much of the credit for the feat was given both at home and abroad to the drive and initiative of West German private enterprise.

The fact that the present regime got its start during an explosion of collective and individual prosperity in this manner had a long-term effect on policy-relevant attitudes and relationships. In the course of about two decades of substantial and steady economic growth the new political order became identified for most West Germans with a thriving capitalist economy that might be tempered, but not too much tampered-with, by governmental policymakers. Higher incomes, steady prices, full employment, and abundant surplus resources for mass consumption of goods and services were linked to the expansion of domestic production and foreign trade. And here close cooperation among governmental agencies, big business, and trade unions was thought to be of critical importance. The structural switches had been thrown and policy choices locked into courses of action that promised to keep the capitalist economic train on track at maximum safe speed.

During the Golden Age of West German prosperity an increasingly affluent population became accustomed to unprecedented high standards of material comfort. Consider, for example, that households with refrigerators increased from 9 to 98 percent

4. Between 1950 and 1961, the output of goods and services expanded by 123 percent, industrial production by 162 percent, and per capita income by 152 percent. The number of employed persons increased by a third between 1950 and 1963, and wages and salaries 115 percent between 1949 and 1964.

between 1953 and 1979 and those with at least one automobile from 8 to 71 percent. Households with at least one television set grew from 32 to 94 percent between 1962 and 1983, those with a washing machine from 34 to 83 percent, and those with a deep freeze from 3 to 65 percent. Working people came to enjoy longer paid vacation and their rising incomes allowed ever larger numbers of West Germans to spend their holidays in foreign countries. Increasingly generous social welfare arrangements assured that West Germans without their own means of adequate support shared in the prosperity. The relatively few who were unemployed and those who were unable to work for reasons of health or age were provided with incomes and services that kept even the poorest West German well above the official poverty level in most other countries.

To both West Germans and admiring or envious foreigners, it seemed for quite a time that rising prosperity was "The Never-Ending Story" of the Federal Republic—to use the title of a best-selling West German fairy-tale book. Its political leaders were expected to sustain their country's economic growth through appropriate domestic and foreign policies and thus provide for still greater personal affluence and collective economic power. These leaders, for their part, were attuned to an intimate relationship between changes in economic conditions and changes in the political order and correspondingly sensitive to developments at home and abroad that might threaten the material foundations of the prevailing regime.

Economic growth, stability, and security are still generally considered necessary, though not altogether sufficient conditions for the smooth operation of the political system. However, such conditions have been far less favorable in recent times than during the salad days of the 1960s. Economic growth declined drastically in the 1970s and threatened to stagnate through the 1980s. Mass unemployment made a comeback and by 1984 had climbed to almost 10 percent of the work force, a level unknown since the beginnings of the Federal Republic.

West German policymakers would dearly like to achieve a strong and lasting economic recovery without politically unsettling conflicts but this may prove difficult, if not impossible. Key industrial sectors, such as steel, have been weakened by obsolescent equipment and foreign competition and it appears that the degree of modernization and reorientation of the economy needed for sustained growth may involve long-term unemployment and social dislocation for many West Germans.[5]

POLITICAL SOCIOLOGY

Interrelated and frequently overlapping social distinctions are of major importance in the political life of the Federal Republic. Continuity and change in the relative significance of different aspects of social relations are reflected in voting patterns, in the activities of parties and interest groups, in the kinds of policies that are demanded and supported, and in the policies that prevail at the governmental level.

Some of these distinctions are based on birth: sex, age, family background, nativity, and religion. Others are based on acquired characteristics: residence, occupation, income, and education. Some of them have come to carry less weight in politics, other have remained significant or become more important. Religious distinctions in particular, matter far less today than twenty or thirty years ago.

Nominally the West German population is almost equally divided between Protestants and Roman Catholics. Under the prevailing laws most people are born into one or the other faith; it is marked on their birth certificates and, unless they legally opt out, they will pay a tax to their church for the rest of their lives. But religious identification is no longer a major source of political cleavage. Organized religion continues to exercise considerable influence in some policy areas, especially on matters relating to public morals and the constitutional obligation of the state to safeguard the sanctity of marriage and the family. However, when

5. In this connection see "Down to Earth: A Survey of the West German Economy," *The Economist* February 4, 1984; John Tagliabue, "The Twilight of the Industrial Ruhr," *New York Times*, November 27, 1983.

it comes to partisan alignments and the selection of policymakers, religious distinctions are today clearly subordinate to secular differences such as occupation, income, or age.

Occupational Patterns

In the early years of the Federal Republic it seemed for a time that profound changes in the political order were accompanied by equally basic changes in the social order. Widespread poverty and general social dislocation in the wake of World War II suggested that far more social and political equality would now prevail. Former members of the upper strata were reduced in social status and former members of the lower strata elevated. An American sociologist found social mobility to be very high in the mid 1950s and a German colleague saw "a relative[ly] equal and uniform social class" emerging from a "far advanced breakdown of social distinctions."[6] In view of 72 percent of the respondents in a 1958 opinion poll, a capable child of poor parents no longer faced serious obstacles to social advancement. A poll of young West German adults taken fifteen years later presented a very different picture: 72 percent of the respondents now thought that an individual's future station in life was virtually determined by his parents' occupation and his family background.

The leveling of social differences turned out to be not nearly as far-reaching as it had seemed in the early years. Economic recovery reestablished a distinct social hierarchy; what had been taken to be an almost revolutionary transformation of West German society proved to be a continuation of long-range evolutionary changes extending over different regimes. Technological developments have produced a high rate of both upward and downward social status mobility for individuals over the last fifty years—about as much as in the United States—but on the whole the chances for

6. See Morris Janowitz, "Social Stratification and Mobility in West Germany," *American Journal of Sociology* (July 1958) 64:6–24, and Helmut Schelsky, "Elements of Social Stability," *German Social Science Digest* (Hamburg: Claasens, 1955), p. 115.

social advancement from the lower strata have not changed appreciably.[7]

About half of the people of the Federal Republic work for their living. As indicated in table 3.4, the general characteristics of the working population are much like those in other countries with a similar political and economic order. Two interconnected trends that have accompanied the evolution of the prevailing regime are of particular political significance—a decline in family and self-employment and a growth of employment in white-collar service occupations.

Between 1950 and 1982 the proportion of the working population engaged in agriculture and related activities dropped from 22 to less than 6 percent, and employment in the service sector

TABLE 3.4

Profile of Working Population in Major Non-Communist Industrial Countries

	G.F.R.	U.K.	FRANCE	JAPAN	U.S.
Civilian working population, 1982					
Percentage of total population	43.8	46.4	42.1	48.8	47.5
Percentage of male population	49.4	51.1	45.5	58.9	51.7
Percentage of female population	38.6	41.1	38.8	39.0	43.5
Distribution by economic sectors, 1982[a]					
Agricultural[b]	5.5	2.7	8.4	9.7	3.6
Industrial[c]	42.7	34.7	34.6	34.9	28.4
Service[d]	51.8	62.6	57.0	55.4	68.0

Source: Statistical Office of the European Communities, *Basic Statistics of the Community,* *1982–1983,* p. 112.
[a] Data in rounded off percentages.
[b] Includes forestry, hunting, and fishing.
[c] Includes mining, manufacturing, and construction.
[d] Includes trade, finance, transport, and utilities.

7. See Gerhard Kleining, "Soziale Mobilität in der Bundesrepublik Deutschland," *Kölner Zeitschrift für Soziologie* (1975), pp. 96–119, 273–292.

increased from 33 to 52 percent. The great decline in the percentage of self-employed and assisting family workers shown in
table 3.5 is largely accounted for by fewer persons deriving their

TABLE 3.5

Shifts in Form of Employment in the Republic of Germany 1950–1982
(as percentage of total employed)

	1950	1982
Self-employed and assisting family workers	31.4	11.8
Wage earners	48.6	41.3
Salaried employees	15.8	38.3
Civil servants	4.2	8.7
Total	100.0	100.0

Source: For 1982; *Statistisches Jahrbuch für die Bundesrepublik Deutschland, 1983*, p. 97. For 1950:
Die Zeit, January 9, 1976, citing data from the Federal Statistical Office.

principal income from the operation of small family farms or
shops and other independent business enterprises. And it was just
this element which traditionally constituted the mass of the politically most conservative groups in Germany. The growth of employment in private and public service occupations, expecially in
clerical and administrative jobs, has had a countervailing political
effect. For it is particularly from younger and better educated
people in these occupations that the proponents of political
change in West German society have received disproportionate
support in recent years.

Forecasts indicate that manual employment in industrial production will further decline, but that employment will continue to
grow in nonmanual service occupations. These trends are typical
for a technologically advanced society and are largely attributable
to increasing automation and the economic advantages of large-
scale operations in a mass-consumption economy.

Income Patterns

As in the United States, personal incomes in the Federal Republic
are derived primarily from employment, pensions, and profits.
Most persons rely either directly or indirectly on wages and salaries

to meet their living expenses; about 17 percent depend on pension payments; and only a small minority receives most of its income from investments in property and business ventures.

On the average, the people of the Federal Republic are today more prosperous than those in most other countries, and all income groups are appreciably better off than in the early years of the present regime. Income from employment increased by 147 percent in the Golden Age between 1960 and 1970, and income from profits by 83 percent. Over the last decade or two the average income of West Germans has grown more slowly, but it has generally kept up with rising prices.

Average income figures do not, however, tell the whole story; they tend to obscure the persistent relative deprivation of different income groups. Although everybody's income has gone up over the years, everybody has not benefited equally from an expanding per capita income. Government policies have over the years served to diminish once very large income differences, particularly between the very rich and the very poor. There are now more of the former and fewer of the latter than twenty or thirty years ago, but the very rich have also become richer and the very poor poorer. The distribution of personal income after taxes has on the whole become somewhat more evenhanded. Still, in the early 1980s 75 percent of the self-employed and 65 percent of salaried white-collar employees received more, but 75 percent of wage-earners less than the average after-tax income. Moreover, inequalities in the distribution of personal wealth have changed hardly at all, with a few having the most. In 1981, according to reliable studies, 3 percent of West German households owned 40 percent of all private property, whereas 30 percent of households owned less than 2 percent.

In the view of radical critics of the present socioeconomic and political order these disparities testify to the social injustices inherent in a capitalist economy. In the opinion of its more conservative supporters they merely reflect variations in monetary rewards for different levels of achievement in an open, competitive society.

In some respects, certainly, present conditions seem to offer considerable opportunities for getting ahead to those who will seize them. Traditional barriers to socioeconomic advancement are fewer and far less rigid than they once were in Germany and still are in many other countries. Religious discrimination in employment has pretty well disappeared and a title of nobility is no longer an "open sesame" to high positions. Still, significant inequalities remain in the structure of opportunities. Ambition alone is not enough to move a person from a lower to a higher level of income and social status; one also needs the necessary resources— skill, wealth, or better yet, both—and these are unequally distributed.

From the top to the bottom of the contemporary social pyramid we find a recurring theme: highly valued occupational skills will bring monetary and status rewards, and wealth will beget more wealth. Or, to put it another way, those who have more of what it takes get more of what is wanted. Persons who have large funds to invest in profitable real estate and business ventures can earn more than individuals who depend primarily on wages, salaries, or pension payments. They are economically more secure in a time of rising prices and better able to see their children through a long period of educational training for the best jobs. And in a technologically advanced economy, white-collar workers who have much needed skills are paid more than industrial workers who do not, and individuals with investments in growth enterprises receive more than those who work in declining sectors of the economy. Moreover, differences in occupational income and status are reproduced in old age and survivor pensions under West German law. Highly paid managers may thus expect to receive many times over the retirement pay of clerical workers, and civil servants will get much better benefits than public employees who do not hold civil service status.

Such disparities in the size, sources, and benefits of personal incomes have been at the bottom of most domestic political issues. According to its Basic Law, the Federal Republic is "a democratic and social" state. But just how this declaration should be interpreted and implemented, to what extent and in what manner public policy should assure everybody of a "fair share" of the monetary and nonmonetary fruits of national prosperity, divides political factions. Reduced to its essentials, the problem is to strike the right balance between political and economic democracy, and between technological progress and social justice.

The people who have profited the most from the present social order are quite naturally content to leave well enough alone. Conservative business leaders and their political allies point with pride to the Federal Republic's overall material accomplishments—particularly in drawing unfavorable comparisons with living conditions in the Communist German Democratic Republic. Their message to those further down in the socioeconomic hierarchy is that all of us Germans here are a lot better off than those over there.

At the opposite extreme are the proponents of radical change. In their view, to compare conditions in the Federal Republic with those in earlier times and other countries is either irrelevant or pernicious. To them this begs a pressing policy question: How can we achieve substantially greater social equality here and now? The answer, they claim is a drastic redistribution of economic power and benefits.

Most of the dominant political leaders now take a far more moderate, centrist position. Many will grant that more could be done to lessen socioeconomic inequities. But they are not prepared to carry reforms to the point of changing basic societal and economic structures that would drastically alter the prevailing political order.

Educational Patterns

In the Federal Republic, as in the United States, political interest, social status, and earning power are closely related to schooling. A good education is virtually essential for the more prestigious and better-paying jobs. And the better educated a person, the more likely he or she is to feel capable of influencing the course of public policy, and to take part in politics.

A child's future occupational career is ordinarily settled quite early by parents and educational authorities. After four years of common primary schooling students are sorted out for one or

another type of secondary education on the basis of past performance and apparent promise. Roughly one out of four are sent to
the most prestigious and generously financed of the secondary
schools, the Gymnasium, for a nine-year course of study in subjects
needed for admission to university. About an equal proportion go
to the *Realschule*, the closest to an American high school, for some
six years of academic and prevocational study. This will qualify
them to move on to vocational schools for skilled white-collar
employees, such as computer operators, laboratory technicians,
and nurses. Most other primary school students are dispatched to
a third-type of secondary school, the *Hauptschule*, for five more
years of compulsory basic education. Those who make it to grad-
uation qualify for a four-year apprenticeship program of on-the-
job training and once-a-week occupational schooling that equips
them to become skilled manual workers, sales persons, secretaries
and the like. Those who do not finish have to settle for less desirable
jobs and are particularly disadvantaged in times of mass
unemployment.

In effect West Germany's secondary schools, like those of most
other Western countries, serve to prepare their students for stratified socioeconomic positions in adult life. Various efforts designed
to merge the three-track system into one like the comprehensive
high-school system of the United States have not gotten very far.
Only four percent of secondary students were attending such
Gesamtschulen in the early 1980s and much further growth seemed
unlikely. In most parts of the Federal Republic politicians, parents,
and educators have preferred to keep the more discriminating
traditional system of selection.

A general education in a *Hauptschule* is generally considered
appropriate for children who need, or want, or cannot absorb a
greater amount of formal learning. But more and more West
German parents have wanted a better education for their offsprings. The proportion of secondary school students getting just
a basic education thus dropped from 72 to 47 percent between
1955 and 1981. On the other hand, the proportion receiving more
advanced prevocational training in the *Realschule* went up from

13 to 26 percent and proportion getting a pre-university education in the Gymnasium from 15 to 27 percent.

The impact of these changes is just beginning to become evident in West German society. In politics they point to the emergence of better educated voters, notably among the offsprings of manual workers and among women. In so far as they extend to higher education they have already become evident in larger mass support for unconventional political groups among university students and graduates.

Until the 1960s only about 5 percent of secondary school graduates went on to institutions of higher learning; in 1984 it was more than 20 percent. The number of students in universities and professional schools is today four times what it was just two decades ago and a far larger proportion, some 40 percent, are women. There are also more children of manual workers getting a higher education; in 1982 they constituted 16 percent of West German university students, compared to 11 percent in 1973. While this is still far less than in the United States, it is a good deal more than in Britain (10%) and other Western countries. But for the most part the increase in university students is accounted for by more offsprings of middle-income white-collar employees going to the Gymnasium and then to university.

Now that a free higher education is no longer just the privilege of a select few it also no longer guarantees a good job in business, the civil service, or one of the professions. University departments providing training for a career in medicine, law, or some other popular field are overcrowded and have had to restrict admission drastically. Students may have to wait for several years to enter their chosen field, if they get in at all, and may run out of money before they can finish their studies. About half of West German university students are provided for by their families, but the rest depend on government loans, which have been reduced, and on part-time work, which has been harder to come by in a time of mass unemployment. A tighter labor market has lowered the job expectations of university graduates and put them in competition with young people who have less schooling but are better trained for positions requiring special skills. An increasing number of university students and graduates have therefore sought work as apprentices in commerce and industry, making it more difficult for less well educated West Germans to get such on-the-job vocational training.

The Status of Women

Equal rights for men and women is a cardinal principle of the constitutional order of the Federal Republic; according to the Basic Law "no one is to be prejudiced or favored because of gender." Public policy has been directed toward the complete emancipation of women from their traditionally inferior position in German society.

A vast number of laws have been passed to eradicate all sex discrimination in fact as well as form. Husbands no longer have the legal right to govern the family and control its property: wives no longer need their husbands' permission to take a job. Divorce settlements no longer favor the male, and sex discrimination in education and employment have been outlawed. Women are entitled to six weeks of paid vacation before and after childbirth and to more equitable opportunities for on-the-job training for the better jobs.

Social change has, however, lagged behind public policy. The notion that husband and wife should have equal rights in a marriage has been gradually accepted, especially among younger people. But a lot of men still hold to the time-honored belief that women belong in the home as mothers and housewives, and all too many women, in the view of West German feminists, accept these traditional roles with varying degrees of enthusiasm or resignation. Politically influential women's organizations—as in the United States—are virtually nonexistent in the Federal Republic, and women liberationists are still considered oddities even by members of their own sex.

The lag between formal rules and actual practice is particularly notable in the status of employed women. Most of these come from and marry into lower social strata, are relatively poorly educated, and hold jobs because they need the money. Women from more affluent homes are usually better educated and more likely not to take jobs at all or to quit them when they marry. Consequently, most women who work start as and remain unskilled and semiskilled workers at the bottom of the occupational ladder—usually in blue-collar or, more often, clerical occupations requiring little or no vocational training.

Some recent surveys indicate that these patterns are gradually changing as a new generation of better-educated women enters the labor market. In the mid-1980s, however, there were as yet only about half as many women as men in managerial positions, but four times as many in more lowly white-collar jobs. Top positions in the public as well as private sector remained largely a male preserve. Not many women held leading posts as judges or university professors, only one out of ten members of the national parliament were women, and women were not prominent in the upper echelons of the civil service and West German corporations.

Sex discrimination is less pronounced when it comes to equal pay for equal work—due in no small part to changes in public policy. Increasingly women doing the same kind of work as men have received the same pay, something which is still quite unusual in other Western countries. In the Federal Republic the after-tax income of women, like that of men, has risen substantially in two decades (see table 3.6). The fact that their earnings have on the average not kept pace with the overall increase in real wages and salaries is largely due to the pronounced overrepresentation of women in lower-paying jobs.

TABLE 3.6

Shifts in Distribution of Income from Employment by Sex, 1964–1982

	NET MONTHLY INCOME (IN DM)							
	UNDER 800		800–1199		1200–1800		OVER 1800	
	MEN	WOMEN	MEN	WOMEN	MEN	WOMEN	MEN	WOMEN
1964	62%	90%	31%	9%	5%	1%	2%	—
1972	19	70	46	22	24	6	11	2%
1982	8	29	5	25	31	30	56	15

Source: *Statistisches Jahrbuch für die Bundesrepublik Deutschland, 1974*, p. 143; *1983*, p. 101.

In West German politics sex distinctions have gradually lost their former importance for electoral behavior. Thus, the vote of women has not reflected greater pressure for equality. Still, it may in time lend more support to feminist demands should the gender gap in socioeconomic status persist. The men who presently dominate the political scene in the Federal Republic are manifestly against all forms of sex discrimination, but they also have not gone out of their way to bring women into top leadership positions.

The Alien Underclass

Close to 2 million foreign workers—along with about an equal number of their dependents—have stirred a good deal of public controversy in the Federal Republic. The economies of a number of other advanced industrial countries in Western Europe—notably France, Belgium, and Switzerland—also have come to depend on foreign labor from less-developed Mediterranean countries. In West Germany, as elsewhere, mass unemployment has in recent times aggravated social rifts between natives and aliens. However, special factors complicate the political issues raised by so large an alien population in the Federal Republic.

To begin with, too many migrants came from too many countries in too short a time to be easily integrated into a state that lacked a distinct national identity of its own. And then the Federal Republic became the only Western country where a shrinking native population confronts a growing alien one. For more than a decade deaths have exceeded births among its citizens, whereas the reverse has held for non-citizens. Foreigners now constitute more than 7 percent of the West German population, and demographers predict that it could be close to 12 percent by the year 2000 if current trends continue.

No one forsaw this back in the 1960s when expansionist economic policies led to a shortage of native labor—particularly in labor-extensive enterprises where labor-saving technological changes were not feasible. For every person seeking a job, there were on the average four or five vacancies, most of them in menial occupations shunned by West Germans. The policy response to this problem was the importation of "guest workers"—an official euphemism designed to avoid unpleasant associations with the slave laborers brought in by the Nazis from captive countries. By 1972, foreign workers comprised 11 percent of the labor force— a tenfold increase in a decade. Key export industries, such as automobile production, came to depend on them for unskilled and semiskilled labor. In many cities foreigners provided most menial services, such as collecting garbage and burying the dead.

Economically, this arrangement proved for some years to be mutually beneficial. Foreign workers could earn much higher wages in West Germany than in their native countries. In addition, they were eligible to receive unemployment compensation and other welfare benefits. At the same time they contributed to the economic well-being of the West Germans. Their tax payments and those of employers drawing profits from their labor provided money for public expenditure. Their contributions to the social security system subsidized West German pension and welfare benefits.

What was an economically beneficial arrangement produced, however, less desirable social consequences. Foreign workers and their families—a third of them Turks, the rest mostly Yugoslavs, Greeks, Spaniards, and Italians—have become largely social outcasts at the bottom of the West German status hierarchy. Many speak little German, live in crowded "guest workers' ghettos," pay exorbitant rents for dilapidated housing, and are limited to social contacts with their own kind. Moreover, since they do not enjoy the same political rights as West Germans, they have little or no say about policies affecting their future in the Federal Republic.

Particularly in cities with large concentrations of foreigners (as many as one out of five employees and one out of four school children in highly industrialized areas), their local hosts tend to view them as extra burdens on already overtaxed public services. A good many West Germans especially dislike the alien ways of the Turks and believe that these are more prone to commit crimes than West Germans.

In 1982 a young Turkish woman burned herself to death in Hamburg in protest against the hostility shown her compatriots.

On the whole foreign workers have, however, received better treatment from West German policymakers than they have gotten in other European countries. But as social relations between native and aliens have gone from bad to worse with increasing unemployment, the policymakers have come under increasing pressure from public opinion to halt or, better yet, reverse the flow of immigrants. This has proven rather difficult.

Every proposal to deal with the matter has encountered telling counterarguments. For instance, the suggestion that only foreign workers without dependents be admitted, as in Switzerland, has encountered the argument that this would only make their social integration more difficult. A proposal for a wider dispersion of the alien population in order to reduce social tension has been resisted by employers of foreign workers who would have to relocate their operations.

The Federal Government, attempting to stem the tide, has forbidden West German employers to bring more foreign workers into the country. It has also sponsored a repatriation program that has provided Turks in particular with generous financial inducement to go home and stay there. The impact has been modest, though the rate of unemployment among foreign workers has been twice that of West Germans. Most of them are evidently unwilling to leave the relatively rich country where they have by now lived for many years, where they have brought their families, and where their children feel more at home than in their parents' native land.

While West German authorities have not encouraged foreigners to overstay their welcome, they also have avoided forced expulsion. Aliens may apply for permanent residence after five years in the Federal Republic and for citizenship after eight. Note, however, that though half of the foreign workers had lived in the Federal Republic for more than a decade by the mid-1980s, only three out of a thousand had been naturalized. Whether this was more because most were not interested in West German citizenship or more because it was denied to them by the authorities is an open question.

What can and might be done by public authorities is not just a domestic issue; foreign workers involve foreign relations. For example, efforts to reverse the flow of Turkish migrants has involved the West Germans in difficult negotiations with the Turkish government. And the Federal Republic can not legally block the entry of workers from poorer countries in the European Community, notably Greece, and, Spain and Portugal. They can, however, deny them permanent residence.

THE EXTERNAL SETTING

Foreign relations intrude on domestic politics in every country in this age of electronic warfare, interlocking national economies, and global mass communications. But in few, if any, major industrial states are internal and external affairs as closely enmeshed as in the Federal Republic. Here governmental and nongovernmental relations with other states, with supranational organizations, and with multinational corporations cast a tightly woven net over policy processes. Its strands extend down to local politics and far beyond the borders of the Federal Republic to remote areas of the world that trade with West Germany.

British and Japanese politics reflect centuries of insular isolation, whereas West German politics show an intensive involvement in the wars, commerce, and cultural exchanges of continental Europe over the last 2,000 years. In France a traditional sense of national exclusiveness still colors domestic and foreign policy processes, but policy in the Federal Republic is much more a product of changing international conditions. And although the size and resources of the United States have provided Americans with a sense of military security and economic independence, West Germans closely identify their welfare with external circumstances largely beyond the control of their own policymakers.

The Maintenance of Peace

Peace in Central Europe has been a primary and undisputed principle of West German policy that transcends constitutional and treaty limitations on the use of force by the Federal Republic.

Memories of past wars and destruction and fears of future cata-
clysms have deprived West Germans of any taste for military ventures and for leaders who might involve them in such. They neither
possess nor seek nuclear arms to deter or repel an attack, knowing
that a few such weapons could wipe out their population. Yet they
are also keenly aware that here their leaders have had to adapt to
international developments.

The two Germanies have been focal points in the shifting patterns of East-West and, above all, Soviet-American relations. Nowhere else have the two superpowers confronted each other as
immediately and continuously over the last four decades, and nowhere else has there been as massive a concentration of awesome
military power at the command of foreign governments. The Federal Republic has come to be the keystone of the American-dom-
inated NATO alliance and the German Democratic Republic that
of the Soviet-controlled Warsaw Pact. The leaders of both superpowers have considered their countries' defense and political interests bound up with the military security of their respective
German allies.

Most West Germans want the protection afforded by the Western
military alliance, but they do not want to risk involvement in war.
Time and again an anxious public has dreaded that a clash between the superpowers in this or some other part of the world
might suddenly unleash the forces of its destruction. The question
of what might be done to reduce the risk has provoked a good deal
of controversy. Some groups favor an international arms control
agreement that would lead to the gradual withdrawal of all foreign
forces and weapons from Central Europe. Others maintain that
American forces in the Federal Republic provide an essential guar-
antee against Soviet aggression or nuclear blackmail. A small neutralist minority—particularly on the extreme left of the political
spectrum—asserts that the notion of a Soviet threat is a myth
designed to uphold the power of American and West German
ruling groups in the Federal Republic.

Over the years, varying perceptions of West German security
needs have conditioned the course and tenor of these domestic
controversies and the reactions of the mass public. The greater

the fear of a Soviet attack, the greater too have been the feelings of military weakness and dependency on American protection. Conversely, the greater the sense of security from aggression, the greater has been the ready willingness to support disarmament proposals. But, in the last analysis, peace and security for the Federal Republic are generally believed to rest first on the maintenance of a worldwide balance of terror between the superpowers, and second on a Soviet-American understanding to preserve stability in Central Europe.

In this context, West German policymakers have had few options and little maneuverability. Their opportunities for pursuing an independent course of action have been particularly restricted in periods of high tension in East-West relations and greater in times of lowered tension.

A climate of high tension prevailed during the early years of the Federal Republic in the era of the Cold War. The failure of the United States and the Soviet Union to find a mutually acceptable solution to the "German Problem" and increasing friction between them in other parts of the world led to the rearmament of their two hostile German client states. American demands for a German military contribution to the "defense of the West" overrode the objections of a substantial minority in West Germany; the Federal Republic was locked into the NATO alliance; and German reunification became, in effect, a dead issue. West German troops joined those of their new allies in guarding the eastern frontier against the troops of the Soviet Union and its German cohorts. West German governments embraced the prevailing American hard line against concessions to the Soviet Union and so did most West German voters. As it happened, every federal election from 1949 until 1965 was preceded by a Cold War crisis and a majority of the electorate responded by supporting the ticket they believed to be most acceptable to the United States.

The easing of East-West tensions from the mid-1960s onward allowed a new set of West German policymakers to seek an accommodation with the Communist states of Eastern Europe. As a first step they met Soviet demands for the Federal Republic's adherence to the nuclear test ban and nuclear nonproliferation treaties, which reaffirmed West Germany's status as a minor military power. This step opened the way for a series of treaties in the early 1970s that "normalized" relations with Russia and its allies. With these agreements, the West German leaders formally accepted the political order and territorial arrangements that had emerged in Central Europe in the wake of World War II, above all the division of Germany and the incorporation of some of its former territories into Poland and the Soviet Union. Public opinion turned with the tide. Opponents of the new "eastern policy" (Ostpolitik) were overwhelmed in the federal election of 1972 and its proponents given a strong endorsement.

The late 1960s have proven to be something of a watershed between two eras in West German foreign policy. Relations with the United States and other military partners are troubled more than formerly by disagreement over the Federal Republic's role in the Western alliance. Whereas Americans have wanted West Germans to stand with them in a worldwide confrontation with the Soviet Union, West Germans have been more concerned with preservation of peace and stability in Central Europe through arms limitation agreements with the Soviet Union. On the other hand, West German relations with the Communist countries of Eastern Europe, while not exactly cordial, are no longer highly controversial and charged with emotions. Both sides have, in particular, come to place a good deal of value on their economic ties.

The Need for Trade

The Federal Republic's leading position in world trade is a measure of its economic strength as well as its economic vulnerability. West Germany plays a key role in international commerce and finance, but it is also highly susceptible to external political and economic developments that might undercut its vital trade ties and foreign investments.

The Federal Republic ranks second only to the United States in exports and imports (see table 3.7). Exports represent only a relatively small share of American production, but they constitute about a third of West German. Moreover, for West Germany—

TABLE 3.7

Comparison of Major Trading Countries

	G.F.R.	U.S.	JAPAN	FRANCE	U.K.	TOTAL
Exports as percentage of GDP (1981)	25.7	8.0	13.4	17.8	21.2	—
Percentage of world exports (1982)	9.7	11.6	7.6	5.1	5.5	39.5
Percentage of world imports (1982)	8.1	12.8	6.9	6.0	5.4	39.2

Source: Statistical Office of the European Communities, *Basic Statistics of the Community,* *1982–1983*, pp. 269, 271, 273.

even more than for Japan and Great Britain—the need and competition for the sale of industrial goods in foreign market is far more important than for the United States. Whereas substantial part of American exports is made up of agricultural products, those of the Federal Republic consist largely of manufactured products. More than half of its industrial production has been devoted to exports, mostly machinery, motor vehicles, and chemical products.

Imports are also far more crucial in the West German than in the American economy. Key industries in general and export industries in particular require basic foreign raw materials, such as copper and iron. In contrast to France, the Federal Republic has become increasingly dependent on agricultural imports; in contrast to Britain, it has no significant natural gas and oil resources that might diminish its reliance on foreign energy supplies; and in contrast to Japan, it has imported a substantial amount of foreign labor as we noted. For other industrialized countries and less developed nations West Germany has become a leading customer for semi-finished products and many consumer goods, such as cars, home appliances, and clothing. Foreign investments have continued to pour into the West German economy, mostly from other European countries and the United States (see table 3.8).

Foreign trade is both an objective and an instrument of West German public policies. In international relations it concerns not merely questions posed by economic cooperation and competition

TABLE 3.8

Foreign Trade and Investment Partners of the Federal Republic

COUNTRIES	TRADE 1983		INVESTMENTS 1981	
	PERCENTAGE OF GOODS EXPORTED FROM G.F.R. (DM 432.3 BILL. = 100%)	PERCENTAGE OF GOODS IMPORTED INTO G.F.R. (DM 390.4 BILL. = 100%)	PERCENTAGE OF FOREIGN INVEST- MENTS OF G.F.R. (DM 84 BILL. = 100%)	PERCENTAGE OF FOREIGN INVEST- MENTS IN G.F.R. (DM 61.7 BILL. = 100%)
U.S.	7.5	19.7	22.7	33.5
France	12.8	11.4	8.8	6.0
Netherlands	8.7	12.3	5.3	13.0
U.K.	8.1	6.9	3.4	12.3
Belgium-Luxemburg	7.3	7.1	9.8	5.6
Italy	7.4	8.0	2.9	1.0
Switzerland	5.2	3.6	7.3	15.2
Austria	5.1	3.2	2.7	n.a.
Sweden	2.6	2.1	7.3	15.2
USSR	2.5	3.0	n.a.	n.a.

Source: Calculated from data of the Federal Economic Ministry reported in *Die Zeit* May 14, 1982, and March 30, 1984.

with other states but diplomatic and military problems. In domestic politics, both specific interest group demands and more general ideological and socioeconomic cleavages are involved.

It is a generally accepted policy principle that West German economic strength, growth, and prosperity rest largely on favorable competitive conditions in world markets. The need for policies that will provide ready access to foreign customers and suppliers has been beyond dispute. All West German governments, whatever their partisan complexion, have sought to remove impediments to trade expansion. But what particular policies should be pursued to promote favorable trade conditions and obtain the best deal— and with whom and for whom—has occasionally engendered a good deal of political controversy. For example, some groups have favored international agreements that would bring in more and cheaper imports, whereas others have opposed them for fear that they would injure domestic producers. Political disputes have arisen over foreign policy priorities, especially when economic, military, and ideological objectives conflict. For example, should the need for intimate military ties with the United States override economic differences with that country? Should the Federal Republic make trade concessions to Communist countries for the sake of improved political relations? And should West Germany forgo arms exports to Arab countries because they would displease Israel?

The most important economic partners of the Federal Republic are other Western democracies, above all the United States and members of the European Community (see tables 3.8 and 3.9). The ties with the United States have been largely financial. American capital has played a major role in the Federal Republic ever since its establishment; more recent large West German investments in the United States do not loom nearly as important in the much bigger American economy. In West Germany's ties with fel-

TABLE 3.9
Direction of West German Trade, 1960–1982

	PERCENTAGE OF EXPORTS			PERCENTAGE OF IMPORTS		
	1960	1973	1982	1960	1973	1982
EC Countries[a]	29	46	47	29	51	48
United States	8	8	6	14	8	7
Other Non-Communist industrial	36	26	23	27	18	20
European Communist[b]	4	6	5	4	4	5
G.D.R. (East Germany)	2	2	2	2	2	2
Other countries	21	12	17	24	17	18
Total	100	100	100	100	100	100

Source: Calculated from data in *Statistisches Jahrbuch für die Bundesrepublik Deutschland, 1974,* pp. 306–310; German Information Center (New York) *Bulletin,* August 1983.
[a] European Community: in 1960, France, Italy, Belgium, Netherlands, Luxemburg; in 1973 also Great Britain, Ireland, and Denmark; in 1982 also Greece.
[b] USSR, Poland, Czechoslovakia, Romania, Hungary, Bulgaria.

low members of the European Community (EC) trade in commodities and in services—banking, transportation, insurance, and the like—is more significant.

Such trade increased vastly in the 1960s, in large part due to the abolition of internal custom barriers and the introduction of a Common Market tariff on imports from outside countries, and because the West Germans were cut off by the Cold War from former markets and suppliers in East Germany and Eastern Europe. As a result Common Market countries are now the most important customers and suppliers of the Federal Republic. At the same time, sales to and purchases from West Germany are also of great economic significance for those countries.

These interdependent ties have reinforced the effect of joint European Community policies on West German economic and political relations at home. For example, EC agricultural policies have catalyzed the decline in the number and political influence of West German farmers. West German policymakers, in turn, have sought wider and deeper EC ties. The government of the Federal Republic promoted and welcomed the inclusion of Britain, Denmark, and Ireland on the grounds that this would strengthen the viability and political potential of the Common Market. And it has pushed for closer collaboration among the member states in finding solutions to mutual economic problems, such as their relations with less developed countries and their differences with the United States and Japan on trade and monetary issues.

The changes in the external military and political environment that led in the early 1970s to improved diplomatic relations between West Germany and the Communist states of Eastern Europe also added a potentially significant economic element to that environment. In previous years the patterns of trade had conformed closely to prevailing East-West cleavages. Compared to the Federal Republic's extensive commercial relations with the United States and other Western industrial countries, trade with the Soviet Union and its East European allies has not been very important for the West German economy. More recently, however, West German policymakers have sought political as well as economic benefits for their country through more extensive and intensive trade relations with the Communist countries.

For their part, the Communist governments have been most ready to cooperate. Sophisticated West German industrial products and technical assistance—and bank loans to pay for them— are very much sought after in the Soviet Union and the rest of Eastern Europe. The Federal Republic has furnished the largest share of Western imports flowing into COMECON—the East European counterpart of the Common Market—including about a third of Soviet imports from non-Communist countries. Ideological differences have not stood in the way of such collaborative ventures with capitalist West German business firms as the construction of a pipeline that delivers natural gas from Russian oil fields to the Federal Republic. Under current commercial agreements, West German industry is to provide its Russian customers in coming years with substantially more steel and chemical products and advanced technology; the Federal Republic, in return, is to receive more much-needed fuel and critical raw materials from the Soviet Union.

Whether the liberalization of these trade relations and the advance of substantial purchase credits to the East European countries will pay off over the long run is a question that divides West German leaders. Some predict substantial economic benefits in the form of profitable new export markets and sources of raw materials, whereas others question the willingness and ability of the Communist countries to meet West German trade needs. Some expect that more trade will further improve political relations; others fear that it will make the Federal Republic more vulnerable to Soviet pressure and undermine its bonds with Western countries. Depending on their outlook, political and opinion leaders are therefore committed or opposed to more eastern trade, whether as an objective or as an instrument of West German foreign policy. What complicates the issue all the more is that it is inseparable from the course of so-called intra-German relations (relations with the East German Democratic Republic).

The Other Germany

The notion that someday, somehow, the former Reich might be reunified has been a constant theme with many variations in West German politics. The Basic Law calls on "the entire German people. . . to achieve in free self-determination the unity and freedom of Germany" and these words have been sung to different tunes by different singers—sometimes loudly and sometimes softly. By all present indications, reunification is, however, not even a remote possibility.

It has been more than forty years since the old Germany was divided and almost as long since the creation of its two successor states. Former political ties between East and West Germany have been severed and each has developed new and intimate bonds with other states. The Federal Republic has become an integral part of the Western NATO alliance and of the West European Community; the German Democratic Republic has been tightly integrated into the East European Communist bloc. The Democratic Republic is today a key component of the Warsaw Pact military alliance as its forward bastion in Central Europe. It is, moreover, the second largest industrial power after the Soviet Union in the East European economic community and the leading source of industrial products for the other member states. The Soviet Union is East Germany's principal customer, and East German policies are shaped by Soviet policies.

In short, the German Democratic Republic is a cornerstone of the East European Communist system, and Soviet leaders have continually emphasized the necessity of a loyal East Germany for the cohesiveness of that system. The Western associates of the Federal Republic consider West Germany no less important to their side and have shown no enthusiasm for the re-creation of a state in Central Europe that would vastly exceed—in size, population, and economic strength—all but the two superpowers. Constitutional principles notwithstanding, West German policies toward East Germany are therefore restricted.

The Federal Republic's Basic Treaty of 1972 with the Democratic Republic was an important milestone in the relationship between the two Germanies. Over vehement protests from the opposition, the government of Chancellor Willy Brandt abandoned the claim of its predecessors that the Federal Republic was the only legitimate German state and formally recognized a regime that earlier West German governments had repudiated as an illegal instrument of Soviet control over East Germany. According to the Brandt government the agreement was a necessary step in its efforts to "normalize" relations with the East European Communist states and provided the basis for closer collaboration between the two Germanies after two decades of belligerent confrontation.

For the rulers of East Germany, the treaty brought the international acceptance they had long sought. Both Germanies were admitted as equals to the United Nations and the Democratic Republic was recognized as a sovereign state by countries that had previously refused to establish diplomatic relations with it in deference to West German wishes. The treaty also provided a breakthrough from intense mutual hostility to more peaceful coexistence between the two German states. But some basic differences in the outlook of East and West German policymakers still stand in the way of closer political collaboration.

To begin with, West and East German policymakers proceed from very different positions. When the two Germanies joined the United Nations in 1973, Chancellor Brandt emphasized the goal of reunification when he declared "My people live in two states but continue to think of themselves as one nation." But the East German spokesman asserted on the same occasion that "reunification between the German Democratic Republic and the Federal Republic will never be possible." The official West German position is that the Democratic Republic is not a foreign country with a German-speaking population, like Austria, but a part of one—though for the moment politically divided—country. Common historical experiences and cultural characteristics are asserted to be stronger than political rifts between the two regimes, and economic affinity greater than ideological differences. Accordingly, West German policy has emphasized closer cultural and trade associations in what are officially designated "intra-German" rather that international relations with the Democratic Republic.

East German leaders, to the contrary, maintain that theirs is a separate country whose people are first and foremost citizens of a "socialist" state rather than brethren under the political skin of the Germans in the Federal Republic. Accordingly, they consider the political and ideological differences preeminent and emphasize East Germany's ties to other European Communist states—above all the Soviet Union.

The present East German leadership thus shares the view of those West Germans who believe that irreconcilable differences in their regimes will at best permit the two Germanies to live together but not to grow together. Hard-line Communists in the Democratic Republic, like militant anti-Communists in the Federal Republic, consider the very existence of the other political system a threat to their own and believe that German reunification will be possible only if one or the other is overthrown. Vigilance against such an event is the watchword on both sides of the border. Although the East German leadership has given overt and covert financial support to groups in the Federal Republic that want to introduce some if not all the elements of East German socialism, it has taken stringent measures against West German subversion of its own regime. In the face of West German efforts to increase private travel between the two states, the East German government has, for example, maintained severe restrictions on interpersonal contacts, in part to limit defections from the Democratic Republic and in part to keep West German agents out of the Democratic Republic. The border between the two states is heavily guarded on the East German side to prevent unauthorized crossings, and the importation and possession of illegal West German literature draws heavy penalties.

The most prominent symbol of the East German exclusion policy is the Berlin Wall—built in 1961—which divides the former capital of united Germany and cuts off East Berlin, the capital of the Democratic Republic, from West Berlin. The latter is closely linked to the Federal Republic by political and economic ties, but separated from it by 110 miles of East German territory. Its status as a nonsovereign entity under control and protection of the United States, Britain, and France was reaffirmed by a 1971 agreement between these powers and the Soviet Union, but its associations with the Federal Republic remain a point of friction between the two Germanies and their respective allies.[8] West German leaders are determined to preserve these bonds and will, for that reason, do their utmost to maintain the Western guarantees and troops that protect the city against East German efforts to change its status—a factor that plays a key role in the Federal Republic's relations with its allies. The East German leaders, on the other hand, have considered West Berlin a source of covert West German threats to their security and therefore have sought to loosen, if not sever, its ties to the Federal Republic.

None of these factors is necessarily insurmountable. Since the conclusion of the Basic Treaty of 1972 and its affirmation by the West German voters, leaders on both sides have repeatedly demonstrated a strong desire to keep military and political friction between the two Germanies at a minimum. The East German rulers seem to have become more relaxed about their relations with the Federal Republic and the status of West Berlin, and to have been compelled by economic neccessity to seek more material assistance from capitalist West Germany. West Germany policymakers, for their part, have found it politically expedient to shore up the East German economy with trade and financial benefits. An economically more secure Communist regime seems to them more prone to ease dictatorial controls in the Democratic Republic and allow closer social and cultural contacts between the "two states within one German nation."

For the Federal Republic intra-German commerce has amounted to 2 percent or less of its total trade (see table 3.9), and has been of little importance for its economy. For the Democratic Republic, however, it represents most of its trade outside the Communist bloc. The Federal Republic has become its third largest trading partner. Manufactured goods and credit arrangements provided by West Germany have played no small part in placing East Germany among the ten largest industrial countries. East

8. Under the terms of the agreements, West Berliners are represented by officials of the Federal Republic in their relations with foreign countries but by their local government in their relations with the two German states.

German exports to West Berlin and the Federal Republic, exempt from the customs levies of the European Common Market, furnish the Democratic Republic with much needed hard currency for purchases in Western markets.[9]

Whether and how the two Germanies will develop on even more harmonious relationship in the future has far-reaching implications for West German as well as international politics. Can the two rival regimes overcome basic differences or are these differences too deep and the elements for conflict too numerous? Will West Germans continue to see East German Communism as a threat to their own political order and, if so, what kind of policies will be advocated and selected to meet such a challenge? And if it should prove possible to forge closer bonds to the Democratic Republic, how will they be reconciled with the Federal Republic's membership in the Western alliance system and the European Community? If a choice must be made, which ties will appear to be the more important to the West Germans and their leaders?

9. One steady source of West German marks has been a stipulated sum which visitors from the Federal Republic must exchange for East German currency. Another has been the ransom of East German prisoners by the government of the Federal Republic. It has evidently used a secret fund for many years to buy out some 5,000 prisoners annually, paying as much as $10,000 per prisoner.

4

Political Orientations: The Collective Past and the Present Regime

The formal organization of the state and the nature of the policy environment affect political relationships and behavior according to how they are perceived and evaluated by the involved actors. That is, "objective" circumstances are "subjectively" interpreted in line with personal beliefs, values, and sentiments. A social scientist may divide the West German population into classes on the basis of official figures on income or occupational differences. But it takes a sense of class consciousness on the part of that population to translate such statistical distinctions into policy-relevant attitudes and interest alignments.

A West German's view of governmental and nongovernmental components of the political system is correspondingly shaped by his or her orientations toward the state and its regime. In aggregate, such individual orientations form the underlying psychological "climate of opinion" for West German politics, and over time they reflect continuities and changes in common attitudes. Thus, when we speak of "typical" patterns of collective political beliefs, values, and sentiments in the Federal Republic we refer to generalized habits of thought and long-range attitudinal dispositions.

Differences in the policy processes of countries with similar socioeconomic and political structures are often attributed to cultural differences. Decision making under the Japanese parliamentary system, for instance, is said to be particularly slow and cumbersome because cultural norms call for extensive consultation, and ultimate agreement, between opposing factions. And though Americans and British share to a large extent a common legal tradition, their methods of law enforcement are said to differ because Americans are more likely to resort to violence than the British.

Such cultural differences are in turn frequently associated with distinct historical memories transmitted across generations. American politics are said to reflect to this day the divisive legacy of a civil war that occurred more than a hundred years ago; British politics, centuries of constitutional continuity; and French politics, cleavages dating back to the revolution of 1789. The question before us, then, is to what extent and in what manner "unique" historical experiences have a bearing on contemporary West German politics.

HISTORICAL OBJECT LESSONS

West Germans, like other people, perceive and react to contemporary events in terms of past experiences and transmitted history. For example, we noted that memories of past wars and their destructiveness have led to strong pacifist sentiments in the Federal Republic. Such "lessons of history" as West Germans derive from what they believe to have happened in earlier times—what they personally remember and what they have been taught—provide guidelines for their political thoughts and actions. To some degree at least their expectations and their views about present developments represent negative or positive reactions to a shared historical legacy. For some the collective past is rather blurred and forms only vague pictures in their minds. For others it provides sharply engraved images that serve as reference points for their political attitudes and behavior.

For most West Germans, firsthand political experiences do not extend back much further than the lifetime of the Federal Republic. When it was founded, most of its citizens were old enough to remember living under at least one other regime, but by now two out of three were then at most children (see table 4.1). They

TABLE 4.1

*Age Distribution of the West German Population, 1950 and 1981
(in rounded-off percentages)*

	AGE					
YEAR	UNDER 15	15–20	21–44	45–59	60–	TOTAL
1950	23.3	8.7	34.1	19.9	14.0	100.0
1981	17.2	10.3	34.5	18.4	19.6	100.0

Source: *Statistisches Jahrbuch für Bundesrepublik Deutschland, 1983*, p. 62.

must therefore depend on the testimony of others for information about what happened previously. Some of this testimony might come from those who are old enough to remember what they saw and were taught in earlier times. But for the most part, and to an increasing extent, West Germans must rely on written history, especially for information on their collective past before the beginning of the present century.

What sort of clues can West Germans derive from their transmitted past for what they should do and expect in contemporary politics? Perhaps the most basic lesson conveyed by most of their history books is that political controversies can lead to pathological conflicts but that autocracy is no cure. They can learn that the "German people" were divided for centuries by profound cultural differences and fratricidal conflicts and were only briefly united in a single state. The Protestant Reformation of the sixteenth century provoked long and bitter religious wars, and political controversies that extended into the twentieth century; the particularism of innumerable princely states—and the policies of more united countries, such as France and England—prevented the unification of "the Germanies" until it was achieved through war in the late nineteenth century. Then, the industrialization of united Germany led to two military catastrophes and intense political conflicts between rural and urban interests, employers and employees, and ideological factions committed to sharply divergent, exclusive dogmas.

Their history books also tell West Germans that the management of domestic and foreign conflicts became identified with a powerful state, strong executive leadership, weak legislatures, and minimal popular participation in policymaking. Except in some of the German cities, autocracy was the rule and majoritarian government the exception. The principles of government usually exalted the need for political order and stability in the state and assigned the formulation and enforcement of rigid legal norms to paternalistic public authorities. Harmonious relationships among individuals and groups were to be ensured more through suppression than through the free expression of differences, and more through popular compliance with formal rules handed down to them than through a popular consensus based on political bargaining among the people and their elected representatives.

Imperial Germany

A popularly chosen assembly of liberal democratic intellectuals failed to establish a united Germany governed by elected leaders in the mid-nineteenth century. The effort was ridiculed by conservative monarchists and frustrated by their superior military power. When unification finally came in 1871 it was imposed through a policy of "blood and iron" (war and force) identified with Otto von Bismarck, the founding father of Imperial Germany.

Formally a federation and a parliamentary monarchy, the German empire (1871–1918) was in fact a thinly disguised autocracy controlled by the rulers of Prussia, its most powerful member state. Under the constitutional order devised by Bismarck, Prussia's prime minister, and Imperial Germany's "Iron Chancellor," the authoritarian Prussian regime was superimposed on the new political system. The Hohenzollern king of Prussia was also the emperor of Germany, the Prussian military establishment controlled the German armed forces, and the "nonpartisan" Prussian bureaucracy became the classic model for the German civil service. The popularly elected Imperial Diet was for the most part little more than a democratic fig leaf that barely concealed the naked exercise of political power by Prussia's landed aristocrats and big businessmen.

The elitist rule of this civil-military oligarchy was supported by rigid social stratification patterns anchored in law, and legitimated by prevailing political orientations. For nearly half a century Germans were imbued with the notion that only a powerful imperial state could safeguard the unity and survival of their national community and protect it against internal and external enemies. German political and legal philosophy glorified a personified state. Liberty was associated with the freedom of the state from restraints on its organic growth, and not with the freedom of the individual Germans to pursue their private interests. The principal duty of all members of the state was said to be service to the German nation. Political parties intervening between the patriarchal German family and the sovereign state were declared to be unimportant, if not disruptive elements in public affairs. From this point of view public authority was exercised by the executive and administrative officials (Obrigkeit) who served the interests of the state rather than the people. The role assigned to the ordinary citizen was that of the state's law-abiding subject (Untertan).

Over the objections of a small minority of nonconformist liberal democrats and the leaders of the emerging socialist labor movement, every German was taught these principles in the schools of Imperial Germany. Every conscript in its mass armies was indoctrinated with them, clergymen preached them in the churches, and the nationalist conservative press fed them to its readers. The cultural product was a deeply ingrained political orientation that gave support to the Imperial regime. Most Germans either could not or would not see its structural weaknesses and accepted it more or less enthusiastically. The world prestige, military might, and

industrial growth and economic prosperity of Imperial Germany
were taken as proof that its autocratic structures worked as well,
if not better than, Western parliamentary systems.

Contemporary West Germans have been taught that the Imperial regime failed to facilitate the smooth integrations of preindustrial habits of thought and action with those produced by the
industrialization of Germany. At home, cleavages among a plurality of interest groups were obscured rather than alleviated; in
foreign affairs rational calculations yielded to nationalist emotions. Bismarck's design for internal and international conflict
management—tailored to fit the man rather than his formal position—worked reasonably well for the twenty years he was in
charge of its execution. But thereafter the attempt to fuse traditional conservatism with integral nationalism under the auspices
of an autocratic state proved increasingly unequal to internal and
external pressures. The policymaking stratum effectively resisted
domestic demands for democratic reforms and committed the
country to a foreign policy that exceeded its capabilities. The
constitutional order underwent no substantial adaptive changes
until 3 million German lives had been lost in World War I and
defeat was imminent. By then political disintegration had pro-
ceeded too far to reform the system, and the Imperial regime
collapsed in 1918.

Republican Germany

The second attempt to establish a democratic regime in a united
Germany was initiated in 1919 by a popularly elected constitutional assembly meeting in the little town of Weimar. The framers
of the new political order were for the most part democratic socialists and liberals who believed that government should rest on
the consent of the governed and compromise between political
factions. The experiment did not work, and the fourteen years of
the Weimar Republic are presented to contemporary West Germans as an object lesson in the failure of democracy in Germany.
The Weimar regime got off to a bad start. By some accounts it was
a stillbirth. According to others the regime died in infancy because

it lacked the strength to surmount conditions unfavorable to its institutionalization.

With the collapse of the Imperial regime, responsibility for making peace and establishing a new political order was suddenly thrust on its former critics, who had no governmental experience. Confronted by chaotic conditions at home and harsh demands from the victor power, their most immediate concerns were the establishment of their policymaking authority and the revival of a war-shattered economy. And for that they felt compelled to rely on the business leaders and officialdom of Imperial Germany. The Hohenzollern monarchy was abolished, but key positions in the economy, the armed forces, the judiciary, and the public administration remained in the hands of supporters of the old regime. In that sense the so called revolution of 1918 did not produce any basic changes, as the American and French revolutions did, nor did it mark the beginning of a gradual democratization, as did the English revolution of 1688.

The subsequent fourteen years of the Weimar era proved to be only a stormy interlude between two autocracies. The regime was often shaken by insurrections and assassinations directed against the democratic order and by politically destabilizing socioeconomic crises. In calmer times political stability rested on a fragile standoff between traditionalist and modernizing elements among a deeply divided people struggling along the road from a preindustrial to a full-blown industrial society. The complex constitutional arrangements for conflict management worked badly in a highly fragmented political system. The Weimar constitution turned out to be an unsuccessful compromise between libertarian and egalitarian principles, between a unitary and a federal state, between a parliamentary and a presidential system, and between representative and direct democracy.

The formal system of checks and balances required an underlying popular consensus and, even more importantly, a basic willingness among the ruling groups to support the regime and to accept the legitimacy of its rules for the making and implementing of public policies. As it was, no generally acceptable political formula could be found that would overcome deep ideological divisions within the policymaking stratum and reconcile the divergent beliefs, values, and sentiments of encapsulated socioeconomic and religious subcultures.

The still extremely powerful remnants of the preindustrial aristocracy, entrenched in the army and civil service, sought overtly and covertly to restore princely particularism—especially in Bavaria—or the autocratic regime of the Hohenzollern empire. Big business increasingly favored a nationalist autocracy that would suppress the trade unions of the industrial workers and promote German economic imperialism. Leaders of feuding interest associations representing salaried employees, farmers, artisans, and small shopkeepers wanted a strong national government that would save their clientele from the socioeconomic effects of advancing industrialization.

Influential opinion makers—such as journalists, teachers, and clergymen—either were opposed to the Weimar regime from its inception or became alienated because it failed to live up to their perfectionist standards. Their frequently savage criticism implied or declared openly that another, more or less democratic regime could do a better job in meeting governmental responsibility for the welfare of the state, the nation, or the masses. The alleged neglect of such abstractions by Weimar governments was commonly advanced by the self-appointed spokesmen for the army, the judiciary, the public administration, and other governmental and nongovernmental groups to justify their opposition to the democratic constitutional order and their frequent defiance of the elected political leaders of the republic.

Party governments were unstable during the Weimar Republic and constantly shifting single-issue parliamentary coalitions proved to be brittle alignments. In fourteen years there were twenty-one national governments, most of which did not last more than six months, and eight national elections in which no party ever won an absolute parliamentary majority. The leaders of the large number of parliamentary parties were deeply divided over the proper scope, form, and functions of state and government and could not agree on enduring solutions to pressing policy problems.

Instead of producing compromise agreements on controversial issues, the Weimar regime intensified friction among socioeconomic, religious, and political factions. The liberal democratic alternative to an authoritarian system became increasingly discredited in the eyes of Germans who had learned to look to the state for authoritative guidance and expected its leaders to ensure order and harmony in society. The average citizen shunned the participant roles which were provided for him by the Weimar constitution, except when he was mobilized by political activists to exercise his voting rights in plebiscites and elections.

To an increasing extent these activists were radical opponents of the regime who used their constitutional liberties to bring about its destruction. The Communists on the extreme left promoted political instability in the hope that chaos would lead to a "proletarian" dictatorship; the Nazis on the extreme right pursued a similar strategy toward the establishment of a fascist dictatorship. In the last years of the Weimar Republic these otherwise irreconcilable parties would occasionally join forces against the defenders of the liberal democratic regime, most notably the Social Democratic party. By November 1932, 17 percent of the voters supported the Communists and 33 percent Hitler's National Socialists.

Perhaps, as some historians have maintained, more time and fewer critical pressures might have allowed the development of more supportive political orientations. As it was, a growing sense of fatalism undermined the determination of the regime's defenders and played into the hands of its opponents. "We were at the mercy of events," the leaders of the Social Democratic party argued when Hitler assumed power in 1933.

Nazi Germany

A highly negative picture of Germany under the dictatorship of Adolf Hitler has been employed by West German opinion leaders to build support for the political system of the Federal Republic. The Nazi regime (1933—45) is invoked as a standard for comparison between a frightful past and a far more congenial present,

and as a warning of what may befall West Germans if they should
fail to give firm allegiance to the present political order. At most
a fifth of them are old enough to draw comparisons on the strength
of personal experiences under both regimes. For those who are
too young to have such firsthand knowledge of Nazi Germany
there is a vast literature of memoirs and historical studies that
demonstrate the evil consequences of blind faith in arbitrary
leadership.

Hitler, it now appears, had nothing but contempt for the German people. But he successfully exploited mass feelings of discontent and strong romantic, escapist sentiments produced by the
cumulative effects of military defeat in World War I and subsequent socioeconomic crises in the Weimar era. He played on these
emotions and integrated them by promising magical escape from
national humiliation and distress; and an increasing number of
Germans came to believe him. As a charismatic leader Hitler
became the symbol of salvation for millions who were alienated
from an increasingly urbanized and industrialized environment,
particularly young people and impoverished small farmers, artisans, and shopkeepers. But though the head of the National Socialist German Labor Party publicly denounced the plutocratic
enemies of "the German national community," he simultaneously
sought and gained the implicit support of business leaders and
other elite groups who wanted a more autocratic form of government than the Weimar regime.

Mass and elite dissatisfaction with the Weimar system finally
came to a head in a severe economic crisis that caused mass unemployment, destitution, and desperation and paved the way for
Hitler's "legal" accession in 1933. The prevailing climate of opinion allowed him to gain "temporary" dictatorial powers that he
claimed he needed to provide full employment, stability, unity, and
order. Hitler's confident cry "Give me four years time and you
won't recognize Germany" held out the hope of satisfying very
diverse values and inspired heterogeneous elements with the idea
that Hitler's "new" Germany would correspond to their particular
vision of what it should and would be like.

Very quickly, a leader who had never obtained the endorsement of a majority of the voters in a free election effected a dramatic shift in political opinion and gained the enthusiastic support of most Germans, primarily on the strength of negative memories of the Weimar regime and utopian expectations about the future. The Protestant Prussian aristocracy had visions of a return to the "glorious times" of the Hohenzollern Empire, while the leaders of the Roman Catholic church were encouraged to accept the Nazi regime by its treaty with the Vatican, granting their church privileges that they had sought in vain from Weimar governments. The paramilitary storm troopers who had fought Hitler's street battles expected to take control of the army, while the old military elite looked forward to building a new military establishment unencumbered by the "fetters" placed on German rearmament under the Weimar regime. Leading industrialists were cheered by the abolition of trade unions, while small businessmen and farmers expected that their interests would be served by the elimination of "Jewish capitalists" from German economic life. Nationalists were stirred by Hitler's spectacular successes in foreign policy, and anti-Communists applauded his destruction of the left-wing parties. Senior civil servants welcomed the elimination of parliamentary controls and the concentration of executive power in one hand, while young people looked to Hitler to realize their romantic dreams of a new German society released from the formalistic restraints of the past.

Hitler skillfully exploited this euphoric mood to consolidate his power. He destroyed the parties and interest associations of the Weimar Republic and transformed surviving formal structures into instruments of his personal rule. Respected governmental agencies like the public administration and the judiciary, as well as the "unofficial" terror and propaganda apparatus of the Nazi movement, were used to eliminate or gravely weaken competing groups, such as the churches and the aristocratic officer corps, which might deny the leader the absolute loyalty of his subjects. Big business was the notable exception in this process of "coordination" and was left pretty much unscathed to build Hitler's war machine.

As soon as Hitler took over he set out to establish a new political

82   POLITICAL ORIENTATIONS

order built around the mythical notion of a German "people's community" from which Jews and other "inferior non-German races" were excluded. As Joseph Goebbels, the head of a newly created Ministry for Propaganda and People's Enlightenment, proclaimed in 1933: "The people shall begin to think uniformly, react uniformly, and put themselves at the disposal of the Government with full sympathy."[1] In the new autocratic "leader-state" all boundaries between state and society, and between political and nonpolitical roles, were to be eradicated. The new political system was to reflect solely the spirit of the national collectivity as articulated by its omnipotent leader. "Hitler is Germany and Germany is Hitler" was the slogan chanted in unison by the thousands at huge, carefully staged rallies and echoed all over the country from millions of loudspeakers. Belligerent nationalism, anti-Semitism, and radical romanticism were incorporated into a rather vague Nationalist Socialist ideology based on Hitler's speeches and writings and focused on the secular godhead.

For twelve years the political attitudes and emotions of the German masses were most effectively shaped by the agents of the Nazi regime. The political orientations taught in schools and in mass organizations, in the conscript army and labor service, in prisons and in concentration camps, established or reinforced hierarchical relationships of strict command and unquestioning obedience. The anti-Semitic image of the Jews, who were made the scapegoats for all ills, became a stereotype that was accepted readily and widely. Though Hitler did not publicize his "final solution of the Jewish problem," not many Germans worried about their Jewish neighbors' disappearance. A few abortive attempts to overthrow Hitler—most notably toward the end when he had lost World War II—did not involve more than a handful of conspirators.

The myth of the leader's unfailing intuition helped to sustain the regime until its destruction by foreign armies. Studies of German civilian and military morale during World War II show that even as bombing attacks were devastating the country and casual-

1. Quoted in Marlis G. Steinert, *Hitlers Krieg und die Deutschen: Stimmung und Haltung der deutschen Bevölkerung im Zweiten Weltkrieg* (Düsseldorf–Vienna: Econ, 1970), p. 30.

ties were mounting into the millions, mass support for the Nazi regime and mass compliance with the commands of its leader maintained domestic stability. Criticism was directed against obviously false propaganda, and against secondary Nazi leaders who were blamed for unpopular actions ordered by Hitler. But until the day of his suicide in 1945, the Führer's personal image remained untarnished in the eyes of most of his subjects. Fervent believers in his magic gifts kept faith to the very end, trusting that their charismatic leader would somehow turn the tide by some miracle or wonder weapon.

After Hitler's fall, West Germans were informed, first by foreign occupation powers and then by their new political leaders, that the supposed unity of the Nazi regime was a most costly illusion created by its monopolistic propaganda machine. They have been taught that the trust which subjects had placed in their autocratic leader was undeserved and that those who willingly danced to his tune ultimately had to pay dearly for it.

The overt totalitarian cohesion of Nazi Germany concealed the failure of its control apparatus to penetrate deeply and radically alter the underlying socioeconomic structure. Not only was the timespan too brief, but the man on the top did not establish the promised "new" Germany. From the beginning to end Nazi policymaking contained pluralist features that limited Hitler's power. Even if he had wanted to, he could not have followed up the atomization of the pre-Nazi organization of political life with enduring new cultural and social patterns. Conflict management was personalized rather than institutionalized, and one-man rule accentuated rather than eliminated competition and conflict among leading members of various hierachical segments of the Nazi system.

Essentially the Hitler dictatorship sought to manage Germany's continuing transition from a preindustrial to an advanced industrial society. But the Führer's erratic and intuitive style of government, as well as the organization of his leadership state, caused destabilizing tensions in Nazi Germany that became more pronounced as its fortunes declined. The one-sidedness of political communications in a system resting on command and obedience, and the dualism of governmental and Nazi party structures, led to widespread uncertainties about what kind of compliant behavior was expected, and to bitter jurisdictional disputes among the elites who were supposed to execute Hitler's orders faithfully.

In every sphere of public life, decision-making authority formally descended from the dictator, in his dual capacity as chief of state and leader of the Nazi movement, to thousands of subordinate Nazi potentates, military commanders, and public administrators. However, these offical lines of command were deliberately obscured and often bypassed by Hitler who had the habit of unexpectedly reversing his previous decisions without explanation. The nature of his regime encouraged not only blind obedience, but "buck-passing." Although Hitler demanded and received the blind trust of the common people, he himself trusted only his dog and his mistress. Even his closest associates labored under the constant threat of sudden disgrace in a regime marked by arbitrary decisions affecting life, liberty, and status. The irrational, emotional, and antiformalist components of the Nazi system precluded the predictable, rational policy processes that are the requisite of a smoothly functioning political system in an industrialized society. "The revolution of nihilism" described by one perceptive observer at an early stage of Hitler's rule led eventually to anarchic conditions in the conduct of government and culminated in complete disintegration in 1945.[2]

The Postwar Era

With the collapse of Hitler's regime in 1945 began the third attempt to establish a liberal democratic Germany. "The year zero," as it came to be called, is now proclaimed as the start of an entirely new political beginning. It brought a great mass awakening from the dreams and nightmares of the Nazi regime, along with a sobering hangover. American, British, and French military governments assumed jurisdiction over what was to become, four

2. Hermann Rauschning, *The Revolution of Nihilism* (New York: Longmans, Green, 1939).

years later, the Federal Republic and set out to teach a disillusioned, cynical people their versions of democracy.

The foreign occupation powers sought above all to remove what they took to be the principal elements of Nazi political and military power. Measures were taken to completely eradicate German authoritarian traditions and and permanently eliminate from positions of status and influence individuals and groups believed to have been prominent in the Nazi regime or indirectly responsible for it. Not only surviving Nazi party leaders, but also civil and military officials, business managers, journalists, and educators considered members of the former ruling elites were purged.

The victors' authoritative decisions were based on a punitive policy toward a people held collectively responsible for the actions of the Nazi regime, and reflected an "enlightened depotism" aimed at preventing future German aggression. War crimes trials, denazification proceedings, educational reforms, dismantling of industrial plants for reparation payments, and the carefully controlled reconstruction of political structures were the means used by the three occupation powers to implement these policies.

At the same time, ostensible anti-Nazis and non-Nazis were encouraged to assume responsibility for the implementation of the military government directives and the gradual development of a Western-type liberal democracy under foreign tutelage. Such benevolent sponsorship, however, did not extend to Germans who had different notions about the best way to create a lasting democratic regime and who demanded more profound socioeconomic changes and a greater part in political reconstruction. The political duty assigned Germans during this period of imposed denazification and democratization was to obey commands, a duty they had become quite used to. Most of them had no difficulty in accepting the directives of their new rulers and adapting to foreign control.

As noted in the preceding chapter, economic recovery and social reorganization began about 1948 and developed rapidly in the following decade, along with the recovery of German political influence. As tensions between Western and Soviet leaders increased, foreign supervision and intervention in West German political affairs decreased. The establishment of the Federal Republic in 1949 terminated Western punitive and tutelary efforts, war crimes trials came to an end, and political decision making was gradually handed over entirely to German leaders. The new policy was to woo the West Germans into a voluntary and intimate partnership against the Soviet bloc by providing them with economic assistance and military protection, and by encouraging anti-Soviet opinion and behavior.

West Germans now learned that they could expect very tangible rewards—such as complete sovereignty, achieved in 1955—in return for demonstrations of their reliability as anti-Communist partners of the West and of the stability of their new political system. Such lessons, combined with the effect of socioeconomic recovery, enormously strengthened the position of leaders who took over the direction of political reconstruction from the Western military governments—above all, Konrad Adenauer, chancellor of the Federal Republic from its inception until 1963. They rallied elite and mass opinion behind their efforts to institutionalize the new regime and give it legitimacy at home as well as abroad.

Whereas the first fifteen postwar years are now recalled as a very demanding and difficult time for most West Germans, the next fifteen are remembered as a period of rising prosperity, political stability, and social progress. The Federal Republic became a leader in European and world politics and was termed a model for less successful Western countries. From about the mid-1970s onward, however, economic stagnation and political unrest gave rise to a less rosy picture and the earlier euphoria was replaced by more pessimistic attitudes about West Germany's future.

The Legacy of the Past

What do West Germans make of their transmitted history and what have they learned from the object lessons presented by former regimes? Have they inherited not just their forebears' land and language but also their political orientations? Do they look back in longing for "the good old days" when Germany was a powerful nation-state?

On the evidence of opinion polls, elections, and similar expressions of public sentiment, West Germans—and particularly young West Germans—appear to have made a conspicuous break with their autocratic past. Unpleasant memories of former regimes provide general support for present political order. Its extremist critics are identified with the antidemocratic forces that destroyed the Weimar Republic; for practically all West Germans the changes advocated by such radicals evidently do not represent desirable alternative arrangements

According to opinion polls three out of four West Germans condemn the Nazi regime without reservations; some—mostly older people—hold that it might not have been so bad had Hitler not persecuted the Jews and brought about World War II. But there is no denying the Holocaust and German culpability for other Nazi crimes. And, in striking contrast to the Weimar era, war and defeat are now widely attributed to the previous regime and its leader, and not to pernicious internal traitors and external enemies or to uncontrollable events.

For most West Germans such evaluations are, however, based on increasingly vague and emotionally detached perceptions of the Nazi era. Occasionally a dramatic confrontation with that past, such as films about the Holocaust on television, will lead to a good deal of public soul-searching. But generally West Germans have become gradually more relaxed and less defensive about what happened under Hitler's rule. As political wounds that still festered at home and abroad during the 1950s and 1960s have healed and ceased to cause pain and discomfort, they have also become less conspicuous scars on the body politic.

In part this is attributable to the passage of time and the disappearance of a generation whose members were directly involved in the Nazi regime as its victims, opponents, or supporters. What in the first two decades of the Federal Republic had been the problem of the "unresolved" Nazi past is thus being resolved by the natural course of events. In part, too, divisive sentiments have waned due to governmental policies designed to put to rest the Nazi legacy of persecution and aggression. The politico-cultural restraints that this legacy had earlier imposed on the "normalization" of domestic and foreign relations have largely been lifted, and in the view of most West Germans the inherited moral debt has been more than paid off through generous restitution payments and territorial adjustments. Accordingly, they no longer think it necessary to make reparations on demand and to refrain from criticizing what they consider Nazi-like actions in other countries.

This diminishing sense of personal identification with the Third Reich may explain a seemingly contradictory phenomenon. In recent years newspaper articles, books, and films about Hitler and his regime have found a wide audience in West Germany. "Insider" accounts are particularly "good copy" for enterprising journalists; not long ago a leading magazine spent millions to buy what turned out to be a fake diary of the late Führer. Some West Germans and foreigners with still vivid recollections of his crimes have found this alarming, fearing a Nazi revival built around a Hitler cult, similar to the Bonapartist legend that allowed a second Napoleon to come to power in France thirty-five years after the fall of the first.

But rather than indicating widespread sentiment for a return to a glorious past, the popularity of such accounts appears to reflect more a morbid curiosity about and horrid fascination with a man pictured as an evil genius by his erstwhile associates. The one-time leader of the Nazi youth movement, for example, described Hitler as "a fabulous monster" and the Führer's former architect wrote of his overpowering personal magnetism. For elderly West Germans who in their youth had blindly worshiped Hitler from afar these revelations by men once close to him may also serve to explain and excuse their own culpability to the younger generations. A German psychiatrist had earlier attributed the Nazi generation's failure to acknowledge its guilt for Hitler and his crimes to "an inability to mourn" and repent. New evidence that the "little people" in Nazi Germany could not have known then what is known now many provide another mode of liberation from the spectres of the past.

For the postwar generations, whose members have no reason to feel personally responsible for what happened, Hitler poses no such problem. Hitlerism stands as a warning symbol for terror and tyranny, but the Führer himself has become a blurred figure some forty years after his suicide. Middle-aged West Germans tend to dismiss him as a deluded autocrat who led his people into catastrophe. Younger people are more prone to place the blame on the entire totalitarian system and right-wing elements that brought it to power.

In contemporary West German politics the legacy of the past is on occasion invoked in the sometimes heated rhetoric of partisan disputes. Staunch proponents of the prevailing system refer to conditions under earlier regimes in order to demonstrate that the present one has provided West Germany with unprecedented freedom, affluence, and tranquility. Radical social critics, on the other hand, use history to show that changes in regimes have produced no appreciable changes in the inequitable distribution of power, benefits, and burdens. Conservatives accuse "left-wing agitators" of seeking to whip up emotional mass support with Nazi-like demagoguery, and they, for their part, are charged by their opponents with using "Gestapo" methods to stifle dissent in the name of law and order.

The purported "lessons of history," however, are preached to a largely indifferent public. For most West Germans the Hitler period and earlier eras represent closed chapters in their collective past and offer few specific guidelines for their views contemporary politics. Some young people have derived a rather depressing sense of historical continuity in postwar Germany from accounts of the seamier side of socioeconomic and political recovery by social critics such as the novelists Heinrich Böll and Günther Grass and the filmmaker Werner Fassbinder. But for most conditions in former times appear to be of little relevance to current political issues and evocations of the past more of a hindrance than a help in dealing with the "here and now." The question for West Germans con-

cerned with their wellbeing—and that of their friends and families—is not so much whether the present is better or worse than
the past, but whether the future will be better or worse than the
present.

THE INSTITUTIONALIZATION
OF THE POLITICAL SYSTEM

When the Federal Republic was established in 1949, the new state
and regime were superimposed on political orientations shaped
by close to a century of mostly autocratic rule in a united Germany,
and the outcome of this grafting operation was by no means certain. As we observed in the second chapter, the new political order
was handed down by the foreign occupation powers and their
German collaborators—ostensibly as a temporary arrangement
pending the reunification of a divided country—and it was not
submitted to the test of a popular referendum. The constitutional
principles of a "democratic and social federal state" remained to
be "bought" by the affected population, and prevailing political
orientations gave no assurance that this would be the case.

The founders of the Federal Republic sought to establish a
supportive consensus by legal engineering. They combined innovative with traditional organizational principles in the Basic Law
and set forth constitutional norms which, they hoped, would in
time lead to the institutionalization of the new regime. The Basic
Law was thus designed to educate as well as regulate West Germans. By following its precepts faithfully they were expected in
time to embrace the constitutional order wholeheartedly as the
only conceivable way of dealing with public policy matters.

These efforts to reshape political orientations seem to have
borne fruit. In striking contrast to the dissension that doomed the
Weimar Republic, both leading and supporting players appear
today to accept the legitimacy of the constitutional order not just
in theory but in practice. The game of politics is played in the
Federal Republic pretty much as the formal rules say it should be
played. Expressions of dissatisfaction focus mostly on particular
features of the political system rather than on the entire system.

And it also seems that on the whole West German attitudes toward the legally constituted state and regime have come to transcend purely nominal commitments and to incorporate more enduring attachments.

Conceptions of the State

Political reconstruction in the early years of the Federal Republic, like economic reconstruction, was not so much an entirely new beginning as a process of reorganization and, to some extent, restoration. As in the initial phase of the Weimar Republic, the new political leadership considered it above all necessary to provide for orderly legal procedures in the state. But this time the shattering of earlier authority patterns—begun by Hitler and carried forward by the occupation powers—as well as a more favorable climate of elite and mass opinion, made it easier to institute a new Rechtstaat, a state governed under law rather than by capricious rulers. In the German political tradition the rule of law over men was identified with legal principles that accentuated highly formalized and hierarchical authority relationships in the organization of the state, and explicit, as well as comprehensive codes of political conduct.

The incorporation of these notions into the constitutional theory and practice of the new political order appears to have greatly facilitated the acculturation of West Germans to its innovative features. The liberal democratic norms of the Basic Law deemphasize state control over the citizenry and call for public policies that are the product of peaceful bargaining and compromise among law-abiding members of a pluralist society. In this respect the state provides the organizational means for the adoption and enforcement of governmental decisions that flow from the resolution of legitimate conflict. At the same time the Basic Law accommodates the beliefs that the state is more than its parts and that its interests are broader and more enduring than those of particular parties, pressure groups, and politicians. In this sense public authorities are responsible for the collective welfare of present and future citizens of the Federal Republic, and must safeguard societal harmony and stability.

Over the years both concepts of the state have been accommodated in evolving political orientations. West Germans have learned to evaluate the operation of their governmental system in terms of the liberal democratic norms of the Basic Law. They have therefore come to see the choice of policies and policymakers as largely the outcome of an interplay among a plurality of elites, parties, interest associations, and voters. But West Germans still look beyond these groups to the authority of the state as the supreme guardian of law and order and ultimate arbiter of socioeconomic conflicts.

In current West German usage, "the state" has a rather different meaning than it has for Americans. When "the state" is said to do this, or is called on to do that, more often than not the association is with something more than the government and something different from the country. What the state "does" is rather vaguely perceived by most West Germans not so much as an expression of the will of the people but as the action of an abstract organizational entity. It is not an object of love or hate, of feelings of loyalty or alienation; it is something like a giant impersonal corporation with its managers (government), supervisory board of directors (parliament), and administrative staff (civil service). The average citizen appears in this view as a rather poorly informed small stockholder who may elect the directors but not control the management, who may or may not get efficient corporate services, and who gets whatever share of the profits the management considers his due. Members of the policymaking stratum are correspondingly perceived as large stockholders who know more and can do more about corporate policies and, therefore, who receive a disproportionate share of the profits and services. Policy processes are thus evaluated in essentially economic terms, the state distributing goods and services in exchange for payments rendered—such as taxes and other citizenship duties—with some people getting more and some paying more than others.

Though such orientations still retain elements of the traditional German idealization of the state as a guardian and provider, they have become increasingly business-like and pragmatic. The prevailing view of a state under law implies a contractual relationship between state and citizens based on reciprocal legal obligations. West Germans accept the constitutional principle of the supremacy of public over private interest, but in return they expect the state to provide for domestic harmony and stability, for their economic and social welfare, and for their physical security.

Perceptions of Political Authority

In every political system the effective exercise of public authority rests on a mixture of coercive control by the governors and voluntary compliance on the part of the governed. As the ruled comply more readily and habitually with the decisions of their rulers those rulers will have less need for coercive measures.

In the Federal Republic constitutional and legal arrangements for the exercise of political authority by responsible elected and appointed public officials have over the years become imbedded in West German political orientations. Consequently the ruling elites of the policymaking stratum can normally expect popular compliance with the decisions of the executive, legislative, and judicial agencies of the state.

Unlike their forebears, contemporary West Germans do not simply consider it their civic duty to be deferential, passive, and quiescent subjects. The days are past when German leaders could command popular obedience merely by virtue of holding positions of public authority. Younger West Germans feel particularly free to criticize public officials and policies and to voice their objections to governmental laws and regulations they consider unfair or unreasonable. Agents of the state are expected to adhere to the rules of the constitutional order and to meet exacting popular standards of political propriety and efficient performance.

Governmental interference in matters that the Basic Law declares to be none of the business of the state and violations of the legal rights of West Germans by public officials have at times provoked strong and effective public protests. The dockets of the constitutional and administrative courts are always crowded with the complaints of ordinary citizens and private organizations who seek redress for wrongs allegedly committed by public officials. Investigative reporters are continually looking for cases of official malfeasance, and governmental authorities have learned to be very careful of what they do for fear of exposure in the public media. Elected officials have become much more aware of the voters' grievances, and members of the executive branches of the federal, state, and local governments have found it advisable to pay close heed to legislators voicing complaints on behalf of their constituents.

In the last analysis, however, most West Germans accept the legitimacy of the prevailing patterns of political authority. Normative standards for evaluating the political propriety and competence of the rulers have changed and continue to change, and they vary a good deal among different socioeconomic strata, age groups, and partisan alignments. However, the dynamics of change in political attitudes and shifting subcultural cleavages have not led to widespread popular disaffection from the regime and to mass civil disobedience. Quite to the contrary, the longer the regime has been in existence the more firmly have its basic organizational principles defined legitimate authority patterns for the general public.

According to opinion surveys, many West-Germans were rather ambivalent about their new political system until the 1960s; since then practically all appear to have been generally satisfied with it. On the more particular issue of the way democratic processes operate in the Federal Republc public contentment has not been quite as widespread, but still very substantial. As shown in table 4.2 and the first item in table 4.3, about seven out of ten have expressed satisfaction in various surveys—more than in other major liberal democracies—and this favorable evaluation has been made by West German adults of all ages.

Public opinion surveys also indicate that West Germans quite realistically perceive authority relationships in the Federal Republic as rather rigidly dividing the rulers from the ruled. For example, two out of three adults of all ages maintained in 1982 that they had no direct influence over what their government did (see table 4.3)—more than in the United States but the same as in a

TABLE 4.2

Satisfaction with the Way Democracy Works in Own Country, 1973–1983
(mass opinion data in rounded-off percentages)

	1973		1978		1983	
	SATIS-FIED	DISSATIS-FIED	SATIS-FIED	DISSATIS-FIED	SATIS-FIED	DISSATIS-FIED
Federal Republic	44	55	76	19	66	24
Great Britain	44	54	62	31	61	32
France	41	46	49	40	46	43

Source: Commission of the European Communities, *Euro-barometre,* December 1981, December 1983.
Note: "Don't know" and no-answer responses have been omitted from table.

1971 West German poll. Now as then most West Germans believe that major political decisions are made by a few powerful leaders and then handed down to the relatively impotent multitude through governmental channels. Roughly seven out of ten people, and more among the more poorly educated older generations, considered politics beyond their understanding in the early 1980s—about the same proportion as in the United States and Japan (see table 4.3).

Public policymaking in the Federal Republic involves conflict, bargaining, and compromise among manifold leadership groups inside and outside governmental bodies. At that level, as we shall see, the political system serves primarily to reconcile competing policy demands before the authoritative policymakers arrive at a final decision. But most of the people, who are largely excluded from these processes, see the political system principally in terms of its effects—what it does for them and to them. They therefore tend to evaluate the performance of the constitutional order not so much by its democratic principles as by the evident consequences of governmental action or inaction in domestic and foreign affairs.

Perceptions of the Citizen's Roles

To most West Germans the formal rules of the political system today largely define the legitimate roles that an ordinary citizen can and should play in public affairs. In this regard cultural tra-

TABLE 4-3

Political Attitude of Adults by Age Groups in West Germany, the United States, and Japan, 1980–1981

(mass opinion data in rounded-off percentages)

Age Group	All adults			Young adults (18–39 yrs.)			Middle-aged (40–59 yrs.)			Young-old (60–69 yrs.)			Old-old (70 yrs. & over)		
Country	GFR	US	JP	GFR	US	JP	GFR	US	JP	GFR	US	JP	GFR	US	JP
Number in sample	1651	1680	2544	685	762	1190	598	484	928	204	232	266	162	197	160
Q: Are you satisfied with the way democracy works in this country?															
Yes	67	77	52	66	72	50	68	83	52	69	82	59	70	79	52
No	29	21	43	31	27	49	29	16	44	27	16	33	25	14	29
No opinion/answer	3	2	5	3	1	1	3	1	4	4	2	8	5	7	19
Q: Do you believe that people like yourself have no influence over government actions?															
Yes	66	58	67	65	58	70	67	56	66	66	56	63	65	69	49
No	30	41	29	32	42	28	30	44	31	29	43	31	27	31	28
No opinion/answer	4	1	4	3	x	2	3	x	3	5	1	6	8	2	13
Q: Do you consider political affairs beyond your understanding?															
Yes	67	71	76	63	66	76	67	72	75	71	72	78	77	85	73
No	30	28	22	35	33	22	29	28	23	26	28	17	19	14	11
No opinion/answer	3	1	3	2	1	2	4	x	2	3	x	5	4	1	6
Q: Do you consider patriotism the most important obligation of citizenship?															
Yes	53	84	77	44	78	68	55	85	83	63	90	90	71	95	83
No	40	15	20	49	20	30	39	14	14	29	9	7	20	5	4
No opinion/answer	7	1	3	7	2	2	6	1	3	8	1	3	9	x	13

Source: Unpublished survey data from Japanese National Television (NHK).

Note: x = less than 1%.

ditions stressing the need for law and order in state and society have been sustained by the patterns of socioeconomic stratification and the organization of political life in the Federal Republic. As we observed earlier, the founders of the Federal Republic feared that too much popular participation could lead to political instability. Accordingly they formulated constitutional rules for a "representative" democracy in which citizens were to play only intermittent and indirect roles in the choice of governmental policies and policymakers. West Germans have by now learned to accept the legitimacy of these role assignments, though many of them also feel that they should have a greater voice in public affairs.

For most West Germans, but especially for older persons, women, and people living outside the urban centers, their rather formalistic perceptions of the state and its authority relationships inform their sense of political involvement and efficacy. They see little reason to engage in sustained political activities since they believe that they are essentially consumers rather than producers of governmental policies.

Nonetheless, West Germans seem on the whole to be exceptionally interested in politics according to various crossnational attitude surveys—more so than Americans, Frenchmen and Italians, for instance. Why this should be so in light of their sense of political impotence is at first glance a bit puzzling. West German politics have been singularly devoid of the intense ideological conflicts and mass turmoil that are often associated with a high degree of political interest. According to any number of political theories the fact that most contemporary West Germans have received less formal education than Americans should make them less rather than more interested in politics than Americans.

Part of the reason for the apparent gap between a large, politically attentive public and a small, politically active public in the Federal Republic may be the exceptionally high political content of the mass communications media. Extensive coverage of public affairs in the press, radio, and television has made politics something of a spectator sport in West Germany.

But there seem to be more basic reasons. Ordinary citizens may today be poorly motivated to enter the political fray but they want to be seen as attentive to politics. German cultural values have long stressed the possession of knowledge and, over the past four decades increasingly, of political knowledge. Particularly younger people who grew up under the present regime have had it impressed on them by civic educators that mass political ignorance led to mass political impotence under former regimes and that a democratically "competent" citizen is a politically informed citizen. To judge by their responses in opinion polls, West Germans have learned this lesson rather well. Whereas, for example, only one in four adults in a 1952 poll professed to be interested in politics, one out of two did so in a 1983 survey.

A closer examination of such polls indicates, however, that most West Germans are in fact no better informed than most Americans about particular aspects of their political order and find it no less difficult to comprehend the intricacies of public policy processes. As in other representative democracies, the further removed people feel from the centers of decision making, and the less they consider their personal interests to be involved in policy outcomes, the greater is their propensity to be bored by everyday politics. Furthermore, it seems that when West Germans tell a pollster that they are "generally" interested in politics, their responses are more often than not expressions of conformity with what they take to be the norms of democratic citizenship rather than of a belief that they know enough to play the game of politics. Thus 75 percent of the respondents in a 1978 poll considered it a characteristic of a "good democrat" to be well informed about political affairs, but only 47 percent to be active in them.

Public authority in the Federal Republic emanates in the last analysis from the people, according to the Basic Law, and is to be periodically delegated by them to their representatives in elections. Compared to other regimes that provide such opportunities for popular control through entirely voluntary electoral participation the turnout in West Germany has been exceptionally high over the years. Whereas in the United States, for example, only about half of the eligible voters cast their ballots in national elections, in the Federal Republic federal elections have consistently brought practically all qualified voters to the polls. The exercise of the franchise then, would seem to indicate a singularly high sense of popular involvement independent of changing issues and candidates. But here too we find a gap between formal adherence to the constitutional norms of democratic citizenship and perceptions of political efficacy in the way most West Germans perceive their participant roles.

The turnout for federal elections has been even higher than in the turbulent national elections of the last years of the Weimar Republic. But whereas then a high rate of participation was attributable to the mobilization of voters by radical parties opposed to the regime, the reasons and consequences now appear to be entirely different. West German election studies have shown that the campaign rhetoric of contending parties and candidates usually leaves the voters rather cold and that most of them do not believe that casting their ballots matters very much over the long run. The major parties, naturally enough, seek maximum mass support by making every election appear to be crucial, but with few exceptions West German voters have not considered electoral outcomes truly crucial for their own or the country's future. In effect the large turnout in federal elections has enhanced rather than weakened the combined strength of the major parties supporting the present regime and thereby has promoted its institutionalization.

On the whole it appears that the turnout has been high not so much because West Germans believe that their votes determine governmental policies but because they consider it their civic duty to go to the polls. Although social pressure to exercise one's franchise is rather high—particularly in smaller communities where abstentions are more noticeable—the cost is not. Since elections always come on Sundays a voter can spare the time and will not suffer a loss of income. And as legal residence and age automatically entitle every citizen to cast a ballot, there is no need to register, pay a poll tax, or take a qualifying test.

In sum, an electorate which believes that voting has no decisive effect on the way political issues are dealt with by the ruling elites has been extensively but not intensively involved in elections. Popular dissatisfaction with some political developments may produce some shifts in electoral support for the major parties; but usually such shifts have until now reflected comparatively mild protest votes directed against particular policies rather then against the regime.

Political Community

A basic measure of the institutionalization of a state is its citizens' sense of a shared political identity. When the Federal Republic was carved out of the former German Reich, and for some time thereafter, most West Germans did not seem to consider themselves members of a new political community except in a purely formal sense. West Germany was perceived as a geographic expression or an economic system, and its status as a distinct political entity was widely believed to be only a temporary condition pending the reunification of the "German nation."

Over the years a subtle process of political acculturation has produced a greater identification with the Federal Republic. With the integration of the millions of refugees from Eastern Europe, the waning of prospects for reunification, and the absorption of new learning experiences, more and more West Germans have come to identify "Germany" with the Federal Republic rather than the territory of the former Reich. The "flawed sense of national identity," which in earlier years had seemed to many observers a decided obstacle to the institutionalization of the West German state appears to have given way to a national consciousness associated not just with the economic achievements of the Federal Republic, but with its liberal democratic regime. The "normalization" of domestic and foreign relations, particularly with respect to the Nazi past and Communist East Germany, reflected and accelerated this change in the climate of opinion.

Conspicuously missing from this new sense of political community are affective loyalty and feelings of national pride regarding the Federal Republic. West Germans may root for "our team" in international athletic competitions, but few of them think of their country as a beloved "fatherland." Numerous studies have shown them to profess feelings of national pride to a much smaller degree than the citizens of the United States and other modern democracies. In the early 1970s the ruling Social Democrats sought to capture such sentiments with election posters that proclaimed "Germans: we can be proud of our country." But feelings of pride have in fact become even less widespread since those days, according to opinion surveys by the European Community. In 1983 the West Germans ranked lowest among the ten countries of the Community in the extent of national pride among adult citizens.

The intense patriotic attachments to a German nation-state that provided mass support for the Imperial and Nazi regimes have evidently not been transferred to the rump that both the constitution and government pronouncements identify as but a part of the "German nation." Present-day West Germans, particularly young people, reject the notion that patriotism is the most important obligation of citizenship to a much greater extent than Americans and Japanese (see table 4.3). Official efforts to promote communal sentiments through symbols of integration tend to be ignored or rejected. The black, red, and gold flag is recognized and accepted as the emblem of the Federal Republic, but its sight does not move people the way the black, red, and white of Imperial and Nazi Germany once did. The new national holidays are not perceived as "holy" days, but as leisure days that are to be enjoyed rather than celebrated. On such occasions West Germans now prefer skiing in the mountains or basking at the beaches, to parading with fife and drum and listening to patriotic oratory and songs.

By some accounts East Germans may have developed more positive communal sentiments. Their Communist rulers have certainly worked hard to replace the affective ties that linked state and national community in the Third Reich with a new sense of "socialist solidarity" in the Democratic Republic. Its leaders have thus sought to employ traditional symbols of German nationalism—such as the Protestant reformer Martin Luther and the Prussian soldier-king Fredrick the Great—to promote patriotic feel-

ings, along with anticapitalist sentiments, in the schools, the mass
youth organizations, and the conscript military forces of the Communist successor state.

To what extent these endeavors have created more of a fraternal
spirit in East than in West Germany is uncertain. But there is
abundant evidence indicating that the citizens of the two German
states have increasingly come to see each other as different rather
than similar, as more and more of them have grown up in quite
distinct societies. Official West German efforts to maintain at least
some sense of cultural unity seem to have done little to arrest the
divisive process. While the East German rulers have not been able
to keep their subjects from watching "bourgeois" West German
television, they have managed to limit unofficial direct contacts
largely to brief visits between old-age pensioners. Numerous surveys show that fewer and fewer West Germans were born and raised
in East Germany and still have relatives and friends living there,
that hardly anyone in the Federal Republic believes that the two
parts of the former Reich will ever be reunified; and that most
young people perceive the Democratic Republic as a distant, foreign land.

In sum, it appears then that neither the Federal Republic nor
the image of a single German "nation" are today foci of mass
sentiments of political community in West Germany. Some observers believe that this lack of national identity favors allegiances to
a European political community. But the absence of one type of
loyalty does not allow us to infer the presence of another. Rather
vaguely perceived, European integration seems attractive to most
West Germans and in principle receives massive support in both
elite and mass opinion surveys. However, there is little evidence
that these endorsements extend beyond purely pragmatic considerations, such as the perceived instrumental advantages of European economic cooperation. The enthusiasm which idealist young
West Germans showed for a truly supranational community in the
1950s is gone.

In recent years the sudden and unexpected emotional engagement of West Germans in mass movements against war and ecological pollution, and for a greater popular voice in government,

has introduced new parochial orientations into West German politics. These suggest the possible development of more pronounced and more exclusive feelings of political community in the Federal Republic, especially if other countries pursue policies that West Germans find contrary to their military and economic needs. However, it seems a mistake to take these new orientations as indicative of a revival of the sort of romantic nationalism that aroused Germans in the past. They also do not appear to point to the emergence of the kind of flag-waving patriotism that one finds in the United States and most other Western countries. Instead they suggest the consolidation of quite exceptional common feelings of negative identification with one's country.

As the product of war and defeat, the Federal Republic has come to be distinguished in the eyes of many of its citizens more by what it is not politically than by what it is. It is not autocratic like Imperial Germany, not torn by bitter conflicts like Weimar Germany, not savagely destructive like Nazi Germany, and not subservient to a foreign power like Communist East Germany. This negative identification seems to have been reinforced, particularly among well-educated young people, by the conviction that West Germany is at the mercy of forces that its leaders cannot or will not control. In its most extreme form, this view conceives West Germans as an involuntary community of people at the brink of disaster. They are thus thought to be facing an ecological catastrophe arising from the polluting effects of industrial waste, an economic disaster due to anarchic world trade conditions, and military annihilation resulting from the arms race between the superpowers.

THE INCOMING GENERATION

Due to a temporary increase in the birth rate once postwar economic recovery was well under way, an exceptionally large proportion of West Germans—about 20 percent—are today roughly between 15 and 30 years of age. Rather different learning experiences distinguish the incoming generation of political actors from that of their parents and, even more, their grandparents. Its members grew up in an era that witnessed a sharp decline in paternalistic authority patterns in state and society and rapidly rising standards of living in all socioeconomic strata. These young West Germans became accustomed to material affluence in a mass consumption society, to a more carefree life-style than their elders, and to the company of like-minded age peers in their own and other Western countries. An increasing proportion went to the better secondary schools and to university, as we noted earlier. And all of them were the objects of massive civic education efforts by governmental and nongovernmental agencies designed to teach them the "legitimate" rights and responsibilities of citizenship under the constitution of the Federal Republic.

What has been the result of these learning experiences? According to recent studies, the members of the incoming generation are on the whole far more extensively committed to the democratic principles of the present constitutional order than their elders. Almost all oppose any form of authoritarian government and any group or country that seems to favor such a regime. But most of them also judge democratic processes by particularly high standards, and therefore consider the Federal Republic not democratic enough. Critical young people thus charge that older West Germans show too little tolerance for deviant views and behavior, and that leading public officials and politicians fail to adhere to ostensibly democratic rules of proper conduct. For many the Federal Republic is a "democratic and social" state more in constitutional form than in actual fact, and the prevailing political system is too rigidly bureaucratic to accommodate the changing needs of ordinary people.

But while young persons of both sexes want more political change than middle-aged and older West Germans, they usually share the view that the average person has little or no control over public policy. The young are usually even less willing than their elders to engage in regular political activities other than voting. Most of them favor mass demonstrations for what they deem a good cause, and many of them will on occasion even participate. But on the whole young West Germans are too individualistic— or self-centered, if you will—to join an organization for collective political action. Ideological appeals on behalf of political abstractions, such as the public interest, the state, and the nation—leave most of them cold. In so far as young people are interested in politics at all they are likely to be concerned with concrete questions about their prospects for the future.

The optimism and high hopes for the future which prevailed among young West Germans in the late 1960s and early 1970s no longer characterize the mood today. By all accounts many members of the incoming generation are quite pessimistic about what lies ahead, and those who are interested in politics are particularly gloomy. In the light of uncertain economic developments and unsettling technological changes men and women under thirty are not at all sure of finding the sort of job they seek and leading the kind of life they want. The better-educated have reason to fear that much of their schooling may prove to have been for naught, the more poorly educated that they face uneven employment, if not long-term unemployment.

Young West Germans find even greater cause for worry in more general long-run developments. According to a 1981 survey, large numbers believe that they will become the victims of electronic means of mass control, three out of four fear that technological development will bring about the destruction of their ecological environment, and one out of two expect to perish sooner or later in a nuclear holocaust.

For politically attentive members of the now dominant generation of middle-aged West Germans such widespread negative attitudes are much greater cause for alarm than occasional youth riots and "terrorist acts" against the established order. Every year witnesses new inquiries on what's wrong with West German youth by government commissions, legislative committees, and private institutes. Here, after all, are the new voters moving into the electorate and the conscripts and reservists who provide almost all of the manpower for West Germany's vital military contribution to the Western NATO alliance. What particularly troubles present leaders of the Federal Republic is that pessimism about the future is most prevalent among some of the best-educated and politically most interested members of the incoming generation.

5

Politicization and Participation

Who participates when, where, how, and why in West German politics is a matter partly of structured opportunities, partly of personal motivation. The two are closely related. The organization and rules of the West German political system offer several opportunities for legitimate participation. But the perceptions of such opportunities and the inclinations to use them vary.

Relatively few West Germans are constantly involved in public affairs because they need to be or choose to be. Government officials and functionaries of political parties and pressure groups cannot help but be involved, but for most people active participation is the exception rather than the rule. Those who say "I could if I would" lack motivation; they believe they have the competence and the freedom to participate but usually see no reason for doing so. Those who say "I would if I could" consider themselves most, if not all of the time, in no position to take effective political action; the political system, as they see it, does not give them the opportunity. Consequently most full-time political activists in the Federal Republic, as in other countries, are first of all exceptionally motivated by ambition, ideology, and other personal values to assume participant roles. Second, they usually have a particularly high sense of potential or actual political efficacy. They believe themselves sufficiently well situated in the system to realize some, if not all of their objectives in the public arena.

In short, a West German's participation in politics depends not only on his position but his disposition. Differences in the prevailing patterns of participation are in this regard both a source and product of variations in perceived opportunities and motivation.

POLITICIZATION

In the Federal Republic, as elsewhere, attitudes concerning political participation—like other political orientations—are conditioned by the information which people receive about ongoing political developments and by what they have learned previously. From what he personally observes, and from what others tell him, a West German derives an image of his political environment, a sense of his place in that environment, and certain ideas about what he likes and dislikes about it. He learns and may relearn to link his self-perception with his perception of other actors in the political system, to relate his views of proper political roles to theirs, and to discover his policy preferences on various political issues. And he learns to formulate and express his views in terms of an acquired language of political intercourse, and to be more receptive to some political communications than to others.

Differences in political learning make for differences in political attitudes. As we saw in the preceeding chapter, West German views about the past and ongoing political conditions have changed quite a bit over the years and now vary a good deal. Contemporary West Germans will attach positive or negative meaning—or perhaps none at all—to the "lessons of history" and to such concepts as state, authority, and nation, depending on what they have learned and from whom. And while acquired political knowledge has provided some with strong reasons for participating in politics it has instilled in others a sense of political indifference, incompetence, and powerlessness.

Preadult Politicization

A citizen of the Federal Republic gets his first formal opportunity to influence the course of political developments when he turns eighteen and may vote as well as run for an elective public office. At that phase in life a West German's preadult learning experiences are apt to have a more immediate effect on his political outlook and behavior than in later years. They are not only more recent, but normally less complex than subsequent politicizing experiences.

We have very little reliable evidence of the family's influence on West German political orientations. There is some indication that in the Federal Republic, as in other advanced industrial countries, the formative influence of the family is waning. However, the evidence also suggests that family background and home environment may still be of some importance for political learning and differentiation, particularly during the impressionable years of childhood and early adolescence. According to a number of studies, West German children are most likely to develop an interest in politics—and expectations that they will participate in public affairs when they grow up—in homes where political issues are frequently and openly discussed. And, as these studies also show, such discussions are most prevalent in families of the higher social strata, and have the greatest learning effect on the children of parents who are well educated and display a high degree of political knowledge and competence.

When a West German child starts to go to nursery and primary school his or her politicization takes on a new dimension. The child is now directly exposed to learning experiences shaped by public authorities. For the most part these are authorities in the various states of the Federal Republic, above all in the state governments. Teachers are civil servants of the states and the states' educational ministries tell them what to teach. Furthermore, both state and federal governments heavily subsidize nongovernmental organizations—youth groups of the major churches, parties, and trade unions—which are considered to make constructive contributions to the political education of young West Germans.

Preadult political learning in the West German schools is in this respect less diversified than in the United States, but more so than in countries with a more highly centralized educational system such as France and Japan. There are no popularly elected school boards, and local educational authorities have little autonomy. The state governments cooperate to a certain extent in deciding what should be taught by whom and to whom. In the 1970s, for example, they agreed that radical opponents of the present regime should not be permitted to teach any subject. The quality and quantity of political education vary considerably from state to state and school to school. The political complexion of different state governments, the party affiliations and personal preferences of their ministers of culture and educational administrators, the strength of regional traditions, and the relative power of various nongovernmental groups that endeavor to influence educational policies, make for considerable heterogeneity.

Studies on the effect of direct and indirect governmental control over preadult politicization in the Federal Republic have been limited and rather inconclusive. Social research suggests that in open, pluralist, and industrially advanced countries such as West Germany, civic training in school is not a sufficient and, possibly, not even a necessary condition for the development of regime-supportive or, for that matter, regime-opposing attitudes. It may well be far less important than conservatives, liberals, and radicals who battle for control over civic education for the young tend to assume.

Political Learning in Adulthood

As West Germans near and then enter into adulthood the sources of their political learning proliferate and current information becomes more decisive in shaping their political outlook. Thereafter, the nature and extent of continuing politicization for participant roles vary a good deal with age, social background and environment, and personal engagement.

Young adults are on the whole more open to new political learning experiences than older ones. For example they are likely to adopt a wait-and-see attitude before committing themselves to a political association, especially if they come from homes where public affairs were rarely or never discussed and partisan attachments weak. Highly educated members of the upper social strata are likely to be better politically informed and to be correspondingly more open to new learning than the more poorly educated members of the lower strata. And differences in the character and stability of their social environment provide West German adults with extensive and intensive resocializing contacts after their preadult socialization. Travel and geographic mobility, for example, tend to broaden the political mind, as do occupational and social mobility. West Germans who marry within their social strata, who reside and work for most of their lives in the same place, and who are generally rooted in a particular subcultural setting, are also likely to be most constant in their political outlook.

West Germans who make it their business to acquire new knowledge for effective participation are apt to be exposed to a particularly large variety of political communications and relationships—formal as well as informal—and to be especially sensitive to implications of political developments. This has been particularly notable in the careers of elected public officials, such as the self-proclaimed pragmatists who have in recent times played leading participant roles in national and regional politics. In the course of making their way up to the top in governmental and party hierarchies, they have shown themselves highly adaptable to changing environments.

In the Federal Republic, as in the United States, the better informed and more attentive political public is a small but influential minority. Most adults feel they have neither the need nor the ability to stay constantly abreast of political developments and are more likely to tune out than tune in when confronted with information that goes beyond their immediate experiences and concerns. Like most people in other advanced industrial societies, they find it difficult to understand complex domestic and international policy issues. Moreover, in West Germany, as elsewhere, various political groupings use a special language for political communications that in effect excludes outsiders. The esoteric terminology of left-wing radicals, for example, has been largely incomprehensible to the workers they have sought to reeducate. And access to and membership in the West German policymaking stratum require familiarity with a particular form of elite communications. In both instances those on the outside have not only the problem of understanding the in group's language, but the problem of articulating their own values and emotions in a way that will be understood by its members. Poll-takers may try to take the political pulse of the masses, and votes at election time may give some indications of popular political views, but by and large the voice of the ordinary people is heard through those who claim to be their spokesmen.

The conditions of a modern industrial society and the present system's principles of political participation enhance the role of elite opinion makers in shaping the political orientations of the average West German through the mass media. Mass political communications and relations are in this respect essentially structured by formal governmental and nongovernmental organizations. If an average citizen is at all interested in public affairs, he usually relies on information and interpretations provided by trusted and respected sources—notably eminent journalists, civic leaders, professors, and high public officials.

The Mass Media. Political events and actors assume prominence in the eyes of the general public largely on the strength of their exposure by the mass media. The organizers of pressure group demonstrations, for example, have sought to obtain the largest possible media coverage in order to gain mass support for their objectives. The strategic role of the mass media in shaping the informational environment of West Germans—and consequently their perceptions of and reactions to political developments—is beyond dispute. However, for that very reason, who does and should control the media—and for what purpose and to what effect—has been a matter of considerable controversy among leaders and would-be leaders who seek to shape mass opinion in the Federal Republic.

To begin with, all of them see the mass media as a key commu-

nication link between the politically engaged minority of West
Germans and the vast majority of peripheral participants. Furthermore, implicit and explicit political messages transmitted
through the media are taken to have a long-term, cumulative effect
on beliefs, values, and sentiments. That is, leaders as well as led,
governors as well as governed learn to adapt their outlook and
consequent behavior to "political reality" on the basis of information provided through the mass media. And it is generally
assumed that those who manage the media can influence adult
politicization directly and preadult political learning indirectly.
They may act as "gatekeepers" and interpreters of the news they
consider fit to be seen, heard, and printed; they may also act as
powerful partisan advocates and adversaries in the realm of public
policy.

The extent of the particular and long-range influence of diverse
media on the development of mass political orientations in West
Germany is, however, by no means self-evident. Here, too, existing
social research studies offer indications rather than conclusive
answers. They suggest first of all that the media are indeed preeminent agents in the structured flow of political communications.
Secondly, although the effect of information varies with different
media, circumstances, and audiences, it seems on the whole to be
greater than ever before. Finally, it appears that such current
information as ordinary West Germans take from favored media
and consider salient is more likely to reinforce than alter their
prior political dispositions, including their inclination and sense
of opportunity for political participation.

In this regard we need to distinguish between the public and
private mass media; they evidently differ considerably in their
effectiveness. In the mid-1980's just about every West German
home had a television set and at least one radio; in fact, there were
more of these per capita than in any other country outside the
United States. The Federal Republic, like the United States, has
no truly national press (in contrast to France and Britain); there,
as here, surveys have shown that radio and television are for most
people the most frequently used and most trusted sources of

political information. But in West Germany regular broadcasting stations and networks are not even partially private enterprises. All are organized as "nonpartisan" public corporations that are formally under the exclusive jurisdiction of the states and supervised by boards appointed by their governments to represent the major political parties, religious associations, and socioeconomic interest groups.[1]

As in most other areas of public policy, the manifest object of these formal arrangements is to accommodate the polycentric and pluralist elements in West German society within a federalist and representative democratic order. Attempts by the Federal Government to obtain a share of the public broadcasting media have been blocked by the Federal Constitutional Court; private entrepreneurs attempting to break the states' monopoly have thus far been restricted to broadcasting nonpolitical programs over cable television in a few areas of the Federal Republic.

The public media are more than passive agents of political communications, as the Federal Constitutional Court has pointed out. The charters of the public broadcasting corporations stipulate that news reports be accurate and objective and clearly distinguished from interpretive news commentaries. But they also provide that their presentations should not only conform with constitutional and ordinary law, but actively promote mass support for the basic principles of the established regime. Broadcasting stations are for instance specifically directed to emphasize the need for peace, freedom, and international understanding in their programs. And although the representatives of "legitimate" nongovernmental groups—such as legal political parties—have free access to the public media, views that are considered "subversive" by the controlling authorities may not be aired.

Within these limitations, the West German radio and television stations offer their mass audience an exceptionally rich and variegated fare of political information. Opposing viewpoints on key

1. The Federal Government has jurisdiction over broadcasts to foreign countries and "intra-German" programs beamed to the German Democratic Republic.

political issues are presented in frequent panel discussions, and many programs present a critical and, often, highly controversial examination of particular aspects of the present political system.

In comparison with the electronic public media, the impact of privately owned publications on mass political attitudes appears today to be neither as great as some observers wish it would be nor as powerful as others fear it is. In the early 1980's West Germany had some 400 newspapers with a combined sale of more than 24 million copies; according to survey data 90 percent of West Germans over eighteen read at least one daily paper. Comparative studies show that West Germans, unlike Americans, are exceptionally avid newspaper readers. They also indicate that West Germans are more prone than people in other major European countries to read about politics in their daily paper, as well as getting current news accounts from the electronic media (see table 5.1). What is less well known is that the number of independent publications has grown ever smaller, that there has been increasingly less variety in political publications, that the press serves more to entertain than to politicize West Germans, and that the political content of most newspapers focuses on local and regional rather than national and international developments.

Freedom of the press and expression are fundamental citizen-

TABLE 5.1

Mass Media as Sources of Political Information in Major European Countries, 1983 (adult mass opinion data in rounded-off percentages)

	G.F.R.	FRANCE	U.K.	ITALY
Watch the news on television				
every day	64%	63%	84%	65%
never	1	4	1	4
Read the political news in the daily paper				
every day	61	31	52	26
never	5	28	14	27
Listen to the news on the radio				
every day	53	49	56	29
never	3	18	14	34

Source: Commission of the European Communities, *Euro-barometre*, April 1983.

ship rights under the Basic Law; public authorities are enjoined from monopolizing the mass media and manifestly they control not a single newspaper and only a few periodicals. In light of the great influence of the German press in the past the framers of the constitution expected that an independent and pluralist "fourth estate" would play a major part in the future development of mass political attitudes.

Initially there was indeed a great blossoming forth of publications that offered their readers a wide variety of political information. But this proved to be a temporary phenomenon. Economic exigencies forced many to fold and others to be absorbed into a few publishing empires. In 1954 West Germany had 225 newspapers with independent political editorial policies and staff; thirty years later it had only 122, with more than half of these owned by just five publishing houses.

The largest of these is today the house of Axel Springer. Springer puts out virtually all of the Sunday papers, and one out of four adults read his *Bild Zeitung,* the only popular daily with a nationwide readership. Springer's commercial preeminence has led his critics to ascribe to him a great deal of political influence over mass opinion; but there has been little solid evidence to support this belief. The *Bild Zeitung* is a tabloid which gives little space to political matters unless they are sensational, and by all indications most of its readers do not depend on it for political guidance.

Most German newspapers and periodicals are today primarily commercial enterprises and feature items intended to attract a wide range of readers in local and regional advertising markets. About three-fourths of the dailies are local editions of regional newspapers that account for approximately four-fifths of the total circulation and two-thirds of the newspaper readers. As in the United States, independent local dailies have been disappearing, and in about half of the country people get their news about local politics from a single paper. In any case most local papers provide their readers with little political information of any sort and West Germans interested in politics are more likely to rely on regional dailies for news about domestic and foreign affairs.

Journals devoted primarily to political subjects do not have a mass readership, but more than three-fourths of West German adults read one or more of the illustrated weeklies containing political material. The most popular of these—*Quick, Stern, Bunte,* and *Revue*—are, like the *Bild Zeitung,* commercial enterprises designed to attract as many customers as possible for their advertisers. Since competition between them is intense, they seek to scoop each other with sensational political items that will boost their circulation. Along with sex, sports, and gossip about prominent personalities, they feature titillating political revelations, interviews, and commentaries that focus on alleged shortcomings of the political system—such as factional fights and bribery scandals—rather than on its more mundane aspects. Consequently, these periodicals often present a rather negative picture of the system, which does not encourage their readers to participate in public affairs. Opinion surveys indicate, however, that most adults do not consider the illustrated weeklies important sources of political information.

On the whole, then, the average West German gets most of his current political information through the public broadcasting media. Leaders and would-be leaders of mass opinion place correspondingly high value on access to radio and television for getting their messages to the general public. This presents no problem for prominent public officials and major party leaders who endeavor to shape political attitudes and behavior. But dissident elements critical of the dominant political establishment normally find it more difficult to broadcast their views. They therefore tend to seek the attention of the general public through newsworthy political actions, such as spectacular protest demonstrations against the construction of nuclear power plants.

The outlook and behavior of the politically more engaged public are informed far more extensively through various printed media in the private sector, through books as well as newspapers and periodicals. About one in ten West German adults reads one or more of the few supraregional dailies that specifically address themselves to a politically attentive and involved public: the *Frankfurter Allgemeine,* the *Welt,* the *Süddeutsche Zeitung,* and the *Frank-*

furter Rundschau. The first two are more conservative than the others, but all firmly support the present political order. These papers are read by the most influential participants in public affairs and provide a forum for interelite political communications and for airing elite controversies over policy issues. Along with two weeklies, *Die Zeit* and *Der Spiegel,* they both mold and express the views of top West German opinion leaders and policymakers in adversary as well as collaborative relationship.

POLITICAL PARTICIPATION

As we move from political orientations to political behavior let us recall that by our definition politics within countries revolve around the choice of public policies and their implementation. Political participation is in this respect identified with active, though not necessarily successful behavior on the part of individuals and groups directed toward the satisfaction of their values in the realm of public policy. The political efficacy of participating actors is measured correspondingly by their ability to realize their objectives through the promotion, modification, or prevention of governmental policy decisions.

Disparities in the extent of political participation and influence exist in every country. But their specific forms in contemporary West Germany reflect a particular mixture of socioeconomic, cultural, and organizational patterns. Changes in these patterns under the present regime have reduced, but not eliminated the inequitable distribution of participant roles and political power that prevailed under earlier, less democratic German regimes. As in other liberal democratic countries, political stratification in the Federal Republic is based on qualitative differences that modify the egalitarian principles of the constitutional order.

Formally structured distinctions in the opportunities for effective participation in effect reinforce the differences we noted in the participant orientations of higher and lower socioeconomic strata. As a result we have a rather sharp division between a general public that is for the most part only peripherally involved in policymaking and a relatively small political public of more or less active participants. Insofar as ordinary citizens of the Federal Republic have the opportunity to participate, they confine themselves largely to a single role, that of the voter (see table 5.2). Leading members of the political public, on the other hand, frequently hold several organizational positions in the political system, allowing them to play several participant roles simultaneously. A federal minister, for example, is not only a voter, a deputy, the chief of a government department, and a cabinet member; he also usually occupies leading positions in his party and other nongovernmental organizations.

The political public is for its part further stratified. At the top are the policymakers who may on occasion sharply disagree on particular policy issues but share a common understanding of the "proper" rules of the game of politics. Such rules define the limits of intraelite conflicts and provide for processes of conflict management that largely bypass the general public. The ruling elites are in turn recruited from and supported by medium-level par-

TABLE 5.2

The Pyramid of Political Participation in West Germany

POLITICAL STRATUM	PERCENTAGE OF CITIZENRY	DEGREE OF PARTICIPATION
Top-level participants (national elites)	0.002	high
State and federal legislators	0.03	medium-high
Members of local and district councils	0.4	medium
Middle-level functionaries of organizations in politics	0.5	medium
Members of civic action groups	1.0	medium
Active party members	1.0	medium
Members of political parties	5.0	medium-low
Members of organizations in politics	10.0	medium-low
Voters in local elections	50.0	low
Voters in state elections	55.0	low
Voters in federal elections	65.0	low
Eligible electorate	70.0	low
All citizens	100.0	low

Source: Calculated from survey data, membership data, election statistics, and various studies on political participation.

ticipants in governmental bodies and nongovernmental organizations.

The Electorate

In three out of every four years regular local, state, and federal elections offer practically all adult West Germans formal opportunities for intermittent and peripheral participation in politics. Though the ostensible object is usually the choice of local and regional legislators, even nonfederal elections tend, in fact, to have a nationwide import. There are no by-elections for offices that fall vacant, as in the United States and Britain, or popular referenda, as in France. Proposals to increase mass participation through American-type primaries and presidential elections have gotten nowhere.

Periodic local and regional elections are therefore considered of correspondingly greater significance as interim tests of the popularity of national parties and their leaders than in the United States. National party leaders are apt to devote a great deal more effort to winning them and the mass media are likely to attribute greater weight to their outcome than the actual importance of the offices at stake seems to justify.

Although casting their votes gives West Germans a chance to express their preference for policies and policymakers, this form of political participation has limited significance for the recruitment of governmental leaders. Particularly in state and federal elections the electorate has had for the most part only an indirect and not necessarily decisive voice in the selection process. In the first place election laws provide that half—in some states all—of the parliamentary deputies are to be chosen through a system of proportional representation that compels a voter to cast his ballot for a party list rather than a particular candidate. Thus, in federal elections for the lower house of parliament, every voter may cast two ballots, one for a local constituency candidate and a second for a party. Accordingly, only half the federal deputies owe their sets to a direct choice of the voters in single-member districts, as in the United States, Britain, and France. The rest owe them to having been placed high enough on their party's state list of candidates to be elected under a system of proportional representation that allocates the total number of seats in the national legislature in accordance with the second ballot votes captured by the parties in each of the ten states.

A further restriction on the realization of electoral preferences is the so-called five percent clause. The West German system of proportional representation does not discriminate against electoral minorities to the same extent as the winner-take-all procedures in countries with a pure single-member plurality system. However, parties that fail to secure 5 percent of the votes in federal and most state elections obtain no seat at all, and all those who voted for those parties thus have no voice whatever in deciding who is to govern. Finally, under the prevailing parliamentary form of government, the ultimate choice of the legislative and executive leadership rests nominally with the elected deputies, but in fact usually with the leaders of the dominant majorities.[2]

As various West German voting studies have indicated, the consistently high rate of participation in federal elections provides two important elements for the stable operation of the political system. First, there is no sizable reservoir of qualified electors who ordinarily do not vote but might be activated by dramatic events or leaders, as in the last years of the Weimar regime. Beyond the limited and gradual influx of eligible new voters, the present turnout of close to 90 percent of the electorate precludes the possibility of sudden political changes produced by a substantial increase in electoral participation. Though the direction of voters' preferences may change, the extent of participation lends stability to the political system.

Second, present attitudinal and voting patterns suggest that electoral participation is a function of neither intense political engagement nor socioeconomic distinctions. Under earlier German regimes and in other countries increase in turnout has re-

2. The direct popular election of mayors in some of the states is an exception to this practice.

flected greater public involvement in election outcomes. However; most West Germans evidently participate today not so much because they expect their vote to have a significant effect on public policy decisions but because they have learned to see voting as a civic duty. Ordinarily, people with pressing policy demands rely more heavily on other formal pressure groups with direct access to governmental authorities. And whereas turnout in other countries with voluntary electoral participation tends to vary a good deal with socioeconomic background—particularly age, sex, education, income, and place of residence—in the contemporary Federal Republic this factor influences electoral participation hardly at all.

Public participant orientations and organizational structures thus interact to produce a self-fulfilling prophecy. According to the prevailing view, "those on top" largely can and will do what they deem best. Most West Germans, as we have seen, have a low sense of political efficacy and see little point in extending their participation in politics beyond discharging their civic responsibilities as voters. Casting their ballots represents for them a very low commitment to political participation, and electoral arrangements tend to confirm their belief that the average citizen may have some say in the selection of policymakers, but little influence over the choice of specific policy measures. The general public thus has limited opportunities for participation under rules of a representative democracy and is not very highly motivated to make the most of such opportunities or to seek their expansion. Consequently, the ruling elites in the Federal Republic do indeed enjoy a good deal of policymaking autonomy and those who owe their positions to the voters usually interpret their electoral mandates pretty freely.

Middle-Level Participants

Middle-level participants in local, regional, and national politics link the general West German public to the top policymaking stratum, primarily through the media and formal organizations. They constitute about one-tenth of the citizenry and a good part of the well-informed and attentive political public. Middle-level participants include regular members of the peace movement and other loosely organized civic action groups that are engaged in politics on behalf of special causes. Such cause groups have on occasion drawn a good deal of mass support, but their active membership is small (see table 5.2) and for the most part only intermittently recruited into participant roles.

In contrast of the situation in Britain, France, and other European countries, only a very small percentage of the citizens of the Federal Republic belong to a political party. By far the largest proportion of middle-level participants are dues-paying members of compulsory or voluntary interest associations organized primarily for nonpolitical purposes but sporadically involved in pressure group activities. Most of these are occupational associations, and middle-level participants are thus recruited largely from the most extensively organized occupational groups—businessmen, farmers, skilled industrial workers, and professional people such as doctors, lawyers and teachers. They are mostly men, preponderantly middle-aged, and, except for trade unionists, are usually among the better educated, higher income white-collar workers.

Such middle-level participants exert little direct influence on public policymaking. They mainly represent the reserve forces of the political parties and interest associations; occasionally they are mobilized by the leaders of their organizations to lend quantitative support to their policy demands. Rank-and-file party members will be called on at election time to help solicit votes and funds. Labor leaders may summon trade union members to demonstrate their political strength and solidarity in mass demonstrations, and those of farm, religious, and business associations every so often ask their members to press legislators to support or oppose a particular bill.

A small minority of upper middle-level participants plays more active and, sometimes, more influential roles in public affairs. These sub-elites usually are in governmental and non-governmental positions that involve them in the articulation or aggregation of policy demands or in the recruitment of top decision makers. They may be party officials or civil servants whose occupational tasks include such activities, but they may also be interest group functionaries, clergymen, or journalists who devote themselves primarily to nonpolitical matters.

Like the rank and file of middle-level participants, but to a more significant extent, these actors perform a strategic function in the West German political system. They are the links between leaders and followers, governors and governed, and they help balance demands from below with control from above. Insofar as they facilitate two-way political communications between the bottom and top of the political participation pyramid, they help to maintain congruence between claims and supports within the system, and within its political sub-systems. A clergyman or journalist, for example, may not only justify and explain the policymakers' actions to a mass audience, but may also address the top leadership on behalf of inarticulate "public opinion." Similarly, a middle-level party or government official or interest group functionary may not only serve as an instrument of leadership control, but communicate "upstairs" attitudes gathered from his contacts with the general citizenry.

All told, middle-level participants are normally only intermittently involved in public policy processes. With the notable exception of activists within the political parties—a matter we shall consider in the next chapter—they are usually content to let their formal leaders run the system. Participation by the rank-and-file members of the numerous organizations in the pluralist West German society is mostly sporadic, and usually does not provide a particularly strong emotional bond between leaders and followers, or much control from below. Upper middle-level participants may be more continuously and profoundly engaged in politics, but highly formalized and hierarchic organizational structures normally restrict their opportunities for influence on public policy decisions quite severely.

These patterns, too, allow elite policymakers a large degree of autonomy in everyday public affairs; but they also point to a source of potential weakness in the present regime. Responsible and responsive leadership requires open channels of communications not only to the political public but to the general public. Elections and public opinion surveys provide only limited opportunities for the articulation of mass concerns and demands. That is to say, they allow an ordinary West German to express his views and interests only in response to, and in terms of, the questions that are put before him, such as whether he prefers this or that party, policy, or leader.

For these reasons upper middle-level participants are strategically important in the day-to-day operation of the West German political system. Although few in number, they carry a heavy load as they intervene between organized and unorganized citizens and the elites. Cultural patterns and organizational forms tend to assign control rather than representative functions to upper middle-level participants; but democratic procedures require that these people be free to speak as well as to listen and that they be sensitive to demands from below as well as from above. This process of interaction seems to be more extensive today than in earlier years of the Federal Republic. It is not nearly extensive enough, however, for the many West Germans who today want more of a voice in public affairs, but who are unwilling or unable to participate more directly in politics.

Leading Participants

A few thousand elected and appointed, coopted and anointed leaders form the top layer in the political influence and participation hierarchy. As national and subnational decision makers in various areas of public life they not only know a great deal more about the specific operation of the political system than other citizens do, but they can do a great deal more to shape popular demands and support, as well as policy outcomes. Some wield political power on the basis of formal governmental positions, others on the strength of special skills, financial resources, or mass support. Some are widely known; others are active behind the scenes.

The policymaking elite can be divided into two groups. The *manifest political leaders* occupy influential positions that involve continuous participation in public policy processes. The *latent po-*

litical leaders hold positions in the system that call for only intermittent participation but involve considerable potential influence.

Manifest political leaders belong to the policymaking stratum on the strength of their key constitutional and paraconstitutional positions of authority under the terms of the Basic Law. Most obviously they comprise the leaders of the federal and state governments and the Federal Diet. But they also include top administrative officials, military officers, and judges who influence policymaking in an official advisory or direct rule capacity.

In West Germany the top functionaries of the major parties are formally manifest political leaders by virtue of their para-constitutional positions in public affairs. Under Article 21 of the Basic Law, legitimate parties "participate in the formation of the political will of the people." This constitutional provision invests the leaders of both the principal governing and opposition parties with key participant roles even when they do not hold public offices.

Latent political leaders are less obviously and less constantly involved in public affairs. They may use their prominent positions in ostensibly nonpolitical sectors of West German society to influence major policy decisions, but they enter the various policymaking arenas only intermittently. Mass support, financial resources, professional expertise, or a generally recognized status of moral or intellectual authority provide them with access to the manifest leaders, and with the means for exerting influence when a policy decision touches on their particular concerns.

The political power of latent leaders is far more balanced today than under previous German regimes, and their policy interests are more diversified. Industrialists and bankers, employers and labor leaders, and the spokesmen for religious, agricultural, and professional associations often press conflicting demands on government and party officials. Mass media leaders and prominent, politically engaged intellectuals may play influential but also competing roles as they interpret ongoing policy developments for other members of the political public and for the general public.

Only about two thousand of these manifest and latent political leaders have key roles in federal policymaking. Because of the polycentric character of the Federal Republic, its national leadership is geographically more dispersed than that of most other advanced industrial countries. But excellent communications facilities and strong associational ties give the national policymakers easy access to each other and to their respective clienteles, and allow them to participate in nationwide affairs as effectively as if they were all concentrated in a single capital city. Even more important, the development of political life since the establishment of the Federal Republic has focused increasing attention on national policymaking and consequently has drawn key participants deeper into federal politics.

Indirectly the preeminence of federal politics is largely attributable to progressive consolidation of the informational media and economic system. It is a by-product of the concentration of the mass media as well as of the economic dominance of a few industrial, commercial, and banking empires and competing interest associations. More directly, two explicitly political factors have promoted the significance of membership in the national elites.

Our earlier discussion of the policy environment emphasized the Federal Republic's intense involvement in international affairs and the significance of extrasocietal factors in West German politics. More than in the United States, almost all major questions of domestic policy touch on foreign issues. Leading participants in the political system are compelled to contend with such national problems as the dependency of the Federal Republic on foreign trade and military allies. The recognition that international relations have a significance bearing on a broad range of domestic problems has therefore led diverse elite members to seek national political roles involving participation in foreign policymaking.

A second reason for the nationalization of elite political participation is that public benefits and obligations are distributed primarily by agents of the Federal Government. Increasingly, the mobilization, allocation, and control of West German human and physical resources have—in fact if not in form—been placed in the hands of national officeholders; consequently, key participants either occupy such offices or seek access to them. The appropriation of vast federal funds for social welfare services and subsidies to various economic groups have focused the efforts of interest group leaders on appropriate national executive and legislative organs. Federal legislation regulating wages and hours concern business and labor leaders. Roman Catholic and Protestant religious leaders take a keen interest in federal regulations of family life and public morals, such as divorce and abortion laws, and university administrators lobby for federal aid to higher education. In short, in domestic as in foreign policy, influence on decision making requires political participation in prominent national roles.

Who Gets to the Top and How. The processes of leadership recruitment confirm the average West German's belief that it takes a good deal more than a sense of competence to play an influential political role. Although the Basic Law declares for instance that "every German shall be equally eligible for any public office" it qualifies this right by stipulating that he must also have the necessary "aptitude, qualifications, and professional achievements." When it comes to the selection of manifest as well as latent top political leaders, such generally restrictive criteria are translated into rather exclusive standards governing admission to the policymaking stratum.

The social qualifications for elite status have changed very little since the postwar era or economic recovery and political reconstruction. Protestants are no longer as heavily overrepresented as they were then, but religious affiliation is also no longer as important. In today's Federal Republic the structured opportunities for getting to the top favor middle-aged, well-educated males from the higher social strata, much as they do in other Western countries.

Most of the incumbents of top participant positions in West German politics have a university degree, many had fathers with a degree, and few are the children of manual workers (see table 5.3). By far the largest number are the offspring of civil servants, independent businessmen, and self-employed professional people (such as doctors and lawyers). And as we have already noted, there are hardly any women in leading positions—and that includes the

TABLE 5.3

Profile of West Germans in Leading Positions of Public Life, 1981

| | ORGANIZATIONAL SECTOR OF LEADERSHIP POSITION | | | | | | | | |
| | POLITICAL PARTIES | | | PUBLIC ADMIN. | MILITARY | BUSINESS | TRADE UNIONS | MASS MEDIA | ALL SECTORS |
CHARACTERISTICS	SPD	CDU/CSU	FDP						
Age									
Mean age	49	50	51	53	55	54	54	52	53
percent under 45	31	23	32	9	0	9	9	18	15
percent 45–60	63	71	44	72	86	71	75	65	67
percent over 60	6	6	24	19	14	21	16	17	18
Social Background (in percentages)									
Religion									
Protestant	62	45	76	60	70	47	29	42	30
Roman Catholic	13	55	16	28	21	35	26	35	52
Other or none	25	0	8	12	9	18	45	24	18
Univ. degree	55	74	68	94	33	75	8	47	69
Father with univ. degree	16	18	36	32	23	23	8	26	27
Father manual worker	36	14	4	7	0	8	51	6	11
Career	(all 3 parties)								
Mean yrs. in present leadership position	4			5	2	7	9	8	6
Mean yrs. in present sector	12			22	28	26	26	27	23
Percent of entire career spent in present sector	52			90	88	91	73	99	84

Source: Information provided by Ursula Hoffmann-Lange from data collected for Rudolf Wildenmann, Max Kaase, Ursula Hoffmann-Lange et al., "Deutsche Elite Studie, 1981," an unpublished survey of 1,744 persons in leading positions of public life.
Note: Percentges are rounded off. "All sectors" includes leadership positions in the judiciary, churches, universities and other cultural institutions, business and professional associations, and local communities.

leadership of the political parties which, in some other respects, is somewhat more representative of the general citizenry than other elites.

The structure of opportunities for getting to the top also discriminate against young people. Even more than in the United States, and much as in England, France, and Japan, those who aspire to high positions must as a rule bide their time. As indicated by the age and career data in table 5.3, West German leaders are usually in their late forties and early fifties when they achieve elite status and then are likely to stay put for a decade or more. To get ahead in government and politics, as in other careers leading top positions in public policymaking, one must not only be highly motivated but normally have a good deal of patience and endurance. Unless mandatory retirement rules, illness, or electoral defeat compel their withdrawal from elite positions, senior West German leaders are usually no more disposed than their counterparts in other countries to give way to younger men. They are equally apt to maintain that wisdom and sobriety are essential leadership qualities and that these increase with age and experience.

Leading participants in the West German political system usually insist that those who aspire to join or succeed them first pass through an extensive apprenticeship in various middle-level organizational positions. The data on age and career patterns in table 5.3 show that most of these leaders of the early 1980s entered the policymaking stratum by this route. Some followed political career lines in governmental and party hierarchies that culminated in a key position, others became leading political participants after they had made their way to the top in some nonpolitical occupation.

The accumulation of experience has become more important as room at the top has opened up more slowly. Ambitious but inexperienced young men were able to advance rather quickly in the years of socioeconomic and political disorganization and reorganization immediately preceding and following the establishment of the Federal Republic. For example, Franz Josef Strauss, one of the most prominent of today's senior leaders, began his political career immediately after the fall of the Nazi regime when he was thirty; within four years he had become a major party leader and within nine a Federal minister. Self-made business tycoons and mass media leaders, such as Axel Springer, made a similar rapid ascent.

The chances for zooming to the top have been far more limited in recent times. The stable and, sometimes rigid structures of leadership recruitment have stayed the political ambitions of young people willing to work within the established system.

Becoming a leading participant calls finally for occupational skills and organizational ties. Lateral movements between manifest and latent political positions have been the exception and ascent through a series of lesser positions the rule for entry into the policymaking stratum. A national leader is likely to have switched to politics as a vocation before rather than after reaching the top of some nonpolitical hierarchy.

Generally speaking, the more sharply defined the functions of a leading position the more difficult it is for someone who lacks the required skill and expertise to attain it. Note that almost all of the West German leaders in table 5.3 spent their entire career in the organizational sector of the present elite position—except the party leaders. Though party careers have become more professionalized, top positions still demand relatively less technical expertise and more all around skills for managing interpersonal relations than elite positions in other sectors.

In contrast to the general public, leading participants—including high civil servants—usually belong to at least one, if not several nongovernmental organizations involved in policymaking. Even if they are not party leaders they tend to be members of one of the major parties, as well as of various occupational and civic organizations. In the tightly structured West German political system, the aspiring leader with few specific technical skills for getting to the top and staying there normally requires the popular or elite support provided by such formal associational ties. His ascent and influence are measured by the size of such political capital. He may be able to do without popular support—particularly if he holds a nonelective position—but rare indeed is the leader who

makes it to the top of the political pyramid without some benevolent sponsorship from members of the organizational elites.

Organizational bonds are most important in the recruitment of
key public officials, particularly ties to a major party. Since the
establishment of the Federal Republic, political parties have increasingly replaced other structures as routes to manifest political
leadership. Party membership—rather than specific occupational
skills—has become a chief criterion for ministerial posts and,
frequently, for key administrative positions. Federal ministers are
now almost always members of the ruling parties and their delegations in the Federal Diet, although membership is not required
by law. Ministers in the state governments are more often recruited
from outside parliament, but they, too, usually belong to the ruling
parties.

Gender, education, experience, occupational skill, and organizational affiliation are thus the principal sources of upward political mobility in contemporary West Germany. By and large, the
opportunities for getting into the policymaking stratum are considerably less restricted than under earlier German regimes and
in many other countries. Consider, for instance, that Willy
Brandt—the illegitimate son of a salesgirl—could rise to become
the Chancellor of the Federal Republic in 1969. Leading participants are no longer recruited from aristocratic families and a
military caste, as in the Hohenzollern empire, nor must they fit
standards of "racial" and ideological purity, as in Nazi Germany.
They are neither the graduates of a few elite universities—as is
still very much the case in Britain, France, and Japan—nor do they
belong to tight cliques based on informal social bonds and shared
socialization experiences. And in West Germany wealth is not
nearly as much a valuable resource for gaining entry into the
policymaking stratum as it is in the United States.

Elite Homogeneity and Heterogeneity. The most profound differences
between the political system of the Federal Republic and those of
earlier German regimes are to be found at the top layer of active
participants. They go beyond formal changes and extend to the

style of political relationships among West German leaders. The deep elite cleavages of the past have certainly not entirely disappeared, but elite relations are marked today by an unprecedented degree of mutual trust and cooperation.

Leadership groups that formerly were alienated from the prevailing political systems—for example, labor leaders in Imperial Germany and military leaders in Weimar Germany—now identify themselves with the regime and its preservation. No influential group of participants rejects the contemporary constitutional order. It expresses and reinforces broad elite support for political arrangements that generally suit the present leaders and conform to their perceptions of the proper distribution of role assignments in state and society.

Every major leadership group today has a share of policy-making, and the elite political culture allows all key actors some influence as long as they observe the rules of the game. The spokesmen for organized labor are no longer excluded from the ruling establishment. High civil servants and military leaders can no longer ignore or bypass the authority of elected officials but must reconcile their policy demands with those of the representatives of the voters. The federal structure of government prevents national officials from riding roughshod over regional interests—as they once did—and compels them to negotiate with the state governments on most matters of domestic policy. These more inclusive patterns of leadership participation have in turn led various elites to value arrangements that regulate adversary relationships among them without involving the general public.

In this regard the radical critics of these arrangements are essentially correct when they hold that the Federal Republic is ruled by leaders who are united in their commitment to the prevailing system. But the radicals overstate their case in claiming that elite pluralism is simply a useful democratic myth concocted by an ideologically homogeneous ruling class whose members manipulate mass opinion strictly for their own benefit.

Contemporary elite attitudes and relations do reflect a basic, if diffuse, leadership consensus on the legitimacy of a representative system of government and operative rules that provide the top leaders with considerable policymaking autonomy. Fundamental agreement on the proper modes of political conduct and patterns of participation transcends ideological and partisan differences and disagreements on particular policy issues among West German leaders. On the whole, present policymakers give the established political order high marks on its adaptability to changing environmental conditions and its ability to maintain societal harmony by processing diverse policy demands smoothly and efficiently. Incumbent West German leaders are basically attached to the regime and do not want a strongman at the helm dictating what they may or may not do.

At the same time this does not mean that all leaders are unreservedly enthusiastic about every aspect of the working of the political system. Far from it. As we have noted, liberal reformers maintain that the system should produce more socio-economic democracy, whereas conservatives demand that it provide more law and order. Business elites complain that labor leaders have too much influence over public policy and labor complaints about the excessive influence of business leaders. Civil service elites object to the "partisan meddling" of party leaders in their sector and these in turn lash out against the narrow-minded bureaucrats. Federal leaders insist that leaders in the states have too much political power; state leaders insist that they have too little. Such complaints are all too familiar to Americans—the others always seem to wield more influence in public affairs than is their due— but they are not expressions of bitter hostility toward the regime.

In contrast to the authoritarian rule of a single political elite in Nazi Germany and the Communist German Democratic Republic, a fairly balanced pluralism among different sectorial elites prevails today in the Federal Republic. Formally, governmental and legislative elites possess the ultimate authority to determine the course of public policy and to mediate conflicts among other leadership groups, such as employers and trade union leaders or the heads of various hierarchies in the public administration and the military. But by law they may not, and for practical reasons they cannot, ignore other key participants whose interests are likely to be affected by their policy decisions. No matter how great their support among the voters, the responsible governing leaders must seek the consent of other involved key actors in order to assure the effective implementation of their policies. In effect this means that they are unlikely to slight the wishes of influential veto groups among the latent political leaders and will usually try to accommodate them in formulating governmental laws and regulations.

In the West German political system the effectiveness of a governmental leader thus depends largely on his bargaining skills. The great political power of Konrad Adenauer, the long-time Chancellor of the Federal Republic, was ostensibly based on his rather autocratic use of his formal position; but equally important was his immense skill in balancing countervailing elite demands and preventing the formation of strong leadership alignments hostile to him.

The patterns of elite interaction in the realm of public policy are today structured by institutionalized organizational arrangements for delegated authority and limited popular participation. Formal governmental decisions are normally the products of complex, but orderly and stable bargaining processes among diverse groups of key participants. At the local, state, and federal levels, these groups negotiate with each other on the distribution of public benefits and obligations. Policy outputs are usually compromises worked out according to the issues involved, the alignment and strength of contending forces, and the feasible options. Legislative and elective policy choices thus flow as a rule from interelite negotiations among politicians, civil servants, and interest group functionaries.

This balanced interdependence among the elites is promoted by an elaborate network of formal and informal relationships. In large part these relationships are regulated by law, as we shall see in subsequent chapters. But they are facilitated by interelite communications through the newspapers and periodicals for the political public, as well as by direct personal contacts among West German leaders. Above all, there is a network of organizational ties and offices among and within elite sectors, linking governmental and non-governmental leadership groups and, through them, respective subordinates and clienteles.

The Incoming Leadership and Change. Some observers of contemporary West German politics believe that a conflict of generations is developing that will eventually shatter the present patterns of elite collaboration. They see a new generation of political activists coming to the fore that places less emphasis on the need for social harmony and political stability than the present leadership and is more deeply committed to divisive ideologies.

What is the basis for such prognostications? By and large age distinctions in political views do not appear to reflect major ideological cleavages between older and younger West Germans. There seems to be little or no reason for expecting a major generational conflict of the type that contributed to the collapse of the Weimar Republic. Hitler's rise to power was then promoted by his ability to exploit the anticapitalist sentiments of young idealists who were alienated from what they considered the overly materialistic values of their elders and who longed for a less mundane "new order." By comparison, most young people in the Federal Republic generally accept the prevailing political order and reject all proposals for drastic solutions to its perceived shortcomings.

But such comparisons are no longer particularly appropriate and tend to distort indications of political unrest among members of the incoming generations in West German politics. As we noted earlier, young West Germans are on the whole much better educated than their forebears and much more committed to popular participation in democratic politics. And, as we also observed, the best educated of today's incoming generation tend also to be the politically most interested and engaged young people—as well as the most pessimistic about their own and their country's future.

It is from this youthful segment of the political public that many, if not most, of West Germany's future leaders will presumably come. And it is also this element which provides most of the activists for the unconventional political groups and social protest movements that oppose the current ruling establishment. These middle-level participants have served notice on the people who are now in charge that they are not prepared simply to follow in their footsteps and that they have rather different ideas about the purpose and responsibilities of political leadership. Radical critics of the present pluralist system have been most vehement on this score. But more moderate young activists, though ready to work their way to the top through established institutions, also appear unwilling to carry on exactly as the present elites believe best.

Such nonconformist attitudes do not sit well with most of the now dominant middle-aged leaders. These tend to be far more conservative in their political views than the rebellious young activists and much more strongly attached to established policies and procedures. The present top participants generally see themselves as rational policymakers who have no use for "woolly romanticism" and doctrinaire ideologies. Though they may belong to different sectors of the elites, these leaders share what they consider a hard-nosed, pragmatic approach to public policy issues and inter-elite bargaining in domestic and foreign affairs. They place a high premium on achievement and efficent performance, on "inside information" and expert knowledge, and on the need for negotiations and compromise among leading actors in state and society. Although they may not exactly agree on what should be done and who should do it, these middle-aged leaders essentially understand each other better than they do their younger critics.

Most contemporary key actors basically agree that the preservation of fundamental political harmony and stability demands that government policymaking be guided by a sense of moderation and caution. The dominant policymakers hold that what has been achieved must be preserved and what does not seem feasible should not be tried. Unavoidable adjustments to changing circumstances are to be made as gradually as possible to avoid unsettling the basic patterns of West German domestic and foreign relations.

Can and will this basic elite consensus on the way to political system should function be maintained by new leaders? The present rulers of the Federal Republic have certainly sought to ensure such continuity by grooming as their successors men who essentially share their attachment to the prevailing patterns. At the same time they have endeavored to block the ascent of young political dissidents who seem intent on destroying the understandings that now sustain harmonious relations among West German elites. Whether such measures will in the long run suffice to over-come what now seems a trend toward sharper differences over means and ends in West German politics remains to be seen.

Political Participation and Political Stability

The theme of this chapter has been that different forms and degrees of political activism in the Federal Republic depend on personal motivation and structured opportunities. As we have seen, variations in motivation are largely the products of past politicization and current information; opportunities for partici-pation vary for the most part with different positions in state and society.

Close to four decades of elite-controlled institutionalization of political roles have yielded orderly and, on the whole, unspectac-ular relationships between the ruling few and the mass of the ruled under a representative form of democratic government. More West Germans are now interested and involved in politics beyond voting than in the early years of the Federal Republic, and more want a greater voice in policymaking. Indeed, some in-formed observers speak of a "participant revolution" in West Ger-man politics from the grass roots to the national level. But the increased engagement in civic action groups and social movements seems not as extensive and may not be as enduring as such a term implies.

Most citizens of the Federal Republic accept the stratified system of representation by which they are governed and see little purpose in becoming more involved in politics. And contemporary politi-cization and recruitment patterns suggest that the distribution of participants roles is unlikely to undergo major changes in the foreseeable future. The exceptional emphasis that West German leaders put on orderly political relations, and their evident concern about disruptive mass participation, go with the widespread con-viction among the general public that the present constitutional framework provides for essential domestic stability in difficult times for the Federal Republic.

The prevailing political recruitment and participation patterns may make for political tranquility, but they also include a conservative bias that tends to isolate the governing elites from important elements of the political public. Individuals and groups who significantly differ in their experience and attitudes from those now dominant are excluded from the top stratum. Elites essentially committed to the preservation of the status quo are usually not especially receptive to major innovations, or to aspiring leaders who sharply deviate from their own beliefs and values. In the years to come, however, the dynamics of foreign and domestic developments may confront West German policymakers with the need for decisions that might strain popular support for representative democratic government. And then it could become evident that recruitment processes that barred ambitious political activists from leading positions because they lacked the "proper" qualifications and outlook had alienated key groups at the middle level of the political public.

6

Party Politics

Representative democracy in the Federal Republic rests today on a competitive party system, and party government provides West Germans with the measure of its effectiveness.[1] Approvingly or not, they conceive of the present regime as a state controlled by political parties *(Parteienstaat)* and, more particularly, by the leaders of the major parties. The regime of the Hohenzollern Empire, in contrast, is remembered as an autocratic "administrative state" *(Verwaltungstaat)* run by government bureaucrats, that of the Weimar Republic as a state dominated by interest associations *(Verbändestaat)*, and that of Nazi Germany as a dictatorial "leadership state" *(Führerstaat)*.

The constitutional rules of the present regime call merely for governments that are the products of free and open parliamentary

1. A competitive party system depends, first, on regular free and open elections that give the voters periodic opportunities to express their preferences for various parties and their candidates for public office. Second, it requires generally accepted, orderly procedures that (a) allow a legislative majority to assume control over authoritative policymaking structures and (b) assure the opposition inside and outside the legislature that it will continue to have adequate opportunities to obtain such control in the future. In this sense, a party system is not competitive if opposition parties are barred from coming to power by legitimate means and parties are not competitive unless they can participate in elections with reasonable expectations of achieving at least some control over public policymaking.

elections and ultimately accountable to the voters. But in fact governments are formed and led by party elites commanding a majority in West German legislatures and dependent on support within their respective parties.

The preeminent role of political parties in contemporary West German public affairs is based on (a) the organization of the regime, (b) the patterns of competition and collaboration among pluralist party elites wedded to the regime, and (c) the effect of different types of party governments and different forms of interaction between governing leaders and their parties. Formal regulations and the actual style of political intercourse have in this respect combined to shape the relationship between the parties and other components of the Federal Republic's political system— notably the electorate, interest associations, and governmental agencies—as well as relationships among and within the parties. All of these relationships are interdependent; they have been molded by continuous reciprocal adaptation and by patterns of continuity and change in the domestic and international environment for West German politics.

DEVELOPMENT OF THE
PARTY SYSTEM

In such older democracies as the United States and Britain the regime came before the party system and the uninterrupted evolution of governmental structures decided the course of party development. In West Germany, on the other hand, the sharp discontinuities between the present and the Nazi regime reversed the process. The party system was formed before the establishment of the Federal Republic and its constitutional order and party elites therefore had greater influence on the development of new patterns of politics and government.

The leaders of parties licensed by the allied military governments after the collapse of the Third Reich were the principal architects of political reconstruction in West Germany. Summoned by the foreign occupation powers to fill the vacuum left by the elimination of the Nazi leadership, they very quickly became preeminent in public affairs. The remnants of the former elites were for the most part prevented from assuming leading roles by socioeconomic dislocation and allied regulations. Thus, party leaders with little or no involvement in Hitler's totalitarian regime could lay the foundations for a new political order before the creation of the Federal Republic in 1949. By the time the occupation authorities asked them to devise a constitution for a West German state, the leaders had become sufficiently entrenched to forge a regime designed to institutionalize party control over the political system.

The party leaders who wrote the West German constitution incorporated a competitive party system into their design for stable as well as representative governments in a pluralist society. The conditions needed for a well-functioning, democratic party system had been lacking under past German regimes; West Germany did not have the strong historical roots that had long sustained the operation of such a system in the United States and Britain. The authors of the Basic Law and subsequent implementing legislation considered it accordingly all the more essential to give firm legal underpinnings to the party system. Competing "legitimate" parties were by law to be principal instruments for the expression and representation of partisan cleavages in West German society, and a regime-supportive party system was to be the organizational framework for electoral processes and the interplay between party government and opposition inside and outside the legislative chambers.

Contemporary West German politics reflect the structural consequences of this design. To an extent unprecedented in German history, political parties now control the recruitment of elected as well as appointed key public officials and coordinate diverse policy preferences among the political and general publics. In contrast to the situation in former times and in other countries, political parties in the Federal Republic are today not the instruments of particularistic cultural and socioeconomic interest associations, but rather more general linkage structures between state and society. The present patterns of party government and opposition restrict the role of pressure groups and administrative agencies in policymaking, and they also limit as well as shape the role of the electorate. As broadly based electoral organizations, the major parties have served to legitimate regime principles that call for responsive and responsible democratic government; as more narrowly constituted membership organizations, they serve to integrate partisan activists into the political system.

In the light of the numerous and deep political divisions of the past, many of the founding fathers of the regime expected—and many contemporary observers feared—a revival of the highly unstable, multiparty system of the Weimar Republic. As it turned out, the parties that were the largest from the outset obtained between them an increasingly larger proportion of the popular vote and elective offices. The so-called "union parties"—the Christian Democratic Union (CDU) and its Bavarian affiliate, the Christian Social Union (CSU)—only barely outdistanced the Social Democratic party of Germany (SPD) in the first federal election of 1949. Thereafter the CDU/CSU took a commanding lead; in 1957 it became the first party in German history to win an absolute majority of the popular votes. The SPD managed to obtain majorities in subnational elections but advanced more gradually in federal elections and did not score a popular plurality until 1972.

West Germany seemed well on the way to a two-party system. Parliamentary government at the federal, state, and local level had come to mean party governments that consisted mostly or entirely of Christian or Social Democrats. The combined popular vote for the two major parties went from 60 percent in 1949 to 91 percent in 1976 and their share of the seats in the Federal Diet from 67 to 92 percent (see table 6.1). Of the seven other parties in the first Diet only one, the Free Democratic party (FDP) remained—rather precariously—represented in federal and state legislatures. All the others—such as a party claiming to represent the special interests of refugees from Eastern Europe and a sectional Bavarian party—failed to stay in the competition. New parties that sought elective offices—such as the right-wing National Democratic party (NDP) and the German Communist party (DKP)— were unable to reduce the combined strength of the major parties. This pattern held until late 1970s when a new partisan alignment, the Greens, broke into West German party politics. After first

TABLE 6.1

Elections for the Federal Diet, 1949–1983
(percentage distribution of popular vote and seats by party)

	1949	1953	1957	1961	1965	1969	1972	1976	1980	1983
Turn-out	78.5	85.8	87.8	87.7	86.8	86.7	91.2	90.7	88.7	89.5
CDU/CSU										
vote	31.0	45.2	50.2	45.4	47.6	46.1	44.8	48.6	44.5	48.8
seats	34.6	49.9	54.3	48.5	49.4	48.8	45.4	49.2	45.4	49.0
SPD										
vote	29.2	28.8	31.8	36.2	39.3	42.7	45.9	42.6	42.9	38.2
seats	32.6	31.0	34.0	38.1	40.7	45.2	46.4	42.9	43.9	38.8
FDP										
vote	11.9	9.5	7.7	12.8	9.5	5.8	8.4	7.9	10.6	6.9
seats	12.9	9.9	8.2	13.4	9.9	6.0	8.2	7.9	10.7	6.7
Greens										
vote	—	—	—	—	—	—	—	—	1.5	5.6
seats	—	—	—	—	—	—	—	—	—	5.3
Others										
vote	27.9	16.5	10.3	5.6	3.6	5.4	0.9	0.9	0.5	0.5
seats	19.9	9.2	3.5	—	—	—	—	—	—	—

Source: Statistisches Jahrbuch für die Bundesrepublik Deutschland 1950–1983.
Note: Vote is for second ballots cast for party lists.

winning some seats in a number of city councils and then in several state legislatures, the Greens became in 1983 the first new party in thirty years to enter the Federal Diet.

THE PARTY STATE

The Christian and Social Democratic party elites have over the years been able to expand and consolidate their paraconstitutional position in West German politics on the basis of Article 21 of the Basic Law. This provision makes political parties essential intermediaries between the voters and their government in a democratic polity, but limits that function to parties supporting the present form of government. In effect, this formal modification of the classical principles of direct as well as representative democracy has first of all enabled the leaders of the major parties to make these parties the primary foci for electoral choice. Second, it has allowed them to restrict alternative opportunities for political participation and the expression of policy demands.[2]

The specific legal implications of Article 21 and related constitutional provisions have been set forth in numerous laws, administrative regulations, and judicial decisions. In the early 1950s, for example, the Federal Constitutional Court sustained the contention of a government led by Christian Democrats that a right-wing party and an earlier version of the present Communist party should be outlawed as "antidemocratic" organizations. These rulings served to warn other groups critical of the regime that they risked a similar fate if they overstepped the boundaries of "legitimate" opposition. Laws sponsored jointly by the Christian and Social Democratic elites in the late 1960s have imposed severe restrictions on the formation and survival of new parties. These parties must have "democratic" objectives and structure and must publicly account for their activities and major sources of income; new parties also lose their legal status if they do not participate in any federal or state election in the space of six years. The political activities of interest associations and civic action groups have been similarly limited by laws that restrict their ability to influence governmental policymaking by penetrating or bypassing the major parties.

Beyond these restrictive rules, Article 21 has enabled the CDU/ CSU and SPD elites to derive tangible benefits from their preeminent position in the party system. As the leaders of the principal governing parties, they have been able to exercise the power of patronage appointments to top positions in the public broadcasting media, the judiciary, the Federal Bank and state banks, and the public administration.

The politicization of the public service has been a key element in the development of the West German party state. In 1981, according to a representative survey, close to 65 percent of top officials in the Federal administration and almost 85 percent of those in the civil service of the states belonged to one of the leading parties. Other than in Britain, key West German civil servants are

2. The integral role of the party state in West German politics is particularly well presented in the works of Kenneth Dyson. See, for instance his "Party Government and Party State" in H. Doring and G. Smith, eds., *Party Government and Political Culture in Western Germany* (New York: St. Martin's Press, 1982), pp. 77–100.

classified as "political officials" of party governments, subject to appointment and removal by their ministers and entitled to a pension. And unlike ordinary civil servants in the United States, those in the Federal Republic usually need not resign to run for and serve in an elective office. Members of the Federal Diet who come from the public service—about a third of the deputies in recent times—must only temporarily retire and retain the right to go back with their former rank once they leave office.

A second advantage enjoyed by the major party elites is that they have far greater access to the public and private media of mass communications than the leaders of other political organizations. As spokesmen for the government or major opposition party, they make frequent appearances on television and, as representatives of the major parties, they receive more of the free time allocated to the parties during election campaigns.

A third advantage is financial. West German parties get most of their income from membership dues, private contributions, and public funds. The major parties get most of this income, allowing them to support organizational and promotional activities that are beyond the means of the smaller parties. For example, the latter simply cannot afford the expensive services of public relations firms and polling organizations, which have become ever more important in West German electoral campaigns.

The information in table 6.2 indicates how much the reported income of the principal parties has increased in recent times and where it has generally come from.[3] For the SPD, the party with the largest membership dues remain the biggest source of income. The CDU and its CSU affiliate in Bavaria continue to depend more heavily on private donations, mostly from businessmen and corporations. The small FDP has needed such contributions from the private sector most of all.

These funds have not been suffcient to let the dominant parties meet their constitutional responsibilities according to their lead-

3. West German parties are required by the Basic Law to provide a public accounting on the size and general sources of their regular income. However, small private contributions need not be reported but are tax-deductible for the donors while legal loopholes have permitted the parties to conceal details on large contributions. Trade unions are specifically enjoined from giving financial aid to political parties.

TABLE 6.2
Funding of Political Parties, 1973 and 1982

	INCOME (IN MILLION DM)	MEMBER- SHIP DUES	PUBLIC FUNDS	PRIVATE CONTRIBU- TIONS	LOANS AND INCOME FROM PROPERTY
		SOURCES OF FUNDS (IN ROUNDED-OFF PERCENTAGES)			
CDU					
1973	72.4	39.0%	14.5%	40.3%	6.2%
1982	120.4	44.4	25.7	17.3	12.5
CSU					
1973	13.0	32.9	19.5	26.9	20.7
1982	32.4	25.3	23.1	21.9	29.6
SPD					
1973	76.8	68.2	16.3	7.6	7.9
1982	117.6	59.2	28.3	6.9	5.5
FDP					
1973	13.8	24.8	14.0	45.8	15.4
1982	22.4	23.2	24.6	46.9	5.4
Greens					
1981	2.7	33.2	17.5	21.2	26.7

Source: Calculated from data in Inter Nationes, *Parteien in der Bundesrepublik Deutschland*, S.O. 1-75 and S.O. 1-83. For Greens, *Fischer Weltalmanach, 1984*, p. 314.

ers. They have therefore increasingly drawn on public funds for shaping "the political will of the people" under Article 21 of the Basic Law. In addition to public grants for campaign expenditures and parliamentary salaries the four so-called establishment parties receive substantial but unspecified sums for their "civil education" activities.[4]

4. Under the West German Campaign Finance Law, parties—rather than candidates—draw funds from the public treasury for some of their campaign expenses if they receive more than 0.5 percent of the vote in federal elections. (Similar regulations exist in the various states). By this provision nine out of the fourteen parties fielding candidates in the 1983 federal election were denied public funds for their campaign. Such subsidies are advanced before an election on the basis of a party's votes in the previous election. If it gains votes the party will get more money after the election, but if it loses votes it must repay an appropriate amount to the public treasury. New and minor parties find it correspondingly more difficult than the large, established parties to borrow money before an election, and the smaller their competitive chances the greater the rate of interest on such high risk loans is likely to be.

Regulations affecting the nomination and election of parliamentary candidates have provided the established parties with another competitive advantage. Sponsored by the CDU/CSU and SPD elites, they have made it difficult for independent and minor party candidates to win and retain seats in the federal and state legislatures.

A candidate must first of all be nominated by a legitimate political party according to proper legal procedures. This stipulation prevents persons who are not sponsored by such a party from entering the race. Under the prevailing system for federal elections, an individual may then run as a constituency candidate, or as a candidate on a party list in the states, or both. As you may recall, a constituency candidate who captures a plurality on the first ballot in a single-member district will, however, not get the seat unless his party has won at least 5 percent of all valid votes or two additional constituencies (see page 119). The list candidates of a party that meets these qualifications will not be elected unless they are placed high enough on its list in the state to benefit from the ultimate proportional allocation of seats on the basis of second-ballot votes for the various parties. Either way the candidates of small parties face greater hurdles than those of the major ones.

In short, when it comes to minor parties, there are limits to the system of proportional representation in federal and state legislatures. These limits, in effect, tend to restrain electors from voting for the constituency candidates and the lists of parties that appear unlikely to gain representation; at the same time they enhance the representation of the major parties, because votes for parties that do not make the race are not counted in the distribution of legislative seats. For these reasons the success of the Greens in overcoming such formidable barriers in the late 1970s and early 1980s seemed all the more impressive to some observers and alarming to others.

A fifth advantage enjoyed by the major parties and, more particularly, their leaders has stemmed from the rules of legislative organization and procedures in various West German parliaments. Under the standing orders of the Federal Diet all key legislative posts and all committee assignments are reserved for members of properly constituted parliamentary parties (Fraktionen) and dis-

tributed by the leaders in proportion to their party's strength in
the chamber. A deputy will thus be excluded from the most important policy processes in the legislature if his party's delegation
constitutes less than 5 percent of its membership or if the leaders
blackball him.

Such arrangements have promoted the party state in the legislative arena, both by discouraging interest associations from supporting independent deputies and by strengthening cohesion
within the parliamentary parties. The leaders of a large one can
use the threat of explusion to keep dissidents in line and the
members of a small one are held together by the threshold for
getting positions on legislative committees.

The Basic Law allows a deputy to resign from his parliamentary
party but retain his seat; when several did so in 1972, it produced
a deadlock in the Federal Diet and that led to new elections. But,
in the absence of a situation where every vote is crucial, a deputy
who quits or is expelled from his parliamentary party and does
not join another will have little or no influence in the chamber and
is unlikely to be reelected. It is therefore not surprising that from
1972 to 1985 only three members of the Federal Diet left their
parliamentary party between elections without giving up their
seats.

Parties and Voters

Earlier we examined West German electoral processes in terms of
general political orientation and participation patterns; now let us
take a closer look at the specific relationship between parties and
voters. Most voters, as we noted, have a low sense of involvement
and influence in politics. Electoral turnout has nevertheless been
much higher than in other representative democracies, such as
Britain. But in the Federal Republic, as in Britain, voting as such
has normally been more the product of a sense of civic obligation
than of a deep concern with the outcome of elections. Under these
conditions the West German parties have not so much needed to
get their supporters to the polls—but to translate a propensity to
vote into ballots for their candidates.

The electoral choices of West German voters have largely been shaped by three interdependent factors: (a) the organization of representative government in the Federal Republic; (b) the partisan dispositions of the voters; and (c) the strategy and tactics employed by the parties to gain new votes without losing those of past supporters. Together these elements have over the years interacted with gradual, unspectacular changes in the environment for West German politics to produce fairly stable voting patterns.

The operative rules of the political system structure and limit of opportunities of West German voters to elect whom they please when they please. Elections ordinarily are held at regular intervals determined by the lawmakers; but they may come before their appointed time if a parliament is dissolved, as the Federal Diet was in 1972 and 1983. Except in some local elections, the voters cannot choose their governmental leaders directly; they can only opt for or against the parliamentary candidates of legitimate political parties. Votes for minor parties are likely to be wasted on unsuccessful candidates. The electorate has furthermore no immediate influence on nominating processes; in the absence of open primaries, it can only accept or reject as its deputies party candidates designated by a small number of active party members and functionaries.

In Federal Diet elections, as we have seen, half of the seats go to the victors in single-member constituency races, and the rest are apportioned among state list candidates according to their ranking and the electoral strength of their parties. Most West Germans cast their two ballots in federal elections as a single vote for or against a party and its designated governmental leaders. A constituency candidate's personal attractiveness is consequently less important to the voters than what he stands for. This applies even more to list candidates who get on the ticket as the representatives of social groups and interests, such as women, young people, and clergymen.

A choice between the major competitive parties has offered West German voters only rather general and limited alternatives among governmental policies and policymakers. Both the CDU/CSU and SPD have been above all electoral organizations for the broadest possible alignment of partisan supporters; their rival campaign appeals have accordingly been pitched to what their leaders take to be the lowest common denominator of political differences and preferences of the moment in a pluralist society.

In this connection it is worthwhile to recall several points that came up in previous chapters. One is that the so-called Old Middle Class of self-employed farmers, shopkeepers, and professionals has grown smaller whereas the New Middle Class of salaried white-collar employees in public and private service jobs has been increasing. A second point is that the incoming generation of young West German voters is on the whole much better educated and more firmly attached to the present form of government than the elderly outgoing generation. A third point is that most West German voters rate the performance of governing party leaders not so much by their adherence to abstract democratic principles as by their actions or inaction on issues which voters relate to their own well-being and that of their families. Last, we observed that the leaders of the major parties have given careful consideration to these instrumental standards of the voters in competing for their favor.

The Christian Democrats have managed to get most of the votes in every federal election but one since the establishment of the Federal Republic (see table 6.1). In national politics and, to a lesser extent, in state and local politics, they have been far more successful than their Social Democratic rivals in consistently capturing the support of a broad spectrum of voters in a changing electorate.

Both of the major parties have drawn most of their votes from more or less constant supporters. The most loyal electors of the conservative and emphatically "Christian'" CDU/CSU have been middle-aged and older members of the diminishing Old Middle Class. Some of them are devout Protestants living in the rural areas of northern Germany; most are men and, especially, women who live and regularly attend church in one of the small towns or villages of predominantly Roman Catholic southern Germany.

The most consistent supporters of the more reform-minded and decidedly secular SPD have been skilled blue-collar workers, often in declining industries such as coal and steel. Loyal Social Democratic voters are found mostly in the densely urbanized areas of the northern and central parts of the country; they are likely to belong to a trade union and to associate mostly with men and women who share their "working class" background and moderate political opinions.

For this relatively small core of firm SPD voters their party stands for social progress and the interests of the working people, the Christian Democrats for big business and reaction. For the not much larger nucleus of constant CDU/CSU supporters, on the other hand, the SPD is almost as much of a "red" menace to all they hold dear as the radical groups to the left of it. For both groups of loyalists voting habits are not necessarily the only, or even the principal, bases of party constancy. The most consistent supporters of the major West German parties are also apt to be their most faithful supporters. That is, they are voters who implicitly trust the party of their choice to do what is right and necessary according to their beliefs, feelings, and values. They vote for their party—rather than against another—because they are strongly attached to it for ideological and sentimental reasons. For these staunch loyalists, the strength of a symbolic attachment to the party and its leaders may override any dissatisfaction with the party's performance in and out of government.

In their election campaigns the leading parties have gone beyond this group of ever-faithful partisans and sought to mobilize a less-dedicated but much larger group of regular supporters. Altogether at least one-half but probably no more than two-thirds of the West German electorate consists of more or less constant voters, and most of these have supported the Christian Democrats. However, the proportion of constant voters has evidently been getting smaller. As in the United States and other Western democracies, there is an increasing number of independents who now vote for one party and then for another. Competition between the major West German parties has therefore come to focus more than formerly on winning the support of such floating voters in national and subnational elections.

The partisan preferences of these floating voters are more

closely linked to current political issues than those of party loyalists and are accordingly more sensitive to short-term changes in the policy environment. Their choice of party is largely determined by their personal involvement in political developments and their corresponding perception and evaluation of what different party governments can and should do about them. The Christian Democrats, for example, have been especially identified with the preservation of law and order and military security, and with greater competence than the Social Democrats in dealing with such major economic problems as lagging foreign trade and inflation. When these issues have been dominant in West German politics, voters in general and independent voters in particular have tended to favor the CDU/CSU. The Social Democrats, on the other hand, have been more closely associated with social reforms and the reduction of East–West tensions in Central Europe. When such matters have coincided with the wishes of independent voters, such voters have been more apt to favor the SPD. As in the United States, the competition for votes in the electoral marketplace is therefore largely informed by what the major party leaders take to be the prevailing mood of floating voters.

Independent voters in the Federal Republic are likely to be younger and better educated than constant voters, to have had more variegated politicizing experiences, and to live and work in more heterogeneous sociocultural settings. They are usually geographically and socially mobile persons who have worked at various jobs. Many commute between factories or offices in urban centers where they associate with fellow employees and take orders from their bosses, and suburban homes where they relax with their families. When it comes to choice of party, such voters are therefore more likely to be subject to a larger variety of incongruent, if not conflicting, pressures than those exposed to a more homogeneous social environment, and to be less firm in their partisan allegiances.

Significantly, shifting party preferences and ticket splitting have become particularly pronounced with well educated, middle-income, salaried white-collar employees in the major metropolitan centers; in other words, the same sort of people who are also disproportionately represented among what we termed the political public. From about the mid-1950s onward, their votes floated increasingly to the SPD and, to a lesser extent, the FDP and proved decisive for the victory of the reformist Social-Liberal Coalition in the 1969 and 1972 federal elections. Subsequently, the direction of these floating votes was reversed and moved toward the CDU/CSU, largely because of deteriorating economic conditions and a more conservative climate of political opinion. By the 1983 federal election the Christian Democrats had won over enough independent voters from the New Middle Class to score their greatest victory over the Social Democrats in almost thirty years.

Distinctions between social and economic groups are now much less important for the relationship between parties and voters than in earlier times and in other European democracies. For example, the votes of unorganized workers and white-collar employees are divided between the two major parties pretty much as those of the electorate in general; most trade-union members still favor the SPD, but their share of the electorate has been diminishing. Partisan differences based on traditional sex and religious distinctions have also waned. Most of the women's vote no longer goes invariably to the Christian Democrats. And the significance of religious affiliation in an electorate nominally divided almost equally into Protestants and Roman Catholics is not nearly as important as it used to be. Catholics still vote more extensively for the Christian Democrats than Protestants—especially in southern Germany, where they are in the majority. But the traditional appeal of the CDU/CSU for the support of all Christians, whatever their occupation and income, is no longer particularly effective, except among a diminishing number of devout members of both major religious groups.

Government by Party Elites

Policymaking has been more of a "positive sum" than a "zero sum" game among West German party leaders. That is, key participants have not normally ended up as outright winners or losers, but have tended to derive at least some benefits from interparty and intraparty bargaining processes. One reason is that the party system as a whole has not been sharply polarized into incompatible camps; this has permitted Christian, Social, and Free Democrats to join together in various mutually beneficial combinations at the federal, state, and local levels of government. A second reason is that party government has as a rule not only meant coalitions among different parties, but elite coalitions within the major parties. A third reason is that policymaking activities are not as centralized under the prevailing constitutional order as they are in such unitary states as Britain and France.

In contrast to the present British system, the outcome of a single parliamentary election has not allowed national West German party governments to determine policies for the entire country. The division of public powers between the executive and legislature and between the central and state governments provides the leaders of a strong and united opposition party with extensive opportunities for influencing national policies. Thus, when one of the major parties has controlled the executive branch of the Federal Government, the other has been able to modify if not block legislation on the strength of a large representation in the Federal Diet, or control of a majority of the votes of the state governments in the Federal Council, or both. And much as in the American two-party system, regional party leaders who are not members of the national executive and legislature have frequently played key roles in the formulation of national policies.

At election time the major party elites have fought against each other and accentuated their differences; between elections, their joint desire to make the present system work under conditions dictated by the policy environment has impelled them to seek parliamentary compromise solutions to partisan conflicts. This desire has been especially notable with respect to constitutional amendments to the Basic Law—requiring a two-thirds majority in both houses of the Federal parliament—but it has also applied to a good deal of bargaining over ordinary legislation. Many of the laws passed by federal as well as state parliaments have been the product of informal "behind-the-scenes" agreements among leaders of nominally opposing parties. Such forms of conflict resolution have been all the more important when public opinion and governing coalition parties have been sharply divided on policy issues; for instance, the 1965 law extending the statute of limitations on the prosecution of Nazi crimes could not have been passed without a de facto coalition between the governing CDU/CSU and the opposition SPD.

In the light of this customary pattern, astute observers of West German politics were all the more surprised when a parliamentary deadlock over the 1972 treaty with the Communist German Democratic Republic could not be resolved and the government had to appeal to the electorate to break it. For the first time in almost a quarter of a century the voters were asked to settle what their representatives could not decide for them; and decide they did by providing the governing SPD and FDP with more than enough votes to get the treaty through the Diet.

In federal and subnational politics, party government has been shaped by two rather different concepts of the relationships between the head of the government and the governing party elites. One is characterized by the autonomous and authoritative leader of an executive-centered elite coalition who dominates his party and considers it his instrument. In the other, the formal chief of government is, in fact, the chairman of a team of more or less coequal party leaders, and party elites inside and outside the legislature may play a much greater role in fashioning government policy. At different times and different settings, the prevailing relationship has been determined by the personality and style of performance of the governing leader, and by the power alignments among and within the political parties. Variations on both types are exemplified by party government from 1949 to 1982 under the first five chancellors of the Federal Republic.

A Christian Democrat, Konrad Adenauer (1949-1963), put into effect the concept of a government leader who dominates his party and uses it to control an executive-centered coalition of party elites. At the time, the proponents of a more liberal parliamentary system considered his "chancellor democracy" too autocratic and arbitrary; it now appears that Adenauer's highly popular leadership made a significant contribution to the institutionalization of party government. Chancellor democracy was congruent with cultural traditions of strong executive authority in the state and served to integrate West Germans into their new political system during a difficult period of socioeconomic and political reconstruction.

In the fourteen years of the Adenauer era the CDU/CSU attained a position of hegemony in the West German party system, and its fortunes were closely tied to the popularity of the chancellor. Adenauer managed to establish and generally to maintain a tight reign over the Christian Democrats by skillfully combining his roles as chief of the federal government, chairman of the party, and leader of an interparty parliamentary coalition. Formally distinct, these roles—along with those of Adenauer's subordinates—became in practice all but indistinguishable. Major policy decisions were often made by Adenauer alone, or in consultation with the members of a small "kitchen cabinet" of trusted ministers, key civil servants, and party lieutenants; on such occasions the regular cabinet, Diet deputies, and national CDU organs ratified rather than determined governmental policy. As the supreme arbitrator between legislative and administrative elites between party and interest group leaders, Adenauer relied primarily on his assistants in the Chancellor's Office to see to it that his objectives were realized.

After Adenauer, party governments became more collegial, with party elites in the federal legislature and the states playing a more important role in fashioning coalition policies. Initially a Christian Democrat, Ludwig Erhard (1963–66), presided over a brittle alignment of the CDU/CSU and the Free Democrats. Erhard could not give West Germans in general, and the Christian Democrats in particular, the strong, authoritative leadership that they had come to expect after fourteen years of chancellor democracy under Adenauer. He did not have the prestige and skill that had allowed Adenauer to resist or vitiate competing policy demands and control factional disputes, and he permitted contending interests far greater autonomy and himself less. This turned out to be his undoing.

Erhard attempted to exercise authority in his government and party by playing the part of a "people's cancellor" above partisan strife, something like the plebiscite presidency which Charles de Gaulle had then established for himself in France. But though such a posture may have helped Erhard to lead his party to victory in the 1965 election, it was not an appropriate role for a federal chancellor in the evolving West German party state. Erhard was unable to check increasing factionalism in the CDU/CSU elite. He was publicly criticized as an inept and weak chancellor by leaders of his own party, especially by Adenauer whom he characteristically allowed to remain as national chairman for some time before reluctantly assuming the position himself. The still immense prestige of the former chancellor helped to seal Erhard's fate after he completely lost control over the Christian Democratic elite; it decided, against his wishes, to form a Grand Coalition with the principal opposition party, the SPD.

Collective government by collaborating party elites shaped the political style of Kurt Kiesinger, the Christian Democratic chancellor of the Grand Coalition (1966–69). It brought together the principal leaders of the two major parties in the name of maximum political stability and harmony in a time of economic difficulties. In contrast to the Erhard government, the Grand Coalition made party authority identical with governmental authority. For all practical purposes, there was no longer an opposition in the federal parliament; the Free Democratic party, with only 8 percent of the seats in the Federal Diet and no veto power in the Federal Council, could do little to influence policymaking. Many West German and foreign observers therefore believed the Grand Coalition to have seriously delayed, if not blocked, the institutionalization of a truly competitive party system.

In fact, this unprecedented form of collaboration between the major party elites was a temporary marriage of convenience. The Christian Democratic leaders hoped that as a result they would win either an absolute parliamentary majority in the next federal election or, at least, a large enough plurality to dominate the next government. The Social Democratic leaders overrode protests in their party with the argument that they had at long last gained an opportunity to eradicate the popular image of the SPD as a permanent opposition party in national affairs; it would now be able to establish its legitimacy and capacity to govern the country.

The partners in the Grand Coalition were bound together by a carefully drawn coalition contract which balanced their formal authority and responsibilities and provided for informal arrangements to iron out differences over government policy. For example, the chancellorship went to the party chairman of the Christian Democrats, Kiesinger, but the chairman of the Social Democrats, Willy Brandt, became deputy chancellor and foreign minister; other posts were similarly apportioned between the two parties. Government measures were decided on by interministerial consultations within or, more often, outside the cabinet, and legislative strategies were worked out in frequent meetings with the governing parties' parliamentary leaders.

In these circumstances Chancellor Kiesinger was, in effect, something like a board chairman who is at most first among equals. He was severely restrained in using the preeminent formal powers that were his under the Basic Law and did not enjoy Adenauer's autonomy in the choice of ministers and the determination of governmental policy. The composition of the government as well as its actions had to satisfy the need for balance and collegial unity in a heterogeneous coalition of independently powerful leaders. These, in turn, had to contend with party opponents who charged them with putting "opportunistic" considerations ahead of party principles. And although neither the Christian Democrats nor the Social Democrats could govern alone, both parties were strong enough to form an alternative coalition with the Free Democrats if their policy differences proved irreconcilable.

Kiesinger was thus a weaker leader of his government and party than was Adenauer, but he was also a more astute politician than Erhard. As chancellor, he acted primarily as a discreet mediator among his colleagues in the government; as the chairman of his party, he sought to use his personal charm and considerable political skills to mollify Christian Democratic critics of the Grand Coalition. He did both rather well, but evidently at the cost of muting his "chancellor effect" on the electorate's choice of party.

The prestige attached to the incumbent chancellor had contributed to electoral victories of the CDU/CSU in the days of Adenauer and Erhard, but it was not enough of a magnet in 1969 to give the party the parliamentary majority it had sought. The SPD still came in only second best, though with more votes than ever before. The Grand Coalition had, however, done its intended service for the Social Democratic leaders; they were unwilling to continue as the junior partners, and found the Free Democrats eager to join them in an alternative "Social-Liberal" Coalition. For the first time in the twenty years since the establishment of the Fedeal Republic, the SPD became the principal governing party and the CDU/CSU the opposition party in the federal parliament. The precedent of the Grand Coalition survived as a model for future "crisis" governments by party elites.

The Social-Liberal Coalition was once again a marriage of convenience, though a more enduring one than the Grand Coalition. It was confirmed and strengthened by the 1972 federal election, which gave the Social Democrats for the first time a parliamentary plurality but not a majority. Subsequent gains by the Christian Democrats in state elections accentuated the interdependence of the coalition parties. The SPD needed the FDP to remain the senior governing party and the FDP needed the SPD to stem the apparent trend toward a two-party system. These considerations strongly influenced the collaborative association among leaders of the two parties in the federal as well as various state governments; and they entered into the relationship between these leaders and the functionaries and members of their respective parties. In both cases the basic theme was that the Social Democrats and Free Democrats had to swim together lest they sink together in turbulent political waters and that their common predicament called for mutual assistance in elections and reciprocal concessions on policy differences.

For most of the chancellorship of Willy Brandt (1969–74), foreign policy issues were in the forefront, making collaboration fairly easy. The SPD and the FDP elites were both determined to "normalize" the relationship between the Federal Republic and the Communist countries of Eastern Europe, above all the German Democratic Republic, and fought together to overcome the opposition of the CDU/CSU. As long as foreign policy was preeminent in West Germany, Brandt was in his element. He drew on his worldwide prestige as a statesman to play the role of a conciliator in domestic and foreign affairs and left more mundane party problems to other Social Democratic leaders. He took pride in his rather easygoing style of leadership, which worked well enough in international and coalition politics, but was less effective in dealing with growing intraparty conflicts in the SPD. Brandt kept rather loose reigns on the party in his capacity as its chairman and maintained a tolerant view toward young militants who wanted to transform the party into a more radical "vanguard of the working class." More moderate Social Democratic leaders vainly sought to induce Brandt to keep the radical wing in line and to curb activities they considered harmful to the party and its reinformist program.

Brandt, like Adenauer and Erhard, was more or less eased out of the chancellorship by fellow party leaders, rather than being deposed by an election or a "positive" vote of no confidence in the Diet. He resigned in 1974 when one of his closest assistants was arrested as an East German agent. But by all accounts key members of the Social Democratic elites made no move to stop him and were not particularly distressed to see him go. In their view Brandt has ceased to be an asset to the party in its electoral battles with the CDU/CSU. They believed that he was unable to deal forcefully with increasingly pressing domestic economic issues; off the record, some of Brandt's most bitter critics in the SPD held that he was too much of a moralizer to be a good politician and that he had turned himself into a living monument to the foreign policy achievements that had won him the Nobel Peace Prize. In any event, Brandt was not considered an indispensable chancellor, not least because a successor was readily at hand in the person of Helmut Schmidt.

As the new SPD chancellor of the Social-Liberal Coalition, Schmidt (1974–1982) evidently took Adenauer for his model. His political style marked him as a highly pragmatic and, sometimes, ruthless man of action. In the government and the Federal Diet he sought to establish himself as the dominant personality of an executive-centered coalition; in the Social Democratic party he assumed a hard line toward the radical left wing and insisted that it accept his more conservative position in socioeconomic matters. Although Brandt remained the SPD's chairman, Chancellor Schmidt quickly became its leading figure in the eyes of the electorate. In fact, his personal popularity came to exceed that of his party.

Schmidt stayed in office longer than any chancellor since Adenauer. But his apparent efforts to emulate Adenauer as an authoritative and autonomous leader of a governing coalition of party elites proved increasingly unsuited to developing patterns of partisan alignments within as well as outside his Social Democratic party.

Schmidt's accession coincided with the first major long-term downturn in the West German economy since the establishment of the Federal Republic, and he gave first priority to drastic measures for renewed economic growth. His Social-Liberal government cut back on social programs, which suited the Free Democratic leaders and their associates among the business elite more than SPD and labor union leaders outside the government. There was a widening gap between domestic and foreign programs advocated by Schmidt's party and the policies followed by a popular chancellor on whom that party seemed to depend for electoral success and governing power.

The CDU/CSU made a strong nationwide comeback in the 1976 federal election and Schmidt was reelected chancellor of a weaker Social-Liberal coalition by just a one-vote margin in the new Federal Diet. There followed six more years of increasingly bitter strife between a chancellor intent on maintaining an executive-centered alignment of party, business, and labor leaders, and unhappy Social Democrats who felt that the chancellor was demanding more loyalty from SPD parliamentary deputies than was his due in a democratic party. In 1980 Schmidt led the Social-Liberal coalition to its fourth electoral victory, but soon after it began to crumble under mounting opposition from business leaders on the one hand and critical SPD leaders on the other. The FDP finally switched partners in 1982 and formed a new coalition government with the CDU/CSU under the chairman and parliamentary leader of the Christian Democrats, Helmut Kohl.

INTRAPARTY RELATIONS

Relations among West German elites—and especially those among the party elites—shape and are shaped by relationships within the major parties. As in other countries, intraparty relationships involve of course many elements—from the momentary effects of particular issues, and the personalities and associations of particular individuals, to the more general and enduring patterns of the political system and policy environment. Two interdependent factors are however exceptionally important.

The first is a party's proximity to the levers of public authority in the Federal Republic. Do its leaders have a great deal of influence over policymaking, or only some influence, or none at all? Is the party represented in legislative bodies and, if so, is it a governing or opposition party? If it is a governing party, at what level do its leaders wield public authority, and how firmly and in what form? For example, do they command majorities in only one or both houses of the Federal parliament? Are they out of power in national politics but in control of key state governments? Are they able to rule alone or do they depend on cooperation of coalition partners? If they depend on cooperation, how solid is the alliance? And what are a party's chances for retaining or obtaining government power in the next election? A strong governing party may be able to manipulate public policy on behalf of its electoral strategy whereas a weak one is more apt to provide opposition parties with opportunities to score electoral gains. On the whole, the greater the present or prospective influence of particular party leaders on public policymaking the greater, too, is likely to be their influence within their party.

The second major factor is the dual character of the major West German parties. Like American parties, they are electoral organizations for directly or indirectly recruiting leading public officials; but they are also mass organizations of dues-paying party members, like most European parties. As electoral organizations the principal West German parties are integral parts of the political order and jointly link the representative components of the state to the pluralist components of an advanced industrial society. As mass membership organizations, however, they stand apart and are associated with opposing partisan viewpoints and philosophies. As competing electoral parties the CDU/CSU and SPD try to appeal to a wide range of values, sentiments, and policy demands and to unite behind their banners the largest possible alignment of voters. In this respect, their activities are aimed outward to gain the support of diverse interest groups and to project a favorable image to a broad and heterogeneous electoral public. But as membership parties, they are committed to particularistic ideologies and programs that may not necessarily appeal to outsiders. In this respect the major West German parties are internally oriented and their character is defined by intraparty relationships among leaders, middle-level activists, and rank-and-file members.

The role of the electoral party is measured numerically in terms of votes gained or lost; that of the membership party qualitatively in terms of its effect on the selection and actions of political leaders. Here we need to notice first of all that though party membership has increased in recent years it still does not include more than one out of twenty West German voters. Second, the ratio of members to voters varies a good deal among the parties (see table 6.3). Both the Christian and the Social Democrats have a relatively large proportion of members among their voters,

TABLE 6.3

Party Members and Voters, 1983 (in thousands)

	SPD	CDU	CSU	FDP	GREENS	TOTAL
Members	940	732	182	86	25	1,965
Voters[a]	14,866	14,857	4,140	2,706	2,165	38,734
Ratio members to voters	1:16	1:20	1:23	1:31	1:87	1:20

Source: Calculated from data in *Der Fischer Weltalmanach, 1984,* pp. 282, 311.
[a] Second-ballot votes in federal election.

whereas the Free Democrats and, even more, the Greens form not so much mass membership parties as so-called cadre parties. Third, there are far more nominal than active party members. These may have been recruited by relatives or friends, or joined to obtain or retain a public service job in the West German party state: beyond paying their dues regularly nominal members will usually participate only sporadically in party affairs.

For most of the time and in places where its influence is most telling, the membership party consists in effect of a small core of political activists. These probably make up no more than one percent of the voters, but they tend to be far more engaged and committed political partisans than most West Germans. To the extent that they have been united on their party's principles and objectives they have given strength to its leadership; insofar as they have been deeply divided on this score they have weakened it. To some degree all of the party elites have had to contend with intraparty tensions arising from conflicts between their party's internal and external relations, and from efforts to reconcile the purposes of an ideologically diffuse electoral party with those of a programmatically cohesive membership party. Generally they have managed to deal with such problems, through compromise where necessary and party discipline where possible. Both forms of conflict resolution are facilitated by the formal requirements for the organization of legitimate political parties in West Germany.

Parties of Representation

The democratic framework for intraparty relations is defined by public law and derivative party statutes, and in both of the major parties it corresponds to the federal and representative structure of the West German state. The regular party organizations are composed of interlocking local, regional, state, and national components; in addition there are special sections for young members, women, and occupational groups. The affiliated union parties, the Christian Democratic Union and the Bavarian Christian Social Union, maintain separate party establishments all the way up into the Federal Parliament; both include federated suborganizations representing particular interest groups, such as the major churches, agricultural and business associations, and organized labor.

Representative leadership in the established parties rests nominally on authority delegated from below, but in fact largely on oligarchic control by party elites. Federal party organs are formally supreme, but they depend on autonomous parliamentary parties and regional organizations to implement their decisions. And although the tasks of various party units and officials are formally divided along horizontal and vertical lines, they are normally connected through a hierarchic network of party functionaries who occupy several positions simultaneously.

Executive committees elected at periodic party meetings essentially run the regular organization at different levels. As a rule, local party chapters provide the ordinary members with their only opportunity to participate directly in party deliberations because all higher party organs are representative bodies. By law local organizations must be small enough to permit such grassroots participation, but frequently the membership is too dispersed or too small to warrant a local chapter. Local party meetings are furthermore usually poorly attended and dominated by a few active party members. Most of these leaders will be local government officials and seasoned, nonsalaried party functionaries who place each other on the local executive committee, and represent the party in communal elections and the local membership on higher party bodies.

Beyond nominating constituency candidates for state and national elections local leaders play on the whole only minor roles in wider party affairs. For party activists in state and federal politics the lcoal chapters are principally a source of grassroots support; for the party organization they are the reservoir for unpaid campaign workers at election time; for ordinary party members they offer a means of access to public officeholders of their party who may intercede on their behalf with governmental agencies.

Regional party organs, in contrast to the local chapters, are key arenas for intraparty relations. They vary in size but normally include several state and federal electoral districts and a hundred or more local units. Delegates to regional party conventions elect the regional party chairman and executive committee and regional representatives to state and national party congresses.

It is at the regional level that the functions of the electoral party and the membership party intersect most significantly and middle-level activists become particularly important. This is the point at which intraparty alignments, and the influence of affiliated and outside interest groups, primarily enter into the choice of candidates and platforms for the electoral party and into crucial deliberations on ideological programs for the membership party. It is also the key organizational level for the conduct of the most intense personal campaign activities in state and federal elections—canvassing, mass meetings, and the like. Lastly, it is the level at which incumbent party leaders maintain—and aspiring leaders seek to obtain—a strong power base for prominent roles in state and federal politics. Members and likely members of the top party elites usually command the support of one or more large regional organizations.

The stepwise contraction of membership representation by leading party activists continues upward through the state to the national level. At conventions of the state party, delegates from the regional organizations elect the state chairman and executive committee, select and rank the party's list of candidates for state and federal elections, and designate their choice for chief of the state government. These proceedings are normally controlled by the regional party elites, though they may occasionally involve a good deal of conflict and bargaining among party factions and spokesmen for socioeconomic interest groups. The designated head of the state government is usually the incumbent government leader or the chairman of the state party and should the party win the next state election, the choice of the party convention is customarily binding on its state diet deputies, though constitutionally they are free to elect whom they please. Should the chief of a governing state party resign between elections his successor will be chosen by the leader of the parliamentary party with the advice and consent of the state executive committee. The strength of the ties between these two party organs will vary with differences in the nature of intra- and interparty relations in various states; since there is usually a large overlap in membership, serious conflicts between the leadership of the parliamentary party and of the party organization on the outside are unlikely unless they are controlled by opposing party factions.

The national organization of the Social Democrats is formally more centralized and integrated than that of the Christian and Free Democrats and a great deal more so than that of the Greens. It still incorporates vestiges of the encapsulated and disciplined "proletarian" membership party that was established more than a hundred years ago and became the model for Lenin's Bolshevik party and its Communist offshoots throughout the world. The national CDU organization, on the other hand, dates back only to the founding of the Federal Republic and still shows its origins as a heterogenous union of regional electoral parties established just a few years earlier. The more decentralized structure of the national CDU also reflects the greater diversity of its constituent and affiliated groups and their resistance to efforts to create a more thoroughly integrated federal party.

Under the party statutes of the SPD and CDU, the representatives of the regional organizations to the national convention speak for the entire membership and form the supreme decision-making body for the party as a whole. However, since most of their authority is delegated to the national executive committee, and most of their decisions serve only to ratify those taken elsewhere, the actual power of the convention delegates is more nominal than real.

National party conventions in West Germany are usually pretty dull. Hundreds of resolutions may be introduced, especially at SPD conventions—but normally few will pass if they are opposed by the top leadership. For the most part between 300 and 400 delegates meeting biannually for four or five days can do little more than listen to lengthy speeches and place their stamp of approval on proposals presented by key party activists. The proceedings will be dominated by national leaders and the leaders of the strongest regional organizations and votes will reflect subnational party alignments.

Nonetheless these conventions serve two important functions in the CDU and SPD. One is focused on the external relations of the electoral party. National conventions are usually held just before a federal or state election and are designed to draw wide public attention to a party's electoral candidates and platforms; before a federal election they dramatize the selection of a candidate for chancellor and demonstrate the party's solidarity behind its choice. National conventions also provide an internally oriented, integrative function for the membership party. They legitimate the authority of the national party leadership through the election or reelection of the party's chairman, vice-chairmen, and other members of the national executive committee. They may also adopt a party program and resolutions stating general principles that are supposed to establish fundamental guidelines for the membership party and its legislative and governmental representatives.[5]

Between conventions, the CDU's and SPD's national executive committees and especially their presidiums act as the top decision-making bodies for the membership party at the federal level. In a way, these bodies resemble the Federal Council of the state governments in the constitutional organization of the Federal Republic. They fuse separate components of the party leadership and link national and subnational party organs. In the SPD as well as in the CDU the national executive committees consist of top government leaders, legislative leaders, and regional functionaries, and reflect the balance of power among various intraparty elite alignments.

The national chairman is the official leader of the membership party and is its principal public spokesman. His formal powers are

5. Such programs and resolutions have played a far more important role in the SPD than the CDU/CSU and FDP. The 1959 Godesberg Program of the SPD thus provided the doctrinal basis for a new course of the national electoral party by discarding practically all of the Marxist ideology of the traditional membership party. SPD leaders could thereafter meet left-wing criticism of their allegedly "opportunistic" electoral tactics and coalition arrangements by reference to appropriate chapters and verses in the party's Basic Program.

quite limited in both the CDU and SPD. At meetings of the national executive committee and presidium his vote counts for no more than those of the other members, and he may find himself in a minority. The extent of the national chairman's real influence in intraparty relations depends on the unity among the top party elites, on his personal authority and political skill, and on the power he may derive from other offices.

The first chairman of the CDU, Chancellor Adenauer, used his governmental position, his personal authority, and his great political skills to dominate the federal party; he was less influential at lower levels and left politics in the states pretty much to regional CDU leaders in exchange for their support. The second chairman, Chancellor Erhard, was unable to play a similar role, as we noted, and had to give way to Kiesinger, previously a CDU state chieftain and minister president. While he was chancellor, Kiesinger held his own in his capacity of party chairman by mediating among other members of the CDU elite. He was, however, compelled to quit as party chairman when he failed to retain the chancellorship in 1969. His successor was the leader of the CDU opposition in the Federal Diet, Rainer Barzel, who had to resign in 1972 when he proved unable to recapture the chancellorship for the union parties.

Helmut Kohl, the man who followed Barzel as party chairman, was neither chancellor nor leader of the CDU in the Diet but a powerful state government and party leader. As the chancellor-designate of the CDU and CSU in the 1976 federal election Kohl was also unable to lead the affiliated parties back to national power. But unlike Kiesinger and Barzel, he retained the chairmanship of his party and remained a viable candidate for the chancellorship. He sought to enhance his chances in this respect by moving from the position of a state government leader to that of leader of the CDU opposition in the Federal Diet. This kept Kohl in the national spotlight, though he had temporarily to stand aside for the 1980 election when the Bavarian CSU leader Franz Josef Strauss made an unsuccessful run for the chancellorship. As the chairman as well as parliamentary leader of his party Kohl was eventually able to forge a coalition between the CDU/CSU and the FDP and to become federal chancellor in 1982 without new national elections. Like Adenauer and Kiesinger before him, Chancellor Kohl held on to the chairmanship of his party and included other key CDU and CSU leaders in his government.

The SPD, as a more cohesive membership party, has been less volatile in the choice of party chairman. At this writing, only three men have held the position; two of these died in office, and all of them became chairman without a contest. The post-Nazi chairman of the party, Kurt Schumacher, kept a tight reign on the party organization in his dual roles as head of the membership party and leader of the principal opposition party in the Federal Diet. When Schumacher died in 1952, his former deputy Erich Ollenhauer succeeded him in both posts. Ollenhauer lacked his predecessor's personal leadership authority in the membership party; he was above all a loyal organization man whom other senior SPD functionaries considered one of their own. Even before his death Ollenhauer let another man assume the leadership of the electoral party as the SPD's candidate for chancellor. That man was Willy Brandt, then Lord Mayor of West Berlin.

Brandt remained a state government leader when he was elected party chairman in 1963; and he kept the party chairmanship when he resigned as federal chancellor in 1974. Thereafter, the national SPD leadership was divided for six years among Brandt, the chairman of the membership party, Chancellor Helmut Schmidt, the leader of the electoral party, and Herbert Wehner, the chairman of the parliamentary party. This exceptional triad arrangement worked better than expected during a period of considerable friction in the principal governing party. However, with Wehner's retirement in 1980 and Schmidt's loss of the chancellorship two years later, long-time SPD chairman Brandt was left free to play the role of a conciliating senior leader for the principal opposition party in the mid-1980s.

In sum, then, effective control over the national organizations of the major parties has rested with an intraparty elite consisting of the top federal and state government leaders, legislative leaders, and key party functionaries. Most regional leaders have played more important roles in the affairs of the Federal party than federal leaders in those of the state parties—especially when a party has been out of power in the national level and in power in the subnational level. At both levels, authoritative public policy-making by governing party leaders has moreover been shaped more by factors outside the party organization than by official partisan policy objectives. Insofar as the membership party provides for the constitutional expression of the "political will of the people," it does so primarily through the selection of their parliamentary representatives.

Choosing Representatives for the People

According to the majoritarian priciples of the West German parliamentary system, competing parties propose and the voters decide who is to represent the people in legislative bodies and who will govern. But as in other representative democracies, the choice of the voters is largely preempted by the decisions of relatively few political activists. And the processes of candidate selection in the principal parties favor the renomination of incumbent legislators.

There are no primaries, as we noted, and the voters are asked to cast two ballots in a Federal election. Most candidates for the Federal Diet are first chosen by local party activists to contest a constituency seat and then placed and ranked on the state lists of the parties by the secret votes of delegates to regional nominating conventions.

Who gets to run in a safe or in a marginal "swing" district and who gets on a state list and how close to the top is thus usually decided by top- and middle-level activists in the regional organizations and only indirectly by ordinary members of the mass membership party. When a constituency candidate who is also on the list captures a district, a list candidate who would otherwise not have made it will move up and get a seat as well—provided his party is entitled to it under the distributional rules for proportional representation of the voters. And when death or resignation open up a place in a parliamentary party, it is filled by the person who came closest to winning on the corresponding state list of that party in the preceeding election. On the other hand, a district candidate who is well placed on the list of a party which surmounts the five percent barrier for representation is likely to make it into the Diet even if defeated in a constituency seat.[6] For that reason, a constituency candidate who faces unfavorable odds in his district will almost always strive for a more promising list slot at the regional nominating conventions. If he is a prominent member of the state party he will ordinarily be successful; if not, his list position will depend on the votes he can obtain from the convention delegates. A nomination contest will usually involve a good deal of jockeying and bargaining among various intraparty factions and competing interest groups that are trying to get their people into the Federal Diet.

The national party headquarters in Bonn coordinates federal election campaigns in the states; it has, however, little or no influence on the selection of candidates for the Federal Diet. Governing party leaders are likely to be more successful than opposition leaders in promoting the nomination of individuals whom they consider particularly qualified for the legislature, such as financial experts and other specialists on public policy matters. But if they press too hard, their efforts are apt to be counterproductive; regional and local party leaders jealously guard their power of nomination and have often gone out of their way to reject candidates favored by national party leaders. Even Chancellor Adenauer lacked sufficient influence to overcome this problem, and his efforts to introduce additional national party lists got nowhere. In federal parliamentary activities, government as well as opposition leaders depend therefore all the more on intraparty discipline and elite collaboration. And in pushing for a particular course of action in the Federal Diet they have to consider that its members

6. Although the proportional allocation of all parliamentary seats is based on (second-ballot) votes for electoral lists in the states, the more constituencies a party captures directly the less secure is a low place on these lists. If the SPD is entitled to 200 seats and has won 100 constituencies, the latter number will then be deducted from the former and only 100 SPD list candidates will get into the Diet. By the same token, if the party should win only 50 constituencies, 150 list candidates will get seats.

are tied to sponsors and clients in the constituency and state organizations of the membership party.

PARTY STATE, PARTY SYSTEM, AND PARTY GOVERNMENT

We began this chapter with the observation that party competition and party government are basic elements of the contemporary regime in West Germany. In conclusion let us consider three questions arising from what we have noted about political parties in the Federal Republic. How solidly is the party state imbedded in the political order? How stable is the prevailing party system? How important is it which set of party leaders form the government?

The West German party state is a peculiar hybrid that provides the formal as well as functional framework for representative government in a pluralist society. The Basic Law, as we saw earlier (chapters 2 and 4), combines liberal democratic principles that endorse partisan conflicts over power in the state with the traditional notion in German public law that the state and its interests are more enduring and comprehensive than partisan organizations and their particular concerns. The democratic state is thus supposed to serve rather than dominate its citizens, and public authority is to be based on the will of the electorate. Democratic parties serve to legitimate that authority under the constitution by providing all citizens with opportunities for participation and representation in politics.

The party state also provides the framework for collaboration among the leading players in West German politics. We noted previously (chapter 4) that West Germans tend to consider the state akin to a corporation with different sets of governing managers making policy in the name of the citizen stockholders. And we also observed (chapter 5) that leadership at the management level of the state involves a network of people occupying top positions in the public and private sector. The principal parties are key political linkage structures for the elites in state and society.

In form as well as function the party state rests on a number of necessary conditions. Three are particularly important: the party state demands a delicate balance between its governmental and its partisan elements; it calls for a spirit of trust and cooperation among the dominant elites; and it requires general acquiescence, if not wholehearted support, from party members and voters. On the whole these conditions have been met in West German politics, but strong criticism of the party state by moderate as well as radical members of the political public have lately raised doubts regarding its future.

The criticism advanced by both conservative and liberal commentators is that, in national as well as in regional and local politics, the party state is in effect a state of the leading parties. In this view the CDU/CSU and SPD have gone beyond their proper roles in a representative democracy and have grossly abused the rules of conduct that go with the privileged positions of so-called regime-supportive parties. Massive patronage appointments to public service jobs in the state have undermined the integrity of the civil service, the public media, and the top judiciary according to such criticism. And self-serving laws for funding party activities through the state are said to have undermined respect for parliamentary democracy in West Germany.

More radical opponents of the prevailing party state make some of the same points, but for a different reason. They want to abolish rather than reform it, because in their opinion the party state serves to uphold an undesirable political order. According to this view, the major parties have not taken control of the state but have become its extension into society. In this sense they are "parties of the state" that limit political participation and legitimate oligarchic rule in the name of representative democracy.

In one way or another, quite a few politically concerned West Germans thus consider the prevailing party state more of an obstacle than an aid to a well-functioning democratic system. Perhaps it will undergo modifications in response to changing conditions. Anti-establishment groups, such as the Greens and various "extra-parliamentary" movements, may succeed in their efforts to weaken the strategic roles now played by the regular parties in shaping the political relationship between people and state. Shifts in electoral support could alter current patterns of party patronage and funding. And irreconcilable differences over national policy might sharpen partisan cleavages among the elites and undermine the spirit of collaboration at the top of the party state. But in the last analysis really major changes in the relationship between state and parties seem unlikely in the foreseeable future. The West German party state has evolved into an institution that is so much a basic part of the legitimate political order in the Federal Republic that drastic alterations appear impossible without unravelling the entire system of representative democracy.

If the party state will persist, what about the stability of the West German party system? Current trends suggest that two factors are particularly important on that score. One is the element of inconstancy in the partisan preferences of West German voters and the other is the questionable willingness of some more active and influential participants in politics to sustain moderate forms of party competition and cooperation.

We took note of a decided trend toward a more heterogeneous electorate that includes fewer all-weather party loyalists and more independent voters than formerly. By present indications the major West German parties will increasingly be confronted with voters who are less likely than those in the past to support or oppose a party in terms of their identification with particular social and economic groups and more likely to divide, not as predictably, on the basis of their perception of a party's ability to cope with urgent governmental problems.

Questions about the readiness of more prominent participants to maintain the prevailing pattern, of competition and cooperation arise from a generational turnover in party membership since the 1960s. The newcomers are on the whole much better educated than the oldtimers and they tend to hold relatively secure white-collar jobs in a period of mass unemployment. Many are pragmatic careerists who joined one of the established parties to get ahead in the public service. The politically most active members in this group are usually local or regional party functionaries who have been elected or appointed to some public office. They are the manifestation of a trend toward the increasing professionalization of West German party politics. A second group among this new generation of party activists consists of ideologically more engaged and uncompromising partisans. Its members are likely to be university students, teachers, clergymen, and journalists—rather than professional politicians. And whereas self-styled political realists in the first group tend to put access to governmental power ahead of fealty to party programs, "idealists" in the second group are prone to insist on strict adherence to distinctive political principles. Both types are to be found in each of the parties currently represented in the Federal Diet. The question is which group will set the tone for relations within and between the parties as they confront a more issue-oriented electorate.

At present the strongest stabilizing element in the party system is the CDU/CSU. It remains what has been for most of the history of the Federal Republic: the most popular party, the principal governing party, the favorite party of leading businessmen, and the most deeply entrenched component of the West German party state.

The preeminence of the Christian Democrats was for a time weakened, but never broken, while they were excluded from the Federal government between 1969 and 1982. Not only did they retain control of most state governments and, therefore, of the upper house of the Federal parliament; they also bested the Social Democrats in major urban centers that had long been SPD strongholds. At the same time the CDU and its CSU affiliate in Bavaria managed to modernize and strengthen their state organizations and to double and rejuvenate their membership—without unsettling the carefully balanced interest pluralism and decentralized national structure of the associated union parties.

The Christian Democrats are no longer what they were in Chancellor Adenauer's day, that is, largely devout Catholic farmers and small-town businessmen with traditional conservative values. At most one out of four of today's Christian Democrats was in the CDU or CSU before 1969, and the newcomers tend to be moderately conservative members of the new urban middle class. They can be expected to support party leaders and policies that appeal to a wide range of opinion in the electorate and to reject radical right- as well as left-wing ideologies. Some Christian Democrats occasionally give voice to rather extreme and impassioned views on the need for tight control over subversives and for maintaining strict law and order in society. But on the whole CDU/CSU party activists and officeholders seem to be a sober lot, more interested in enjoying the concrete benefits of political power than in promoting conservative Christian Democratic principles. Factional disputes and rivalries between and within the CDU and CSU are now more subdued than formerly, and generational conflicts do not appear to trouble the Christian Democrats. All told, they seem reasonably united on most domestic and foreign policy issues.

The other major component of the established party system, the Social Democratic party, is a more unstable factor. Its popularity in the country has not been as consistent and, normally, not as great as that of the CDU/CSU. Support for the SPD among West German elites has been far more limited. And internal divisions between pragmatic politicians and principled idealists have been both more profound and more extensive than on the CDU/CSU.

The SPD has always been more of an internally oriented membership party and less of an externally oriented electoral party than the CDU/CSU. Unity among active members of the party has therefore been of greater importance, but it has also been more difficult to achieve and maintain. It has traditionally required more than a common interest in the exercise of political power and called for some kind of binding agreement on Social Democratic principles. The current conflict among Social Democrats over the future course of the principal rival of the CDU/CSU is thus not just a dispute over electoral strategy and tactics and alternative partisan alignments. It concerns the role the SPD will play in West German politics for years to come.

Differences on that score transcend conventional distinctions between left and right wingers in the SPD. Generally speaking, there are two basic positions. One has it that, at least under present conditions, the principal task for Social Democrats is to assure their party strong influence over current public policies. This is more or less the position of those party activists who believe that the SPD cannot successfully compete with the CDU/CSU unless it persuades large numbers of politically moderate, independent voters that Social Democrats can deal more effectively than Christian Democrats with the problems facing West Germany. And they hold that leading SPD office holders would find it difficult to shape public policies if they were to be bound to doctrinaire programs that limited their bargaining autonomy in the party state.

Other Social Democrats consider this a discredited, unprincipled position. They maintain that their party must take on a far more uncompromising and militant role as the principal adversary of the Christian Democrats and their conservative supporters. And to do that the SPD is said to need a distinctive ideological guidance system and firm programmatic principles for its leaders and supporters.

These differences have been accentuated by the electoral successes of the Greens, the most unstable element in the present party system. Their sudden popularity, especially among well-educated and politically concerned younger voters, has been more of a problem for the Social than the Christian Democrats. The radical alternatives to the present order put forward by the Greens have presented SPD leaders with an ideological challenge which they have struggled to absorb without alienating more conservative voters and trade unionists.

The emphatically anti-establishment and unconventional Greens have given rather diffuse expression to the disatisfaction with prevailing patterns in state and society we noted among the incoming generation of the political public. Nationally they constitute a very loosely integrated network of quite disparate groups of dissidents that have managed to take advantage of rising popular discontent with the performance of the regular parties, particularly in state and local politics. The Greens, in contrast to the charter members of party state, are based on grass-roots social movements of unusually idealistic and dedicated amateurs in politics—including an exceptionally large number of women and university students. These part-time activists may be primarily religious pacifists or environmentalists, radical socialists or militant feminists, advocates of a vast social welfare state or anarchists who oppose any state authority. What essentially unites the heterogenoeus elements is their common opposition to the policies identified with the established power structure; what divides them are quite different ideas about their part in West German politics.

The Greens have introduced an unsettling element into a party system that had been considered exceptionally stable and predictable. Possibly they will bring about major changes in the party state and, more particularly, in the relationship between its principal components. But as of now the many uncertain factors concerning the future of the Greens do not permit an assessment of their potential power and long-term impact. For instance, it is unclear how much of their popular support has been due to passing disatisfaction with particular actions and leaders of the established parties, and how much to a more profound revulsion against the prevailing forms of party government. And it remains to be seen whether and how the many ideological factions among the Greens will reconcile their conflicting conceptions of an "alternative" model for West German democracy.

The stability of the West German party system is thus open to question. A number of observers think that it is going through a period of destabilizing changes, a welcome development to some and a troublesome one to others. In this view a system that has been marked by far-reaching consensus on policies and procedures among collaborating governing and opposition leaders is being replaced by one that features more adversarial relations and ideologically diversified positions. But there are also good reasons for believing that the system is not likely to change very much in the foreseeable future. One is that the West German form of representative government and a well-established party state promote inter-party agreement and constrain partisan factionalism. Another is that by past indications the ideological differences of principled party activists tend to be overriden by a practical need for major West German parties to keep their electoral appeals general and their governing policies flexible.

This brings us to our final question: how much does it really matter for public policy which particular party or coalition of parties is in power? By past indications, it matters not nearly as much as the parties competing for votes may claim and their supporters may hope or fear. Party government at the national as well as subnational level has not been the rule of partisan office holders putting into effect specific party programs, but rather policy management by party leaders commanding majorities of party members in the legislature. That does not mean that the political coloration of party governments has, in effect, made no differences at all. Distinctions between governments led by Christian or Social Democrats have been quite notable in social policy, less so in economic policy, and least pronounced in foreign and defense policy. For example, SPD governments have tended to give special emphasis to educational reforms and CDU/CSU governments to law enforcement. But governing leaders of both major parties have pursued conservative fiscal and monetary policies favored by the business community and pushed for more trade with Communist countries. And whereas the Social Democrats in government readily took over the CDU/CSU Western alliance policy which their party had long opposed, the Christian Democrats forgot their once vehement opposition to closer relations with East Germany when they returned to power in 1982.

Barring unlikely major changes in the policy environment such consensual patterns will probably continue for the foreseeable future. The partisan rhetoric of ruling party leaders may conceivably become more contentious under pressure from militant activists among their supporters as well as opponents. However, the expression of divisive philosophical principles seems likely to remain quite subdued in the policies of West Geman party governments. Ideologues in government are constrained not only by the moderate climate of current mass and elite opinion, but by more enduring conditions arising from the geopolitical situation of the Federal Republic, the dictates of its trade-orientated market economy, and the pluralist character of its political system.

7

Pressure Group Politics

In the Federal Republic, as in the United States, responsible public officials are constantly confronted with the necessity for choice among competing demands on a wide range of issues. A pluralist society gives rise to many diverse policy interests, and a regime based on the consent of the governed must provide extensive opportunities for their articulation.[1] However, giving voice to such demands does not ensure their satisfaction. Democratic principles may call for responsive policymakers and policy implementation may be more effective when it takes account of the wishes of the affected population. But no government can accede to all demands, no matter how democratic it may be and how hard it may try to accommodate conflicting interests. The nature of the political system and the dynamics of the policy environment—as well as personal preferences and associations—cause policymakers to be more responsive to some expressed demands than to others

---

1. Interest articulation is the political process through which individuals and groups make overt demands for the satisfaction of their values by the decision makers in a community or state. According to the nature and intensity of their claims, their perception of political alignments, and the access channels which appear available to them, people choose the means of interest articulation that seem most convenient and most likely to obtain the desired results.

and to vary in their susceptibility to pressure from different interest groups.

THE ORGANIZATIONAL IMPERATIVE

The processes of interest articulation and accommodation conform closely to the highly formalized patterns of mass representation and elite interaction that generally prevail in West German politics. The Basic Law, as we have seen, designates the political parties as the principal nongovernmental agents for the coordinated flow of domestic policy demands into the governmental system. Interest associations provide a complementary organizational link between state and society.

The Basic Law does not explicitly recognize interest associations, but it grants all citizens the right to form and join such groups, provided they are not in conflict with the criminal code or "directed against the concept of international understanding." Pressure group politics designed to promote or prevent decisions by authorities of the state are shaped by several factors. First, access to the "right" people is restricted by the sheer size and complexity of the political system and the multiplicity of competing demands for authoritative action or inaction. In this respect, West German conditions for interest articulation are not very different from those in similarly constituted advanced industrial countries. Second, the organizational framework and operative rules of the present regime favor access through carefully regulated legal procedures. These funnel multiple policy demands through screening agents before they get to authoritative decision makers. Third, there are the prevailing political norms, which identify legitimate interest articulation with law-abiding behavior.

For the average West German the opportunities for direct individual endeavors to obtain interest satisfaction from public officials are limited by law. The ordinary citizen may express his demands through his vote, through administrative and judicial agencies of the state, and by personal appeals to political leaders, such as his parliamentary deputy. Some well-placed persons among the nonelites may also have informal access to influential people, through family connections and friends in high places.

But especially in national politics such bonds no longer carry the weight they did under former German regimes and still do in other countries.

Most citizens of the Federal Republic feel that they can do little or nothing to influence political developments, as we noted in chapter 4. But there are also those who believe that ordinary people can have some voice in public affairs if they organize for collective political action. Some of such West Germans have been active in local "citizen initiatives" and other more or less unconventional civic action groups. Far more, though still a minority, belong today to one or more of the regular interest associations. Such organized pressure groups have generally been considered the most adequate means for mitigating the apparent political impotence of the "little man" through collective action.

In contrast to the major parties, the regular West German interest associations are not organizations for the recruitment of policymakers and do not try to gain general control over policymaking. By law and by custom they usually defend and promote the particular interests of social, economic, and cultural segments of the public. They will intermittently seek to influence policymaking and the day-to-day flow of policy demands, but only on certain issues and on behalf of ostensibly nonpartisan interests. Unlike the political parties, these associations thus have special clienteles rather than broad ones. And to the extent that the major parties have become less closely identified with special interests and more concerned with winning votes through the aggregation of many interests, they have also become blunter instruments for the realization of particular policy demands. For that purpose, the pressure group politics of interest associations have consequently become even more important in governmental affairs than previously.

THE REGULAR REPRESENTATION OF ORGANIZED INTERESTS

Regular interest groups come in all shapes and sizes in the Federal Republic. Some are quasigovernmental organizations and others are strictly private associations. Some identify their nonpartisan objectives with causes that are said to be in the general public interest and others clearly demand satisfaction for special interests. The League of German Taxpayers, for example, claims to serve the general welfare in its battle against "wasteful" public expenditures. The activities of such organizations as the Forest Owners Association, on the other hand, openly serve the special interests of a specific clientele.

West German interest associations are more inclusive, more tightly organized, and occupy a more privileged position in public policy processes than their American counterparts. In certain respects their activities are more closely regulated than in the United States; in others, less so. In fact, if not in name, some of the most important associations antedate the present regime; they are elements of socioeconomic and cultural continuity in a country that has been marked by sharp political discontinuities. Lingering identifications with religious, status, and occupational groups— dating back to the Industrial Revolution and beyond—still affect the policy objectives and pressure group activities of the churches and such associations as the League of German Artisans. At the same time, the effect of more recent changes in West German society and politics is reflected in the preeminently material and pragmatic perspectives of most interest group leaders and members and in the style of collective bargaining in contemporary pressure group politics.

The formal rules of representation that prevail in the governmental and party system also apply to the articulation of organized interest. Ostensibly the policy preferences voiced by pressure group leaders reflect those of their clients but often these clients exercise little or no control over their official spokesmen. This is most obvious in the case of the Roman Catholic hierarchy and other appointed functionaries, but it also applies to elected interest group leaders who are only indirectly chosen by the membership.

The extent of the influence of interest group representatives in the councils of government may be based on their personal prestige and connections, on the status of their office, on evidence of mass support for their demands, and on legal and normative criteria endorsing the "proper" representation of elements considered important in West German society—or on any combination of these. Some pressure group leaders may thus gain attention, if not results, as the presumed spokesmen for persons they only nominally represent and who may not even belong to their organizations. Compulsory membership in interest groups or a high degree of solidarity in voluntary associations may allow others to claim solid backing from their constituents.

In federal, as in state and local politics, interest associations endeavor to influence public policies principally by the following methods: (a) assuring themselves of ready access to key points in authoritative decision-making bodies through the recruitment, placement, and sponsorship of public officials sympathetic to their claims; (b) allocating effective authority to those policical positions which are most accessible to them; and (c) having their goals and methods accepted by influential veto groups and, less frequently, by the general public.

How these methods are specifically employed may vary a good deal from group to group and issue to issue. In some cases such activities will be carefully shielded from public view, in others interest group leaders will openly seek to mobilize mass opinion in order to bring pressure to bear on public officials or to replace them. Depending on what they want, when, and from whom, various pressure groups will direct their efforts to different issues and decision makers. For instance, a business organization may concentrate on economic matters subject to federal legislation and seek to influence relevant federal ministries and parliamenary committees; a pressure group associated with the Roman Catholic church, on the other hand, may be primarily interested in educational policies under the jurisdiction of the states and pursue its objectives at the local and regional level.

A detailed description and analysis of the entire network of interest associations in the Federal Republic would take up the remainder of this book. There are hundreds of such organizations—many with overlapping memberships—including at least 800 national ones. However, we will confine our discussion principally to the most influential pressure groups in federal politics. In general the patterns that prevail there are duplicated at lower levels of the political system.

Compulsory and Voluntary Organizations

Some West German interest associations are specifically established by law, in accordance with corporatist principles going back to the Middle Ages, to represent the different concern of various social and economic groups. Prime examples are the occupational "chambers" (*Kammern*), which have their roots in the corporate guilds of former times. Unlike the American chambers of commerce, these are quasi-governmental organizations of public law, which exercise compulsory jurisdiction over their members and are supposed to link key sectors of the economy to the state. Most private producers engaged in agriculture, commerce, and manufacturing, as well as members of the so-called free professions—such as self-employed physicians and lawyers—must belong to appropriate local chambers, which determine and enforce rules of occupational standards and conduct. The leading functionaries of these chambers not only represent their members in pressure group politics, but exercise derivative governmental authority over them.

These multiple economic and political functions give considerable weight to policy demands put forward on behalf of the chambers since their quasiconstitutional status makes them one of the most important associational structures providing for an orderly relationship between the economic and the political systems. To coordinate and articulate common interests, the local chambers in most of the West German states form regional groupings; their national federations in turn are supposed to defend and promote the interests of the constituent chambers at the federal level of government.

Other associations involved in politics are not based on compulsory membership. These include traditional institutional groups explicitly endorsed and supported by public authorities, particularly the major churches, as well as a host of voluntary organizations for the promotion of symbolic causes and material interests. Some are comprehensive associations performing various tasks and pursuing numerous goals, others have a single main purpose. Religious associations, for example, minister not only to the spiritual needs of their members, but engage in educational and social welfare activities regulated by public authorities. Major business and labor organizations are concerned not only with economic problems, but with social and cultural policy matters. On the other hand, many smaller interest associations—such as the Pensioners' League and the League of War Victims—promote the explicit and exclusive political demands of highly particularistic clienteles.

Although such voluntary associations lack the quasigovernmental authority of the occupational chambers, they are also not as tightly controlled by agencies of the state. At the same time, they are less closely associated with the political parties than interest organizations under former German regimes and in other European countries. Under the present regime these interest associations consequently enjoy quite a bit of political autonomy and flexibility as ostensibly nonpartisan pressure groups.

Sometimes a relatively insignificant pressure group may score a success thanks to an intensive publicity campaign, an exceptionally fortuitous combination of circumstances, or a temporary alliance with politically more powerful forces. A touch-and-go electoral battle, for example, may afford the leaders of a small, but tightly organized and united group unusual opportunities to trade their support for desired commitments from party candidates. On the whole, however, the greatest political influence rests with the official and unofficial spokesmen of the large national organizations. Formal and informal interelite channels permit them to exert direct pressure on leading party and governmental functionaries: at the same time, the major interest group elites command substantial resources for applying indirect pressure through influential opinion leaders and expressions of mass support for their demands.

Influence Through Functional Representation

Whereas American public officials may pay attention to the demands of interest group spokesmen if they wish, West German officials are legally bound to do so. As in most European countries, institutionalized rules for the functional representation of pluralist interests allow pressure groups to bypass the political parties and inject themselves directly into policymaking.

Numerous law and administrative regulations give formal sanction and encouragement to the long-established practice of direct contacts between interest associations and agencies of the state. Thus, in all of the states of the Federal Republic various consultative bodies attached to governmental organs transmit interest group wishes to public officials. In Baden-Württemberg, for example, representatives of the principal economic organizations are regular members of the regional planning council. The same is true in the public media: spokesmen for all of the major interest groups sit on the supervisory boards of the states' radio and television networks along with representatives of the principal political parties.

Similar arrangements exist at the federal level of government. The administrative procedures of the various ministries require that when they draft a bill for submission to the legislature—and most laws originate that way—they must consult the official representatives of the appropriate peak interest organizations (*Spitzenverbände*) and consider their wishes. Effective associational interest articulation through such formal channels is further facilitated by numerous ministerial advisory councils of nongovernmental experts connected with interest groups. For example, the West German Council of Economic Experts (Sachverständigenrat) is not a governmental body, in contrast to the American President's Council of Economic Advisers. However, its influence on public policy is more far-reaching since its official task is to provide for the authoritative coordination of public and private economic activities at all levels of government.

Functional representation also provides for the coordinated articulation of nonpartisan sectional and local interests in national pressure group politics. Various subnational governmental units are represented by their respective peak associations. The League of German Cities (Deutscher Städtetag) thus represents the particular interests of large urban municipalities, and the Federation of German Towns and Communities (Deutscher Städte-und Gemeindebund) those of smaller municipalities.

These legal arrangements have two chief consequences. First, they encourage behind-the-scenes interelite bargaining and accommodation among pressure group spokesmen and key public officials. Such institutionalized practices are favored by both sides on the grounds that direct negotiations among functional policy specialists facilitate the orderly processing of interest group demands outside the public arena of partisan controversy and party strife.

Second, these procedures induce the rank-and-file members of interest associations to depend on their formal representatives to obtain satisfaction for their policy demands and compel the constituent organizations of federal peak associations to rely on top interest group elites who have direct access to national policymakers. Here, too, the formal justification for such organizational arrangements is that they provide for the efficient and stable transmission of policy inputs from a pluralist society to the state. The intended object is to prevent the inundation of federal agencies by amorphous individual and group demands and to allow interests to be aggregated and adapted before and while they are considered by executive, legislative, or judicial organs of the Federal Government. From a comparative perspective, as a perceptive observer has noted, West German arrangements for the national representation of functional interests constitute "an especially clear instance in which entirely formal considerations can increase the power of federated groups and their key functionaries and thus have a major effect on the structure of organized interests."[2]

Influence Through Political Representation

Structures for the functional representation of organized interests, as well as the judicial system, permit West German pressure groups to bypass party and governmental channels of political

2. Reinhard Bendix, *Nation Building and Citizenship* (New York: Wiley, 1964), p. 133.

representation. However, these means also limit their opportunities for influencing the formulation of public policies, and most
pressure group leaders therefore try to keep other means available. Experience has taught them that competing interest groups
may neutralize each other, especially if they pursue conflicting
demands by way of the governmental bureaucracy or the judiciary
alone; they have learned that civil servants and the courts may
decide that acceding to pressure group demands would not be in
the public interest or would violate legitimate principles of law
and justice. Moreover, the formal routes of access leading through
the major peak associations frequently compel the constituent
organizations to subordinate their particular demands to those of
the larger federations and generally place smaller interest associations at a disadvantage.

For these reasons pressure group leaders endeavor to develop
and maintain close relationships with the manifest political leaders
who are recruited by and from the major parties. And here the
degree of mutual interdependence, of agreement on basic political
principles, and of reciprocity in the exchange of benefits is all-
important. Party government leads interest group elites to seek
influence over the composition and actions of the political elites
while these, for their part, compete for the allegiances of diverse
elements in a pluralist society. The power of interest group elites
in the political arena will accordingly be enhanced if they can
demonstrate their ability to promote or frustrate the objectives of
particular political leaders, parties, and factions; these, in turn,
will be most accommodating to the demands of those pressure
group leaders they consider most effective.

The specific methods employed by interest association leaders
to influence authoritative policies through political channels vary
a good deal with particular pressure groups, parties, and circumstances, and are frequently obscure. The general public has been
rather critical and suspicious of such activities—even when they
are legal; on several occasions, pressure group politics in election
campaigns have backfired, harming the parties as well as interest
organizations involved. Elected officials and people who want their
jobs therefore try to avoid the political stigma of close identification

with special interests and to conceal their obligations to pressure groups. At the same time, as we have seen, the major parties— and especially the CDU/CSU—provide for the representation of special interests in their organizations and on their electoral tickets and endeavor to accommodate pressure group demands in their programs.

In general, there are four methods through which pressure groups seek to influence party leaders in government and parliament: (a) attempts to obtain direct representation in the major party organizations, particularly among their leaders; (b) attempts to gain access to governing party elites through formal and informal, direct and indirect party contacts; (c) attempts to use party contacts to provide both governing and opposition party leaders with selective information and interpretations on particular policy issues (for example, articles in elite publications and "expert" testimony and memoranda supporting interest group objectives); and (d) offers of electoral assistance to friendly politicians and threats of mobilizing a pressure group's members and financial resources against those who oppose its policy demands.

Electoral pressure group politics today carry less weight than in the early years of the Federal Republic. First of all, interest associations can apparently no longer persuade politicians to quite the same extent that they can deliver the votes of their own members. Second, even the largest and politically most active pressure groups have evidently been unable to induce significant sections of the electorate in general to support their friends and punish their enemies; their publicity campaigns on behalf of particular parties and candidates have thus proven to be rather ineffective. Third, new laws providing public funds for campaign expenses and restricting private contributions have reduced the importance of financial support from pressure groups. Political leaders have consequently been less ready than formerly to accede to the demands of special interests at election time and to compete for their support with preelection legislative gifts.

As these means have lost effectiveness, other means for exerting influence on political leaders have become more important to West German pressure groups. On national issues these involve principally the effective representation of their policy interests by members of the federal government, by the delegations of the state governments in the Federal Council, and by deputies in the Federal Diet. In this respect traditional patterns of functional representation that bypass political parties have been complemented by the marked increase in collaborative interelite relations between manifest and latent political leaders as we noted in chapter 5.

The major interest associations have been particularly successful in placing their spokesmen in authoritative decision-making bodies. Key officials in federal ministries have frequently been recruited from corresponding interest groups and sometimes returned to them after leaving office. For instance, the heads and leading members of the Ministry of Labor usually come from the trade unions and those of the Ministry of Agriculture from the farmers' organizations. Even when the bonds are not so close, federal ministers and their principal subordinates tend to act as the spokesmen of their respective interest group clients in formulating public policies.

Such relationships are considered to be mutually advantageous, and West German government leaders welcome and encourage them for more than narrow partisan reasons. They are thought to furnish the political leaders of the state with expert advice and special information not available through other sources, such as on the secret flow of foreign funds into and out of the private economic sector and on the well-guarded investment plans of West German bankers. These contacts are also believed to provide governmental policymakers with exceptional opportunities for hearing and considering interest group demands and complaints out of the public view. For instance, they are said to be most helpful for weighing the pros and cons of contemplated fiscal measures designed to influence the patterns of wages, prices and profits. Finally, the representation of private interests in the executive branch of the government is thought to be particularly useful for facilitating interelite negotiations prior to a policy decision and for obtaining the cooperation of the affected interest groups in its implementation.

Lobbying is at least as prevalent in West Germany as it is in the United States. Several hundred national organizations maintain offices in the capital city of Bonn to provide them with close contacts between their headquarters and government and party agencies. In West Germany, professional lobbyists are not required to list their names and sponsors in public registers, but they are likely to have better access to federal ministries and legislative bodies if they do. For example, only those interest group spokesmen who are registered with the Federal Diet will normally be allowed to voice their views at public hearings of its committees or be asked to submit written statements. When this regulation was instituted some years ago, all sorts of associations entered their names in the register, from the very largest to some with as few as eight formal members.

On the whole, legislative lobbyists may be less closely controlled than in the United States, but they also have a less significant role in policymaking. In the first place, negotiations on issues involving the major interest associations almost always reach into the top echelons of the peak organizations and the government and focus on direct contacts among corresponding elites. Second, national and subnational legislative organs are less important targets for pressure group politics than in the American federal system, though more so than in such unitary and parliamentary systems as the British. In West Germany, interest group leaders concentrate especially on the executive branch because it is the source of crucial administration regulations and most legislation. Bills introduced by the executive normally become law, whereas bills that originate in the legislature and legislative amendments opposed by the government usually do not.

Interest group representation in West German legislatures is more conspicuous than in the United States. Under the rules of the Diet its members are required to reveal their affiliations with organized pressure groups and on this evidence alone the groups appear to be well represented. Functionaries of business, agricultural, and religious associations are to be found especially among deputies of the CDU/CSU and FDP, whereas trade union officials are likely to be deputies of the SPD. However, the official listings do not mention more covert links to pressure groups, such as those of deputies who may have temporarily severed formal connections but continue to maintain informal interest group ties.

Whether overtly or covertly, such legislative representation of vested interests is particularly pronounced in the committees of the Diet, where most of its policy actions take shape. Through committee assignments, party leaders have enabled various pressure groups to be especially well represented in committees that deal with matters touching on their interests. Most of the legislative maneuvering and bargaining among pressure group spokesmen occurs in the private sessions of these committees and of the corresponding "study groups" *(Arbeitskreise)* of the different parties.

All of this should not lead us to overestimate the effect of pressure group politics in the Diet. West German interest associations must contend not only with the fact that the Federal government normally exercises tighter party control over the Federal Diet than the American executive does over the Congress, but with constitutional provisions that impose tighter limits on the policy-making powers of the Federal parliament. For instance, neither of its two chambers can compel the government to increase its budgetary proposals. Under these conditions interest groups normally turn to parliament only if they cannot receive satisfaction from the executive branch, and then usually to get desired changes in governmental bills rather than entirely different legislation. The significance of legislative pressure group politics is thus measured not so much by the number of interest group representatives in the Diet as by the amendments that become law through its actions. In this respect interest associations have generally been more effective as veto groups than as promotional groups, and they have achieved more minor than major changes in governmental bills.

THE BIG FOUR

As we have said, economic values and, to a diminishing degree, religious values are basic sources of subcultural group identification in the Federal Republic. In pressure group politics these values take the form of organized interests that focus on socio-economic and sociocultural issues (*Wirtschaftspolitik* and *Kulturpolitik*) and are reflected in the preeminence of four major associational constellations: the national producers associations of agriculture, business and labor, and the religious organizations of the Roman Catholic and Protestant churches.

The effective leaders of these associations constitute a large part of what we have called the latent political elites in chapter 5. They exert pressure on the manifest political elites when public policies seem likely to affect their group. Governmental, administrative, and party leaders are usually very attentive to their demands, but especially so if they believe that policy implementation could be stymied by the major interest group elites. In the case of the principal economic associations, effective interest articulation depends largely—though not entirely—on the strength of the shared material objectives of their respective members and on their leaders' commitment to an instrumental, pragmatic view of the state's socioeconomic functions in a dynamic policy environment. In the case of the religious association, effective articulation rests primarily on the persistence and legitimacy of traditional norms that have allowed the religious elites of the two major churches to claim a special role in state and society as the guardians of ethical standards and public morality.

Business Organizations

Big business, tightly organized into national interest associations and dominated by a few men, was the most powerful private interest group in pre-Nazi Germany and played a prominent part in mobilizing the Nazi economy for war. After 1945, the Allied occupation powers sought to diminish the concentration of West German business establishments, but such measures proved to be temporary; with postwar recovery big business regained its preeminent position in both economic and political life.

However, due to the increased specialization and internationalization of the West German economy, the homogeneity of the big business associations is today a matter more of form than of fact. At the same time, however, institutional arrangements and the structure of the German economic system provide greater mutual cooperation among German businessmen than is found among their American counterparts, particularly in the key economic sectors dominated by a few giant commercial and industrial concerns.

The collective political interests of the business community are formally represented by all-inclusive employers associations organized along regional and functional lines. Every employer of more than two or three workers is a member of local and regional chambers of industry and trade, as well as of specific occupational associations, which in turn are organized into federated groups. Nationally these organizations are united in various peak associations—such as the Federal Association of German Bankers—which employ a full-time staff to look after their constituents interests. At the apex of all these groups stands a triumvirate of federated peak associations whose leaders serve as the formal spokesmen for the political demands of the business community as a whole.

The Diet of German Industry and Commerce (Deutscher Industrie-und Handelstag, DIHT), the national peak association of the chambers of industry and trade, is the least involved in federal politics. It does some lobbying and public relations work on behalf of its rather amorphous business clientele and occasionally lends its unofficial support to conservative candidates for public offices. The Federation of German Employers' Associations (Bundesvereinigung der deutschen Arbeitgeberverbände, BDA) is a more active group, particularly as a national spokesman for business on policy matters relating to labor and social issues. As a counterpart to the peak trade union associations, it seeks to promote the political interests of employers through lobbying and public relations work.

The third member of the triumvirate, the Federation of German Industry (Bundesverband der deutschen Industrie, BDI), is politically the most active and influential. Its membership encompasses thirty-nine affiliated national federations representing all branches of German industry and, through them, 98 percent of

German industrial concerns. The Industrial Federation devotes much of its budget to publicity work designed to provide a favorable climate of political opinion for the promotion of its policy interests.

The leaders of the three peak business associations frequently collaborate in national pressure group politics. Cooperation is facilitated by overlapping membership in top organs and a broad but diffuse interelite consensus on the political interests of business relative to those of other societal groups. The presidents and executive directors of the industrial and employers federations sit as observers at one another's board meetings; in fact, in the mid-1970s one man was president of both peak associations. The two organizations jointly sponsor the Institute of German Industry which conducts leadership conferences on policy issues involving business interests and turns out a large volume of research reports and analytical studies on political developments. Several coordinating committees, such as the Joint Committee of German Trade and Industry, provide additional formal links among the top business pressure groups. Many leading members of the peak business associations, moreover, maintain close informal relationships that extend throughout the Federal Republic. Elite business clubs and "luncheon groups" periodically bring them together.[3]

Recent West German elections have indicated that the peak business associations do not command sufficient popular support to mobilize substantial voting power on behalf of their policy demands. Furthermore, they lack the internal solidarity of some smaller promotional groups due to the heterogenity of business interests in a pluralist society. Although their constituent organizations have been able to use contacts with political and administrative elites to promote or block specific policy measures, the three associations have largely confined their joint efforts to more general business objectives. They have thus opposed the expansion of public economic enterprises and the extension of state controls

3. By some accounts it was largely pressure from such informal elite groups that in 1982 induced the leaders of the small FDP to end their alliance with the SPD and form a new coalition government with the CDU/CSU, the partner favored by most of the business community.

over the exchange of goods and services in the private sector. They have also fought against anticartel legislation and regulations designed to curb the power of big business in setting prices and allocating markets, and have lobbied against "codetermination" laws that allow employees to participate in the direction of both public and private enterprises. But apart from such general issues, the business elite has found it difficult to achieve and maintain a united front through the peak associations.

Business associations, like other pressure groups, endeavor to use various routes of access to policymakers. One of these is the Federal parliament. Estimates of the number of Diet deputies with direct or indirect connections to business orgnizations have varied widely; roughly 20 percent have been business managers, independent entrepreneurs, and functionaries of employers' associations, and, over the years, about two-thirds of these deputies have been identified with the interests of industry. By far the largest number have been Christian Democrats, and most have not been members of the business elite. Few top business leaders have sought to get into the legislature, though conservative politicians have often called for more prestigious business representation in the chamber. Most prefer to play a less conspicuous role in public affairs, and those who have sought election have frequently been unable to get nominated even by the CDU/CSU. Business pressure groups have, however, not lacked helpful friends in the Diet, especially among the members of its key economic committees and party study groups. These friends have served as contacts and lobbyists for the employers associations in their relations with the federal executive.

At the national policymaking level, business spokesmen have found it most effective to present their demands directly to the chancellor or, at least, to his closest advisers and key ministers. Practically every chancellor since the establishment of the Federal Republic has relied to some extent on the advice of leading bankers and industrialists. No matter what party has been in power, the minister of finance and his staff have always had close ties to the major banks and their peak association, and the minister of economics and his most immediate subordinates have always been closely associated with leading industrial firms and the Federation of German Industry. At lower levels of the executive branch more highly formalized institutional arrangements—as well as patronage appointments from the business community—have provided access to key members of the civil service. In addition, party channels can promote close relations among top business and governing political leaders, especially if the latter are conservative Christian Democrats or Bavarian Christian Socialists. These tend not only to be particularly sympathetic to the views of the business community and to have been recruited from its ranks, but to be closely associated with the nongovernmental Economic Council (Wirtschaftsrat) which represents most of the leading business establishments in the country. Business leaders who belong to a party are likely to be members of the CDU/CSU, and recent revelations have once again confirmed that most of the overt and covert political contributions from the business community go to Christian Democrats.

Formally and informally, directly and indirectly, individually and collectively, the leaders of big business enterprises and organiztions undoubtedly exercise a great deal of influence over public policy, perhaps more than any other elite in West Germany. Moreover, they form a politically more cohesive group than their counterparts in other capitalist democracies, such as France. But that does not mean that they constitute a dominant power elite or homogeneous ruling class. Not only are countervailing domestic and foreign factors in the policy environment too strong to make this possible, but the contemporary business elite lacks the necessary attributes. In comparison with its predecessors, it contains more economic subgroups with different—and often competing—policy interests on specific issues. The business elite is also now much more international in its composition and outlook than formerly and less disposed to identify its own interests with the national interests of a German state. And the business elite, and particularly its younger members, is no longer committed to exclusive and distinctive big business orientations dividing it sharply from other leadership groups and political elements in the country.

With the passing of the traditional, patriarchic German owner-entrepreneurs (such as the Krupps) and their replacement by the managerial executives of national and multinational corporations, a new outlook has emerged. It rejects a special ideological "ethos" and political "calling" for business leaders in favor of cost and benefit considerations in domestic and foreign economic relations. There is a far greater readiness than formerly to bargain with employee representatives of the so-called social partners without involving public authorities. There is also far greater willingness to rely on political leaders and civil servants for governmental policies that will safeguard private business interests under a "social market economy" of free-enterprise capitalism in a social service state. Various studies have shown that most members of the present business elite believe that they have neither the time nor the skill to devote themselves very much to party politics. As they see it, their task is to make money for themselves and their clients; that of the public policymakers is to provide them with favorable conditions for the pursuit of profits at home and abroad.

Labor Organizations

In terms of numbers employees associations constitute the largest alignment of occupational pressure groups in the Federal Republic. Their membership is, however, far less inclusive than that of the employer associations. In the mid-1980s about 40 percent of the West German work force was organized, a very large proportion in comparison with the situation in other major industrial democracies but a good deal less than in the early years of the Federal Republic. Proportionate membership strength is, however, not an adequate measure of the trade union leadership's qualitative influence over public policy processes. No West German government, whatever its partisan complexion, can today ignore the spokesmen of organized labor; public officials at every level of government depend on their cooperation for the effective implementation of socioeconomic policies.

The strategic role of the labor elite in the contemporary political system is unprecedented in German history for several reasons: (1) Independent employee organizations include a larger percentage of the labor force than under previous regimes (they did not exist in the Nazi era). (2) Socioeconomic developments have greatly increased the importance of the particularly highly organized areas of skilled industrial and public service employment. (3) The membership and leadership of the labor organizations are more unified and integrated into the political system than in former times. Whereas the German labor movement was once deeply split into bitterly feuding Socialist, Communist, Catholic, and liberal trade unions, such ideological divisions no longer exist. As full-fledged members of the policymaking stratum all of the top union leaders not only endorse, but strongly support the present constitutional order.

The rules for representing collective policy demands in effect allow labor leaders to speak for all employees, whether organized or not. Under law no one can be forced to join a union to hold a job. Other than in the United States and Britain, there are no "closed shops" or "union shops" in West Germany—which makes the relatively large extent of voluntary trade union membership all the more impressive. Formal arrangements assume that unorganized labor shares the socioeconomic interests of trade union members; nonmembers thus derive "free-riders" benefits from pressure group achievements. Thus, if organized labor scores gains in social security, fiscal, and wage and hour legislation, in regulations concerning the labor courts for employer-employee disputes, or in extending codetermination laws to more business enterprises, unorganized labor is considered to profit from these accomplishments as well. We have here one more example of West German legal provisions designed to ensure orderly and stable policy processes in a pluralist society through interelite negotiations and bargaining among leaders representing different interests.

In comparison with their counterparts in other non-Communist and industrially advanced countries, West German labor leaders have been able to depend on a very high degree of cohesive rank-and-file support. The trade unions, like other formal nongovernmental associations in the Federal Republic, are required by law to be democratically organized in accordance with the usual graduated methods of representation. Top labor leaders are thus only indirectly elected by the rank-and-file members and only indirectly accountable to them. They have generally been responsive and responsible to the membership, but they also have had a good deal of autonomy in defining and representing the membership's specific policy interests. In this regard their authority has been sustained within their respective unions by the solidarity and discipline of the membership, by strong organizational bonds, and by tight leadership control over middle-level union functionaries and internal media of communications.

The leaders of organized labor have access to many key public officials, both through formal channels of functional and political representation and through informal contacts. Most also command substantial financial resources for the promotion of their policy interests. In addition to income from membership dues, trade unions derive profits from numerous economic enterprises, such as banks, publishing houses, insurance companies, and breweries. These funds support public relations and lobbying activities. They also enable the peak associations and the richest unions to maintain a professional staff of labor lawyers and specialists who furnish labor leaders with expert information and advice on various policy problems. However, under West German law, labor unions are not allowed to give direct financial support to political parties.

The preeminent peak association of organized labor is the German Federation of Trade Unions (Deutscher Gewerkschaftsbund, DGB). In contrast to the divided labor movements of France and Italy, the DGB, with some 7.8 million members (1983), takes in 85 percent of all organized West German workers. It is neither divided into a large number of amalgamated occupational unions, like the British Trade Union Congress, nor split into industrial and craft unions, like the American AFL-CIO. The DGB consists of seventeen large unions, which are organized nationally by economic sectors of employment and then regionally along Land lines.[4] The Federation takes no part in collective bargaining with

4. The Printing and Paper Workers' Union, for example, takes in organized production as well as service workers in the entire publishing trade. When it went on strike in the Summer of 1984 it could thus close down not only printing plants but delivery and clerical services in the newspaper industry.

employers, and its constituent organizations may engage in political activities of their own. The peak association functions primarily as their joint pressure group in federal politics. Its activities
are financed by the member unions, and their leaders collectively
determine DGB positions on national policy issues. The top functionaries of the giant unions that contribute most of the funds and
members to the DGB—the Metal Workers, with 33 percent of the
DGB membership, and the Public Service Workers, with 15 percent—also carry the most weight in its councils and command the
largest voting blocs at its conventions. The Federation's national
chairman has virtually no independent authority and serves primarily as its leading spokesman and chief administrative officer
at the DGB headquarters in Düsseldorf.

Two much smaller peak associations are less inclusive than the
DGB and more closely identified with traditional status distinctions in employment. One is the German Employees Union
(Deutsche Angestelltengewerkschaft, DAG) which split away from
the DGB when the Federal Republic was established. Its founders
held that salaried white-collar employees did not share the outlook
and interests of blue-collar wage earners—who then, as now, pre-
dominated in the DGB—and would be better served by a separate
labor organization. As it turned out, most salaried employees did
not care to join any trade union. Only one in five belongs to one
today, whereas two out of five blue-collar workers are unionized
in the DGB. Most of the unionized white-collar workers are also
in the DGB; merely a third belong to the rival Employees Union,
particularly mid- and high-level employees in the private service
sector.

Among the particularly highly organized employees in the public service sector the civil servants form a minority, as noted in
chapter 2 (see table 2.1). About three out of four belong to the
German Federation of Civil Servants (Deutscher Beamtenbund,
DBB), a peak organization that is formally not a labor union like
the others due to the special legal status of West German civil
servants. Teachers, officials of the public administration, and other
so-called servants of the state may not, like other public service
workers, strike against their employer under West German law.
But they also enjoy much greater job security and far more gen-

erous retirement benefits. Their position in governmental agencies and the heavy overrepresentation of former or temporarily retired civil servants in West German legislatures have enabled the spokesmen for the civil servants to advance the collective interests of this privileged group most effectively through lobbying and quasi-legal trade union tactics. Over the years the leaders of the Civil Servants Federation, like those of the Employees Union, have increasingly discarded the notion of a distinct corporate identity for their members and have come to share the pragmatic political outlook of DGB leaders.

West German labor organizations have generally been more legalistic and less militant in pursuing their political interests than their more class-conscious counterparts in France, Britain, and Italy. The right to strike is guaranteed by the Basic Law, but it has not been used very much in trade union politics. Strikes of any sort tend to arouse popular resentment against organized labor and its leaders have usually considered it neither necessary nor desirable to resort to this ultimate weapon in their pressure group arsenal.[5] Under German labor law they risk heavy financial penalties when they call their members out on strike for political purposes in violation of existing contracts. But such confrontational measures have in any case not suited the institutionalized patterns of regular West German pressure group politics.

The trade union leadership has only on a few occasions used the threat of a strike to back up its demands in the political arena. In 1951, for example, DGB leaders said they would call a general strike if the Federal Government did not push a codetermination law for the coal, iron, and steel industries through parliament; their demand was met. In 1966, the threat of a strike by the Ruhr coal miners induced the Federal Government to arrange for a

5. By comparison with other leading industrial democracies, including the United States, the Federal Republic has had relatively few significant strikes of any kind. Employers as well as trade union leaders have on the whole sought to avoid major tests of strength between capital and labor and to settle major industrial conflicts through well-established negotiating procedures. These normally leave it to the so-called autonomous social partners to arrive at a contractual agreement without direct intervention by government authorities, legislative bodies, or the courts.

settlement underwritten by public subsidies to the mine owners. At other times such threats not only proved less effective, but provoked strong counterproductive public criticism of the unions and their leadership. For instance, in the late 1960s organized labor failed to block legislation providing for the suspension of certain sections of the Basic Law in the event of a "constitutional emergency." The trade unions had to be content with provisions that appeared to safeguard the right to strike. On this, as on other occasions, labor leaders staged mass demonstrations in support of their demands, but for the most part they have preferred to achieve their pressure group objectives through less dramatic interelite negotiations.

The extensive functional and political representation of organized labor under the prevailing regime affords its leaders manifold opportunities to promote their clients' interests out of the public view. In addition to their participation in numerous governmental and quasigovernmental bodies, labor leaders have direct and indirect access to political leaders through the major parties. DGB and other union officials wield influence in the CDU/CSU through the labor wing of the Christian Democrats, though not nearly as much as in the Social Democratic party. Relations between the DGB and SPD functionaries are especially close due to extensive overlap in the membership and objectives of their respective organizations and a corresponding degree of interdependence. Social Democratic government officials have thus been more receptive to demands from the DGB elite than Christian Democratic ones; at the same time, they have been able to use shared policy considerations to temper such demands.

On the face of it organized labor is strongly represented in the Federal Diet. The proportion of trade union members among the legislators has greatly increased since the establishment of the Federal Republic though the proportion of organized workers in the labor force has declined. Only about one in four Federal deputies was a union member in 1949, thirty-five years later it was close to two out of three.

But it would be a mistake to take these figures as a measure of trade union influence over legislation. Not only have practically all laws passed by the Diet originated in the executive branch, but most deputies affiliated with trade unions have been merely nominal members. The proportion of active trade union functionaries who manifestly represent the interest of organized employees in the Federal Diet and, above all, in appropriate parliamentary committees, has notably diminished in recent times and by the mid-1980s amounted to no more than 6 percent of the deputies. Even those do not constitute a solid labor bloc since rivalries among the peak associations and differences in the policy concerns of various trade unions are reflected in differences among their parliamentary spokesmen. In this respect deputies associated with business and agricultural pressure groups have demonstrated more cohesive strength. Employee representatives on both sides of the aisle have occasionally banded together to promote the passage of legislation favored by most trade unions or to block measures opposed by them. But usually such interest alignments have yielded to party divisions between government and opposition deputies in the final vote. Rather than cross party lines and violate party discipline, the friends of organized labor have preferred to promote its cause in the privacy of preliminary intraparty councils and secret parliamentary committee sessions.

For labor leaders, as for other vested interest elites, the primary target for pressure group politics is not the legislative but the executive branch of government. Here parliamentary deputies, party functionaries, and administrative officials affiliated with organized labor have served as its emissaries to the Federal Chancellor's Office and the Ministry of Labor. Such links were significantly extended between 1969 and 1982 when the Social Democrats governed nationally in coalition with the Free Democrats.

That Social-Liberal Coalition—like similarly constituted state governments—pointed up the particular importance of such interelite ties when the SPD is in power but compelled to share control of the executive branch with a partner that is closer to business interests. On the one hand, a Social Democratic majority in the government appeared initially to place the DGB leadership in a much stronger position to advance its policy interests than under previous governments. In the first years of the coalition it thus obtained tax reforms and social welfare legislation opposed by business and its friends in the FDP and managed to keep the Brandt government from limiting wage gains won by the Public Service Workers Union. On the other hand, in the later years of the coalition the commitment of the DGB leaders to the SPD and its increasingly shaky alliance with the economically more conservative FDP imposed ever greater constraints on what they could seek and get from the Schmidt government. The Social Democratic chancellor and ministers now pressed the labor leaders to defer their particularistic demands for higher wages and better social benefits and support the coalition government even though its economic policies seemed to favor business more than labor. The DGB leadership felt compelled to be more or less accommodating in order to keep the SPD in power, but its frustrations produced mounting friction with the governing Social Democrats until the Free Democrats finally put an end to the Social-Liberal Coalition in 1982.

The moderate course pursued by the trade unions for several decades has led foreign observers as well as West German leaders to give organized labor a good deal of credit for the exceptionally high degree of political stability in the Federal Republic. Radical left-wingers inside and outside the labor movement contend, however, that such stability has been maintained by the ruling establishment—including union leaders—at the expense of ordinary working people and for the benefit of big business. In their view, class conflict is inherent in a capitalist state and economy and the "real" interests of labor are not served by the elitist pressure group politics of "labor statesmen." Conservative critics, on the other hand, assert that West German trade union leaders have been corrupted by the acquisition of too much political and economic power for which they are not properly accountable. In this view organized labor and its leaders have thrived largely at the expense of the unorganized majority of less priviledged taxpayers and consumers.

The politics of organized labor, and particularly the relationship between the unions and the parties, may change due to several current developments. One is the apparent trend toward a greater politicization of industrial conflicts. Unfavorable economic developments and, especially, the prospect of long-term mass unemployment due to technological changes, are putting labor leaders on the defensive in their "autonomous" bargaining with management over job security and pension rights. For them, as for business leaders, the role played by the state and its leaders in industrial disputes is therefore taking on a new importance. Both sets of autonomous "social partners" want public officials in charge of the party state who will give all feasible assistance to their side and impose all possible constraints on the other.

Another development that may prove politically significant is the increasing diversification of pressure group concerns within the Trade Union Federation and its component unions. This trend could make it a good deal more difficult for top DGB leaders to act in concert, on political issues where the interests of union members conflict, be it because the nature of their employment differs significantly, or because some hold jobs while others are unemployed or pensioners.

A third notable development is that union membership is also diminishing in West Germany and that its character is changing. The number and proportion of blue-collar union workers with regular jobs has been steadily declining, most notably in the metal working and construction industries that have traditionally been among the most densely organized and greatest sources of union power. At the same time the proportionate weight of better educated white-collar employees in relatively secure public service jobs, such as teaching, has been increasing in the labor movement in general and the Trade Union Federation in particular. Greater losses in DGB membership and more significant changes in its composition could conceivably lead to new, politically debilitating divisions between old-fashioned unionists who want above all economic growth for industrial employment and public service workers who favor environmentalist arguments for constraints on future growth.

Whatever the future may bring, the trade union leadership is likely to remain an important part of the policymaking stratum of the Federal Republic. It has a major stake in the preservation of institutional arrangements that make organized labor an integral component of the established political order and provide its leaders with prominent participant roles in public affairs. The members of a new generaton of labor leaders that is presently coming to the fore are on the whole much better educated and more self-assured than their predecessors in the 1960s and 1970s; top business and political leaders may find them more difficult partners in interelite negotiations. But the newcomers evidently hold to the belief that differences on specific policy issues must not be allowed to disrupt a more fundamental elite consensus on the principles and rules of the prevailing system of regular interest group pluralism. To the new leaders, as to the old, a basically harmonious relationship between the unions and other organizational structures in the country still seems best for the particular interests of labor and for the public interest. Top trade union functionaries thus continue to share the pragmatic outlook of key political, administrative, and business leaders and to consider themselves fully competent to represent the best interests of organized as well as unorganized labor in pressure group politics.

Farmers' Organizations

West German farmers, unlike their American counterparts, have been represented in governmental and quasigovernmental bodies by the spokesmen for complementary rather than rival agrarian pressure groups. All proprietors are required by law to belong to the corporate units of the national League of Agricultural Chambers (Verband der Landwirtschaftskammern). Most of them are also voluntary members of the League of German Farmers (Deutscher Bauernverband) and affiliated with an association of agricultural banks and cooperatives (Deutscher Genossenschaft und Raiffeisenverband). These three peak organizations have formally distinct functions, but their overlapping membership, leadership, and policy demands have united them informally in a farm lobby for the political promotion of agricultural interests.

Throughout the 1950s and well into the 1960s—when a conservative coalition of Christian and Free Democrats controlled the government and both houses of parliament—the farm lobby exercised a great deal of influence over agricultural policies. Its leadershp displayed a remarkable capacity for obtaining tax concessions, guaranteed price supports, and generous subsidies for its clients, but especially for the full-time farmers. These achievements were aided by the ability of the farm lobby to promote and exploit a favorable climate of opinion—especially among the conservative older leaders and supporters of the ruling parties. Many of these considered the regular farmers the mainstay of esteemed traditional virtues in an advanced industrial society and believed that it was therefore the responsibility of public authorities to safeguard a life-style associated with the pastoral tranquility of rural areas.

More pragmatic political considerations were, however, no less important in winning the support of the dominant government and party elites for the demands of the agricultural lobby. The FDP as well as the CDU/CSU depended then heavily on votes in rural districts where the lobby commanded a loyal and cohesive following that strongly supported its efforts to promote the interests of West German farmers against the competing claims of organized labor, big business, and foreign importers of agricultural products. Especially in the northern and southern regions of the Federal Republic, independent farm proprietors and their families were committed to support the farm lobby not only because they shared socioeconomic interests, but because they had a common political outlook derived from the corporate traditions of an exclusive agricultural estate. Older full-time farmers—who were particularly attached to such subcultural "in-group" sentiments—played leading roles in local and regional recruitment organizations of the Christian and Free Democrats and used their influence on behalf of the lobby.

Organized agriculture was "a real power" in pressure group politics, asserted the head of the Farmers League in 1966, because the exceptional unity and qualitative strength of its supporters made up for its numerical and financial inferiority to big business and labor. At the time the claim seemed still valid to most observers but already a bit hollow to a few. Since then it has become increasingly evident that the farm lobby has lost a great deal of the popular and elite support it once enjoyed. In comparison with equivalent organizations in other major advanced industrial countries—notably the United States, France, and Japan—West German agricultural associations have in recent years experienced a particularly precipitous decline in political influence.

Government measures designed to enhance the competitive viability of West German agriculture through the elimination of small and unprofitable enterprises have been a product as well as a source of this decline. As a product, they reflect the delayed political effects of structural socioeconomic changes. The solid support which the farm lobby could once marshal behind its efforts to block or drastically modify public policies was gradually eroded as more and more farmers and children of farmers went into better paying industrial and service occupations. The farming population dropped form more than 5 million in 1950, to about 1.5 million in 1980, and full-time farmers—always the most loyal supporters of the farm lobby—had by then dwindled to half that number.

At the same time, governmental policies have promoted the flight from the land. Under the terms of a European Common Market agreement, small marginal farmers are gradually being eliminated as protectionist agricultural subsidies are reduced. It was indicative of the farm lobby's diminishing effectiveness that its heavy pressure on the government and parliament in Bonn failed in 1984 to delay a cut in such subsidy payments by the Commission of the European Community in Brussels.

The agricultural organizations have clearly lost a good deal of their power with political parties and legislative bodies in the Federal Republic. Inflationary pressures on wages and prices have intensified the unwilliness of business and labor groups to absorb the cost of hidden subsidies to West German farmers. The largely trade-oriented patterns of the West German economy do not favor the counterclaims of agricultural interests, since these tend to raise the competitive costs of industrial exports. But the farm lobby remains nevertheless one of the more important pressure groups, in large part due to its entrenched position in the institutionalized system of regular interest group representation. Official spokesmen for the farmers thus still wield considerable influence over the formulation and implementation of agricultural policies through well-established ties to appropriate executive agencies at the federal and state levels of government.

Religious Organizations

The religious organizations of the Roman Catholic Church and the German Evangelical Church (EKD) make up the fourth constellation of key pressure groups. Separation of church and state as we know it in the United States exists neither in form nor in fact. Religious leaders are more closely involved in public policy processes and their political influence has been more pronounced than in many other advanced industrial countries.

The free exercise of religion is a private matter under the Basic Law, but its organized expression is not. All religious associations are bound by legal regulations, and the two major churches are very special institutions of public law. As such they are subject to the constitutional authority of the state, but they are also entitled to privileged support and protection from the state.

These formal reciprocal arrangements have given West German religious leaders strong reasons, as well as opportunities, for engaging in pressure group activities. In this respect, the effective political representation of their policy demands in legislative bodies has become less important as religious affiliation has played a diminishing role in West German elections. However, the persistence of traditional corporatist principles providing for the functional representation of the major religious groups in public affairs has sustained the influence of religious leaders at the policymaking level.

As we noted earlier, eight out of ten West Germans are under law either certified Protestants or Roman Catholics in roughly equal proportions. Most attend religious services infrequently, if ever. But all of them are required to pay a surcharge of 10 percent or more of their income taxes, which the government turns over to their respective churches. "Opting out," of this arrangement is uncommon and not easy under present laws. According to opinion polls most West Germans would pay little or nothing to their church if it were not for the traditional tax obligation sponsored by the state. The established churches also get a good deal of tax-exempt income from extensive property holdings.

Some of this income is used by the churches for strictly religious activities, but most of it goes into their numerous social services— such as orphanages, nursery schools, hospitals, retirement homes, and sundry charities. Religious organizations have therefore a considerable stake in governmental fiscal policies that affect the size of their chief sources of income and are bound to oppose tax measures that would give them less. At the same time, religious leaders have a major stake in maintaining legal arrangements under which they are neither directly responsible to public authorities for the expenditure of church funds, nor accountable to nominal church members who have no control over the functional representatives of their ostensibly collective religious interests.

In all of the states of the Federal Republic constitutional and other legal provisions call for clerical participation in the formulation and implementation of social and cultural policies. Clergymen have, for example, a voice in the operation of the public educational system and sit on the supervisory boards of the radio and television networks. Similar arrangements for the functional representation of religious interests prevail at the national level of government. Both of the major churches have quasiambassadorial clerical spokesmen in Bonn and furnish information and advice to appropriate federal agencies, particularly the Ministry for Family Affairs. Thus, the formal organization of the political system affords officially recognized religious interests extensive opportunities for presenting their demands to key public officials.

These arrangements have lent legitimacy to clerical pressure group politics, but they do not fully account for the continuing prominence of religious elites in an otherwise increasingly secularized polity. Other factors have come into play here. One appears to be the belief of many West German political leaders that organized religion remains a major stabilizing element in a time of profound social and economic change. Clerical leaders are considered influential opinionmakers by the political elites, and a public pronouncement by a Protestant or Catholic bishop is taken to express more than a strictly personal viewpoint. No major political figure has recently been willing to invite trouble by criticizing the religious establishment, at least not in public. Religious leaders, in turn, try to apply indirect pressure on policymakers through the force of public opinion. Clerical positions on public issues are put forward in sermons, in the mass-circulation religious press, in resolutions and memoranda from the governing bodies of the major churches, and in pastoral letters from the Catholic bishops. Such opinion-molding efforts have been particularly intense at the grassroots level, notably in the small towns and rural areas of Bavaria where Catholic priests often play leading roles in the dominant Christian Social Union.

A less conspicuous factor has been interelite ties between leading clergymen on the one hand and high party functionaries and public officials on the other. Such bonds have been cultivated on both sides because both have found them to be advantageous. Lay leaders of the two principal churches have played important intermediary roles in both of the major parties. These roles have been more evident in the CDU/CSU, but the less emphatically "Christian" SPD has also given prominence to its contacts to the clergy. These interpersonal relations have been facilitated by a network of religious interest associations and nonpartisan institutes affiliated with one or another of the major churches.

The formal representation of religious interests in public affairs provides for absolute parity between Catholics and Protestants. The leadership of organized Catholicism has, however, been by far the more active and militant force in pressure group politics. It has been more united in its political objectives and more determined in their pursuit, and it has commanded a much larger base of dedicated supporters. There are special associations for Catholic employers and Catholic employees, Catholic men and Catholic women, Catholic parents and Catholic youths. Devout members of the church belong to at least one of these supposedly nonpartisan mass organizations, which usually work together in national pressure group politics. The Catholic Bureau and the Catholic Club in Bonn coordinate their activities and the mass circulation Catholic press serves as the medium for internal political communications from the clerical and lay leadership to the members. For the smaller political and elite publics the church sponsors special political publications, and maintains Catholic academies that serve as conference centers for meetings and discussions on current political problems.

Organized Catholicism has generally been a conservative element in West German politics. Most of its leaders have held that Catholic policy interests fared best under governments controlled by the CDU and CSU and have therefore backed the union parties at election time. Devout Catholics have followed suit by voting overwhelmingly for CDU/CSU candidates, as we noted in chapter 5. The clerical hierarchy no longer urges them to do so in pastoral letters, as it did in the early years of the Federal Republic. Most of the leaders of Catholic lay organizations, however, remain consistent supporters of the Christian Democrats.

By all indications Catholic power in West German pressure group politics is diminishing. In certain areas of the Federal Republic, notably in Bavaria, organized Catholicism is likely to remain influential in local and regional politics for some time to come. However, in national politics the erosion of its influence appears irreversible. The Catholic hierarchy has lost a great deal of popular influence in matters of faith as well as politics, especially among young people. Regular church attendance by Catholics under thirty dropped from 59 to 14 percent between 1953 and 1980, according to surveys, while the proportion of those who very rarely or never went to church increased from 21 to 64 percent. On public policy issues where the Catholic bishops have taken a strong stand, as in their opposition to liberalized abortion laws, young Catholics have tended to hold contrary views. However, on matters that are of concern to these, notably international arms control and domestic socioeconomic inequities, the Conference of West German Catholic Bishops has preferred to remain silent—in contrast to the advocacy position adopted by its American counterpart in recent years.

The activities of the Catholic lobby are still colored by vestiges of the bitter battles fought by a religious minority against a ruling Protestant establishment in the former German Reich. Those of the Protestant lobby, on the other hand, reflect a decided break with the traditional union between church and state. The spokesmen for organized Protestantism represent an interest alignment in a pluralist polity that is neither as powerful as big business and labor nor as cohesive as organized Catholicism.

The Protestant Evangelical Church is a predominantly Lutheran confederation of provincial churches that exercise no direct control over affiliated religious interest associations. Its ministers and lay leaders may wield a good deal of individual or collective influence in regional and local politics, but in national affairs they have often lacked a common denominator for their specific policy demands. The orthodox Lutheran clergy has generally favored a course of minimal explicit involvement in partisan politics and has primarily sought to achieve its policy objectives less overtly through the functional representation of Protestant interests. There is a politically outspoken minority, but it has frequently been divided by differences between conservatives and reformers on particular policy issues, such as the liberalization of abortion and divorce laws.

The resulting problem of achieving a concensus within the Protestant elite therefore requires a good deal of preliminary delibertion and consultation. Consequently, when the leadership of the Evangelical Church has spoken out in public it has usually commanded considerable attention among the political and public and elites.

In the late 1960s and early 1970s, for instance, a series of memoranda from the Synod of the EKD called for a more flexible government policy of accommodation with the East European countries, a subject that had previously been taboo in official circles. In the face of bitter opposition from the refugee pressure groups, the collective authority of the Protestant elite contributed significantly to making the issue a matter of legitimate public discussion and thereby smoothed the way for a new phase in West German foreign policy.

Subsequently the Synod addressed itself in 1973, to two highly contentious domestic issues, the legitimate use of violence and the extension of the welfare state. On the former it cautiously allowed that "Christian" principles might justify revolutionary action against an inhumanitarian, oppressive regime, but said that it was to be condemned in a state where human rights were respected and changes were possible by peaceful and democratic means. On the latter the Synod declared that the socioeconomic inequities in an advanced industrial society required that the state provide more adequate social security and public assistance to the socially disadvantaged and physically handicapped, especially old and sick people and poor families with many dependent children.

Protestant political activities have on the whole been wider in scope at the elite level and narrower at the mass level than Catholic ones. Leaders of the Evangelical Church and its affiliated organizations have played prominent roles in the political parties, as well as in the trade unions and the major business associations; Protestant interest associations have at the same time been less partisan in pursuing pressure group objectives than their Catholic counterparts and have collaborated more readily with governments of different political complexions. Conferences at "Evangelical Academies" have brought Protestant theologians together with leaders from other spheres of public life, and with foreign leaders, for free-wheeling discussions on a wide range of current political issues—for instance on ways to overcome international and domestic sources of political tension.

The popular base and authority of the Protestant elite have, however, diminished even more rapidly than those of the Catholic one. Surveys have found that regular church attendance among Protestants under thirty dropped from 13 to 2 percent between 1953 and 1980, while the proportion of those who rarely or never went to church rose from 58 to 84 percent. The vast majority of Protestants evidently expects neither religious nor political guidance from the EKD and its top leaders appear to owe most of their remaining influence in public affairs to the priviledged official position of the Protestant establishment.

The alienation of young Protestants from their church has

served to aggrevate differences within the EKD over its proper role in West German politics. Traditionalists hold that evangelical Protestantism has neglected in fundamental religious roots and should confine itself to conventional pressure group politics that will promote harmony and morality in state and society. A new generation of political activists among the Protestant ministers insists, however, that the clergy is morally obliged to play a prominent part in the unconventional pressure group politics of the so-called new social movements for nuclear disarmament, environmental protections, and socioeconomic changes. Which of these factions will eventually prevail is unclear, but in any event regular Protestant pressure groups are likely to be increasingly less important in West German politics.

CONVENTIONAL AND UNCONVENTIONAL PRESSURE GROUP POLITICS

In the Federal Republic, as in other countries, pressure group politics are both sources and products of authoritative public policies. Governmental actions may reflect interest group demands, they may give rise to such demands, and they may curb pressure on public policies. In West Germany this reciprocal relationship between pressure group inputs and governmental outputs is conditioned by the dynamics of a particular policy environment and by particular patterns of interaction among the general public, specific interest groups, the major parties, and agencies of the state.

As we have seen in this chapter, the legitimate expression of regular pressure group demands is tightly structured in accordance with the representative principles of the present regime. Explicit legal provisions for the functional representation of organized interests connect the principal pressure groups directly to executive agencies of the state; more indirect and informal arrangements provide for the political representation of organized interests in elective bodies through their ties to the major parties.

As we have also noted, regular West German pressure group

politics have been marked by the corporatist vestiges of a preindustrial society. Present patterns reflect progressive and mutual adaptation between the pressure group subsystem and other components of the ongoing political system, a development that has been particularly pronounced in economic policymaking. Though traditional forms of functional interest articulation continue to have some importance, pressure group politics have by and large come to conform to socioeconomic, cultural and political circumstances that are very different from those of previous German regimes.

On the whole, interest organizations are today less closely controlled by the state, less intimately associated with political parties, and more flexible in their pressure group strategies and tactics than formerly. Most are no longer identified with sharply segmented subcultures, and interest group differences normally tend to involve particular policy issues rather than more profound doctrinal disputes. For example, the failure of an emphatically "Christian" trade union movement testifies to the detachment of organized labor from clerical as well as anticlerical ideologies. And as the encapsulated ideological camps of the past have gradually dissolved, tenuous and transitory pressure group coalitions on specific policy issues have become far more common.

The more heterogeneous the membership of an ordinary interest association, the more difficult it is to achieve internal concensus on its policy objectives. For the sake of at least nominal unity, cross-pressures arising from plural interests and competing affiliations must be accommodated by restricting and diluting the areas for collective political action. Particularly in the large peak associations of organized business and labor, the autonomy of the constituent groups has been promoted by different policy concerns. Employer and employee associations in one economic sector may, for instance, join forces to further their common policy interests against those of a similar alignment identified with another sector. The peak business organizations include associations of importers and exporters who may collaborate on some policy issues but compete on others. Occupational interests may sometimes unite public employees organizations on policy matters relating to the salaries and pension rights of their members and at other times lead to conflicts within and between such associations.

Another major feature of conventional pressure group politics is that they exclude most West Germans and involve primarily interelite relations. The organizational rules and actual operation of the prevailing regime have served to institutionalize mutually advantageous exchange relationships among key interest group functionaries, party leaders, and public officials. As noted earlier, bargaining, reciprocal adaptation, and compromise have come to characterize interaction among various elites in a pluralist state and society; these patterns extend across occupationally seg- mented interest groups and make for basically harmonious rela- tionships among their leaders, and between these and the manifest political decision makers.

But though interest group elites may command extensive means for influencing public policies, they are constrained in the demands they can make and the means they can employ to realize them. One reason is the formal and informal "rules of the game" for legitimate pressure group politics. A second reason is that cultural norms place the interest of state and community above those of special vested interests and establish public officials as the legitimate arbitrators among competing pressure group de- mands. There are also cross-cutting popular and elite allegiances, which may override identifications with "nonpartisan" interest groups and induce political participants to disregard such iden- tifications for the sake of partisan objectives or party discipline. And, finally, there is the pluralism of competing elites involved in policy processes, which disperses rather than concentrates the power of organized interests.

These constraints tend to curb the political influence of even the most powerful pressure groups. They normally allow party leaders and high government officials to aggregate, balance, and, if need be, reject pressure group demands in the name of "larger" public interests. And they enable these leaders to avoid commit- ments that would make them the instruments of any particular interest association or interest group alignment. Control over pub- lic policies rests in the last analysis with elected and appointed public officials, and the extensive intrusion of the authority of the state into West German society provides these officials with considerable power to curb pressure group demands.

It would seem then that the prevailing regime provides for effective checks and balances in the relationships between organized interest groups, political parties, and agencies of the state. Indeed, the apparent efficiency of the West German system for the regular representation of organized interests has been compared favorably with less tidy arrangements in other major European democracies. For instance the system has seemed to some observers far more conducive to the harmonized "concertation" of competing interests in state and society than the much more fragmented system of rival social and economic pressure groups in France. And British commentators have seen in the collaborative relationship between business, labor, and government elites in the Federal Republic a better way to deal with the economic problems of capitalist democracies than the more adversarial relationship between management and trade union leaders in their own country.

More critical West Germans, however, do not agree that their regular interest associations are such admirable institutions for the orderly transmission of diverse demands from a pluralist society to a democratic state. Some assert, to the contrary, that the entire pressure group system has gotten out of hand or, at least, that some of its principal components exercise far too much influence at the expense of common public interests, particularly those of people who do not belong to interest associations. Critics of the prevailing arrangements point out that these strongly favor a few private interest groups with "public status" under West German law, whereas the liberal democratic principles of the constitution call for all kinds of voluntary associations to have more or less equal access and influence. Such institutionalized inequities are said to be particularly pronounced where they matter most, on economic policy issues. Here big business, or organized labor, or both—the critics differ on that—are seen as enjoying undue advantages as priviledged "social partners" of the state.

In the Federal Republic, as in other Western democracies, conventional pressure group politics are generally held in rather low esteem by those who are not part of them. As we noted, most West Germans are at best only nominal members of regular interest associations and peripherally involved in their political activities. When influential opinion leaders resort to attacks on the "excessive" power of particular interest groups in the heat of an electoral campaign or a battle over some policy decision, such charges are prone to tie in with popular hostility toward the regular pressure groups system in its entirety. But the most important groups are especially distrusted. Opinion polls show that big business and organized labor are widely believed to wield more influence than they deserve. Such sentiments are not new, but they have been reinforced in recent years by highly publicized revelations of corruption in trade union enterprises and of unsavory financial deals between business leaders and prominent public officials. And as conventional pressure group politics have become more discredited, more unconventional ones have won more approval from the general public.

Unconventional pressure groups are relatively new phenomena in the Federal Republic. As we noted briefly at the beginning of this chapter, some West Germans have in recent times formed "citizen initiatives" and "citizens lobbies" for political action outside the regular parties and interest associations. The number and size of such civic action groups tend to fluctuate a good deal, but on the whole their active membership appears to take in only about one percent of West Germans (see table 5.2). Like various other so-called new social movements in the Federal Republic, such unconventional pressure groups operate outside the established system because they cannot or will not obtain influence through the regular institutional channels for interest representation.

Over the last decade or so civic action groups have proven to be surprisingly effective instruments of unconventional pressure group politics at the grass-roots level. For example, groups of parents have demanded and obtained more public funds for local schools, as well as blocked educational changes mandated by state authorities; neighborhood associations have both prevented and promoted urban renewals projects of municipal governments; and pressure from environmental protection groups has led to tighter local controls over urban pollution and traffic patterns.

Much of the support for the Green party, and a good many of its activists and elected officials, came at first from such irregular civic action groups. However, their effectiveness and scope is quite limited at the local level since municipal and county governments do not have much power in the Federal Republic. As these irregular grass-roots groups became more concerned with regional and national issues they therefore joined forces for unconventional pressure group activities at the state and federal levels. A coalition of like-minded groups thus staged mass protest demonstrations in the late 1970s to prevent the construction of nuclear power plants and waste disposal facilities by various state governments; a similar alignment employed "extra-parliamentary" direct action in an effort to keep the government of Hesse from building a new runway for West Germany's largest airport; and in the early 1980s such activities went national with mass rallies in Bonn and elsewhere to rally public opinion against the stationing of more powerful American nuclear missiles in West Germany.

A good many West German and foreign observers were alarmed by these protests against the decisions and commitments of properly elected public officials. While the demonstrations were on the whole peaceful and legal, their number and size were unprecedented in the Federal Republic. The predicted "Hot Autumn" of 1983 did, however, not materialize; then as now West Germans have not shown the sort of propensity for militant direct action that has been a constant feature of interest group politics in France.

The loosely organized and quite heterogeneous national alignment of irregular cause groups and new social movements constitutes a highly unconventional form of interest aggregation in contemporary West German politics. It provides expression for the varied anti-establishment attitudes that we already noted for members and supporters of the Green party, and it reflects in large part the social discontent, the fears, and the pessimism we observed earlier among well-educated and politically interested young people. The reformist elements in the alignment generally press for more participatory democracy and for relatively moderate changes in current governmental policies; they include most of the peace movement, the environmentalist movement, and proponents of significant social reforms, such as the womens' movement. The ideologically more extreme elements consider the present socioeconomic and political order with its "elitist" institutions beyond reform. They include radical Marxists, as well as utopian anarchists and romantic anti-technocrats of the counterculture "alternative movement." To the extent that these groups come to set the tone for the entire alignment it is likely to move on a collision course with a ruling establishment that is wedded to economic growth under capitalism, to military commitments under the Western NATO alliance, and to representative governmental institutions, parties, and interest associations.

Like the Green party that has given parliamentary expression to many of their demands, the grass-roots civic action groups and new social movements have grown into a political force that can no longer be dismissed by the dominant elites as constituting an unrepresentative minority of discontents given undue prominence by the media. At the same time these unconventional pressure groups do not threaten to topple the established political system, as some conservative critics have asserted; nor do they appear to signal a significant trend in West German socioeconomic and political values for more personal liberty and collective democracy, as sympathetic commentators maintain. Their concrete achievements have been quite modest, especially above the local level of government, and their pressure group activities cannot compare with that of the regular interest associations. The impact of the irregular groups on the political system of the Federal Republic has evidently been more diffuse.

For the elites as well as for the political and general public the extra-parliamentary activities of unconventional pressure groups have become more or less acceptable, if not always legitimate forms of interest articulation and aggregation. These activities have moreover served to thrust previously ignored or neglected issues on the policy agenda of the ruling establishment. West German political leaders and would-be leaders have thus become more sensitive to public concern over environmental pollution and the threat of nuclear annihilation thanks largely to the mobilization of mass opinion by the peace and environmentalist movements.

8

Policymaking

Who makes or should make authoritative policy decisions, for what purposes, in what manner, and to what effect is at the heart of West German politics. As in other countries, disputes on this score are based on conflicting policy premises, conflicting policy preferences, and conflicting evaluations of the outcome of action or inaction on the part of leading public officials. In contemporary West Germany, such controversies range from substantive ideological cleavages between conservative proponents and radical critics of the regime to procedural disputes among and within agencies of the state; they divide voters, parties, and pressure groups, as well as policymakers and would-be policymakers.

The Federal chancellor may make a policy declaration that his government intends to, say, reduce taxes and expenditures in the public sector to provide more investment capital for economic growth and employment in the private sector. The parliamentary opposition is likely to profess to share his concern about a lagging economy, but condemn his program as the wrong way toward a desirable objective. Its spokesmen may contend that it would be better to put more money into public works or into direct subsidies for ailing business enterprises. Other critics may maintain that short-term measures will not solve long-range problems posed by the nature of the West German economy, such as its trade dependency or its capitalist organization. Then, again, they may argue that other issues are even more pressing, for instance, threats to civil liberties or public security.

Because "open government" and free-wheeling debate on public issues are political norms, policy conflicts may sometimes be more visible in the Federal Republic than in other countries. Particularly—but by no means exclusively—around election time, adversaries to policy disputes will bid for public support by vigorously defending their position in parliament, in the mass media, or even in the courts. As a result—and especially when they capture headlines—such controversies often seem more profound and less susceptible to resolution than they are in fact. Then, too, a good many disputes are not only waged but settled out of the public view in party councils, government agencies, and legislative committees. This is all the more likely when policy issues are complex or politically sensitive and when efforts to achieve compromises involve few key decision makers. In these cases differences are likely to surface only when some or all of the participants feel that they have more to gain than to lose by calling them to the public's attention.

In any event, the authoritative resolution of policy conflicts rests ultimately with the organs and agents of the West German state. Constitutional arrangements provide these with legal control over the formulation of public policies and the operation of the contemporary political system enables them to exercise that control. Our principal concern in this chapter will be with national policy issues and their processing by national public officials. Though measures adopted by subnational components of the state may at times have more than a local or even regional effect, policy decisions affecting the entire country are usually made at the federal level of government.

THE CONTEXT FOR POLICYMAKING

The outstanding feature of the present policymaking system is representative and responsible party government, as we have seen. And we also noted that the decisions of governing party leaders are conditioned by demands for and constraints on policy actions. Some of these demands and constraints are the results of legal arrangements that restrict as well as legitimate the activities of public authorities. Others arise from a dynamic policy environment that generates domestic and foreign problems and structures policy responses. These factors, in turn, enter in different forms at various times into patterns of collaboration and conflict among members of the general public, the political public, and the elites of the Federal Republic.

Under the terms of the Basic Law, you will recall from chapter 2, the federal executive and bicameral parliament are assigned primary legal responsibility for translating the policy intentions of leading public officials into authoritative rules, such as changes in the constitution, a treaty, a budget law, or a government decree. Administrative and judicial agencies are charged with interpreting and applying general rules in specific cases (see figure 8.1).

This formal distinction, however, obscures the fact that in West Germany, as in the United States, judicial and administrative bodies may also shape, if not make, policy. Various top federal courts may do so in the process of reviewing executive legal ordinances and administrative regulations, and the Federal Constitutional Court in passing on the compatability of policy measures with the Basic Law. Consider, for example, that certain sections of the federal constitution are not subject to amendment and that for these sections neither the lawmakers nor the voters, but the constitutional court is the final legal authority. The judicial review decisions of the court have repeatedly compelled executive and legislative officials to discard or modify policy measures; such rulings led Chancellor Adenauer to abandon his effort to create a federal television network in the early 1960s and forced the parties in the Federal Diet to come up with a less self-serving campaign finance law in the mid-1960s and a less intrusive law for a national census in the early 1980s. In formulating a law or implementing regulations, policymakers are therefore likely to take into account the reaction of the courts and tailor their measures so they will pass judicial muster.

Similarly, actions taken or not taken by the Federal Bank under

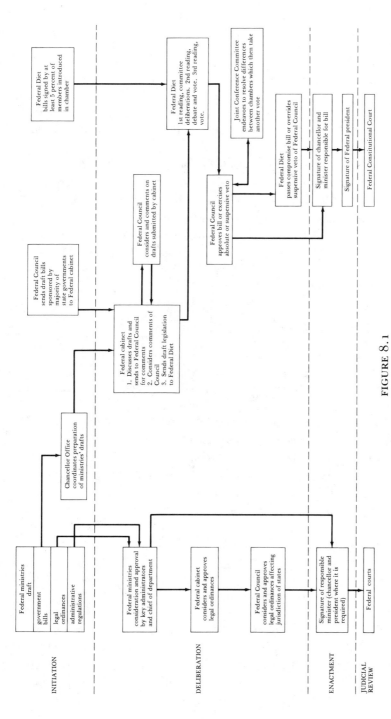

FIGURE 8.1

Formal Federal Rule-Making Procedures

its statutory mandate to sustain monetary stability have often had a decisive effect on the formulation of domestic and foreign policies in the executive branch. And the cumulative spinout of ostensibly policy-implementing activities by federal regulatory agencies, public authorities in the states, and such paraconstitutional bodies as the occupational chambers, have occasionally given a special twist to federal policies that was neither intended nor anticipated by their originators.

How socioeconomic conditions and other environmental factors enter into West German policymaking processes we saw in chapter 3. As we noted there, these shape and are shaped by governmental actions. Available economic resources, for example, influence the size of the federal budget; on the other hand, the allocation of tax assessments and the distribution of public funds affect the amount of money West Germans can put into savings, business investments, and private consumption. In international affairs the Federal Republic's membership in the European Community and the North Atlantic Treaty Organization involve commitments that limit its leaders' freedom of action; and the extent to which they honor these commitments affects in turn West Germany's relationship with its economic and military partners.

Here we need to remember that West German foreign policies are directed toward other states and their governments, whereas domestic policies concern the authoritative distribution of public benefits and obligations within the Federal Republic. This is not just a formal but a practical distinction when it comes to policymaking. Inside the country public officials not only decide who is to get and who is to do what, when, and how; they command extensive means to enforce their decisions. Not so in foreign affairs. There the use of force in support of policy measures is out of the question and West German policymakers are compelled to rely on diplomatic persuasion, economic inducements, and propaganda—and on favorable circumstances—to realize their intentions. Their ability to obtain what they seek may be promoted or hindered by international conditions, but in any event tends to depend on factors largely beyond their control. At the same time we must remember that domestic and foreign affairs are so closely intertwined in West German public affairs that domestic policy issues are frequently colored by foreign policy considerations and foreign policy decisions influenced by domestic policy concerns.

Policymaking in the Federal Republic is finally conditioned by the patterns of political orientations and relations we examined in preceding chapters. These structure the processes of interaction between organs of the state on the one hand, and voters, parties, and pressure groups on the other. It is especially in this respect that public policies in the Federal Republic can be the consequences as well as the sources of political controversies; they may reflect as well as produce domestic demands on and supports for the policymaking system and specific policymakers; they may conform to as well as mold the climate of political opinion and the effective distribution of political resources for influencing policy actions.

The high degree of institutionalization of the present regime and the characteristics of the contemporary political culture enhance the legal authority of public officials; but they also require them to conform closely to establised governmental roles and procedures. As agents of the state these key decision makers are expected by most West Germans to provide for the public welfare and the resolution of policy conflicts within the limits of law and popular consent.

The stratified patterns of political influence permit the general public to express its policy demands and grievances at election time, but largely limit more direct participation in policy formation to the elites and the political public. When it comes to authoritative decisions, West German socioeconomic and political pluralism is primarily reflected in the efforts of government, party, and pressure group leaders to make specific measures conform with their personal preferences or those of their clients. And the management and resolution of attendant policy conflicts on specific issues is usually a matter for negotiations among key public officials and other policymakers. Thus far, at least, there have been few profound interelite conflicts over the nature and direction of public policies. Some issues, such as relations with the German Democratic Republic and other Communist countries, have produced dramatic clashes among West German leaders; however, they have not been the products or causes or irreconcilable conflicts. A high degree of agreement on basic regime principles and procedures, and comparatively well-functioning arrangements for the management of policy disputes, have sustained the collective authority of officiial decision makers.

A substantial part of national policymaking involves automatic procedures and mundane issues that arouse little or no public controversy and concern. A good many governmental measures are designed by civil servants in appropriate executive departments and are routinely approved by their superiors—and, if required, by the Federal cabinet, chancellor, and parliament. Much of the legislation turned out by the Federal Diet and Council has dealt with noncontroversial governmental bills that have been passed as a matter of course with the votes of the opposition as well as ruling parties. Pressure groups, you will remember, are likely to fare best under these circumstances and to find it more difficult to gain their policy objectives when they become embroiled in partisan controversies and in jurisdictional disputes among public authorities.

Still, there have been and will be divisive policy issues that are not very readily disposed of by common agreement. On such issues, the ability of key decision makers to resolve interelite conflicts becomes a crucial prerequisite for the effective implementation of public policies.

ISSUES AND ANSWERS

Policymaking revolves essentially around the decisions of governmental authorities to do or not to do something about public issues, to give priority to some matters, and to handle policy problems one way rather than another. These processes require first of all the identification of policy problems and objectives; second, a ranking by importance; and third, opportunities to choose among alternative courses of action. Thus, if West German officials do not recognize the existence of an issue requiring a policy response, they will not even consider appropriate government measures; if they see some issues as more important than others they will attend to them first; and if they believe that they have no options, their policy response will proceed from this assumption.

Any of these points can pose policy questions that lead to policy conflicts when politically influential West Germans disagree on the answers. To begin with, such disputes may focus on what constitutes a policy problem. For example, there is likely to be little argument if the issues are the preservation of peace and prosperity but a good deal more when it comes to the inequitable distribution of incomes in the Federal Republic. Some policymakers hold that the latter is not a problem, or at least not a public one demanding authoritative reform measures. They therefore oppose laws and regulations that, in their view, constitute unwarranted and harmful interference with the distribution of rewards for private initiative and individual enterprise in a free market economy. Others maintain that income inequality is not a private matter but a policy issue involving the general welfare. For them the question is consequently not whether it is a public problem, but what government authorities should do about it.

Whether the desirable is also possible under prevailing conditions is another question. Here conflicting views of the policy environment can first of all lead to disputes over policy priorities. Thus West German leaders who share policy concerns and objectives may differ on the relative significance of particular public issues and problems.

For example, top West German officials have disagreed in recent years over whether it was more important to curb rising prices or to check mounting unemployment, and to what extent measures to encourage economic growth should take precedence over measures to control industrial pollution and urban congestion. Social Democratic and Free Democratic coalitions have been divided over whether trade union demands for more industrial democracy and income equality were more pressing than threats from the business community that such measures would stifle managerial initiative and profit incentives. Conservative Christian Democrats have insisted that a decline in public morality and civic discipline is a vital policy issue because it threatens to undermine the authority of the

state and its agents. Proponents of immediate socioeconomic reforms, on the other hand, maintain that rising social tensions make
it more urgent to provide for greater equity in the distribution of
opportunities and the allocation of goods and services.

Conflicting perceptions of the international policy environment
have led to similar controversies within the policymaking stratum
over priorities in the conduct of foreign relations. For instance,
policymakers who believe that the Soviet block poses a grave and
sustained threat to the security of the Federal Republic hold that
primary emphasis must be placed on appropriate countermea-
sures, above all joint defense arrangements with the United States
and other NATO allies. Those who consider the danger not as
serious, and the opportunities for mutually beneficial trade relations with the Communist countries more promising, argue that
at least as much stress should be placed on economic
considerations.

But let us say that a sense of common purpose or compelling
environmental circumstances cause West German decision makers
to agree not only on the pressing importance of a public problem,
but on the most desirable policy response. It will then not necessarily follow that there will be no further differences among them
about what should and can be done. Disputes on this score may
arise from conflicting assessments of their freedom of choice, from
conflicting views of appropriate procedures, and from conflicting
perceptions of the consequences of contemplated policy decisions.

Domestic and foreign efforts to influence the output of West
German policymaking organs are predicated on the assumption
that authoritative public officials have at least some choice among
alternative courses of action. At the same time, such endeavors
are usually directed toward narrowing the range of options acceptable to the relevant decision makers and toward persuading
them that the favored decision would also be the best decision. For
example, the efforts of foreign leaders to influence the course of
West German policies have often been aimed at reducing the
choices for West German decision makers to a point where the
actions sought by foreign leaders would seem far more attractive
to them than any conceivable alternative. In domestic politics sim-

ilar strategies are employed by governmental and nongovernmental elites to achieve or prevent particular policy actions by executive, legislative, and judicial bodies.

These efforts are most effective when the ultimate decision makers conclude that other options are out of the question. For instance, most West German leaders today believe that security considerations permit no alternative to close collaboration with the United States; the military and diplomatic benefits for the Federal Republic are said to outweigh the attendant risks, economic costs, and foreign policy constraints.

On the other hand, efforts to influence policy are less effective when the decision makers believe that they have other feasible options and are sharply divided on the extent of their freedom of choice on a particular policy issue. For example, less developed countries have found it difficult to wring economic concessions from the Federal Republic because West German leaders have not thought it absolutely essential to satisfy such demands and have held conflicting views about the necessary extent of foreign aid.

As a rule, West German decision makers seek to increase their room for bargaining maneuvers and conflict regulation by endeavoring to keep options open and extending the range of feasible choices in the formulation of domestic and foreign policies. Chancellor Adenauer was particularly skilled in this respect— both in his negotiations with foreign governments and in his dealings with elite alignments at home—and as a result he was singularly successful in achieving his policy goals.

The issue of options also enters into disputes over how West German policymakers should pursue their objectives. Such disputes may revolve around questions of form and questions of method; more often than not they will involve both.

Controversies on matters of form usually involve conflicting interpretations of constitutional and other legal rules for policymaking. For example, the question of whether a policy measure requires only the approval of the Federal Diet or that of the Federal Council as well can lead to clashes between the two chambers, especially when the opposition in the Diet has enough votes in the Council to block such legislation. Or the point at issue may be a jurisdictional dispute between state and federal authorities, or between departments of the federal executive. Then, too, controversies of this sort may arise over the question of whether formal rules calling for interest group consultation and parliamentary committee deliberations have been properly observed in the course of policy formation.

Disputes over method concern essentially different estimates of what is necessary and what is available to achieve particular policy aims. West German decision makers may want to get at the roots of current economic problems, but if they disagree on where these roots lie they will also disagree on feasible solutions. For example, according to Chancellor Helmut Schmidt, the domestic price inflation of the mid-1970s was primarily attributable to external causes that demanded international solutions through intergovernmental negotiations. However, according to the critics of his economic policies it was a homemade inflation caused by excessive governmental expenditures and could only be cured thorugh a domestic austerity program. But what expenditures should be cut was another question—in effect, a political one. It was answered differently by various party and pressure group leaders in terms of their conflicting political interests and values. That left it to the Schmidt government to come up with an authoritative solution in the form of a budget that made no one happy.

This dispute underscored the fact that controversies over policy methods are inextricably interwoven with conflicting evaluations of their consequences. Some of Chancellor Schmidt's economic consultants argued that if the economy was to get moving again at an optimum rate, social service expenditures would have to be cut to the bone; some of his political advisers insisted, however, that if this were done it would have dire electoral consequences for the chancellor's party, the SPD.

On this point, consider two long-standing disputes relating policy methods to their anticipated consequences. In foreign affairs, one group of policymakers holds that closer trade relations with the German Democratic Republic will lead to a gradual liberalization of its political system; another group maintains that this will only strengthen the Communist regime. In domestic affairs, left-wing Social Democrats assert that tighter state control over private business investments will enhance the efficient mobilization and allocation of economic resources; their conservative opponents predict, however, that such measures will stifle individual initiative and talent and lead to an authoritarian command economy run by a vast and inept government bureaucracy.

In short, arguments over the choice of methods are conditioned by differences over their expected effects. Among West German policymakers disputes of this sort usually focus on three questions. One is whether formal decisions can be effectively implemented. For example, government leaders have in the past been divided over the feasibility of wage and price controls for checking inflation. A second question is whether a proposed policy action may be counterproductive—or, at least, too risky to chance. Thus arguments in favor of wage and price controls were met with counterarguments that such measures would only intensify inflationary pressures through a black market. A third question is whether efforts to deal with one set of issues may not create problems in other spheres of policymaking. For instance, suggestions that domestic economic difficulties might be eased by reducing military expenditures have invariably run up against predictions that such reductions would expose the Federal Republic to Soviet blackmail and antagonize its allies. Similar policy controversies have been provoked by friction between government endeavors to sustain the Federal Republic's strong competitive position in world markets and simultaneous diplomatic efforts to maintain close political relations with the United States and fellow members of the European Community.

All told, then, West German policymaking is subject to controversies over means and ends. On such occasions arguments for and against one or another course of action are presented and disputed in terms of "if-then" propositions that point policy deliberations toward a future state of affairs. In this section we have emphasized some major conflict issues, but we must not forget that many less conspicuous and less broad-gauged problems also pose policy questions. How they are authoritatively answered, if not settled, depends largely on who is involved, under what circumstances, and with what considerations in mind.

THE EXECUTIVE ARENA

The management of the national policy agenda—and of attendant policy conflicts—rests first and foremost in the hands of top officials of the Federal Government. Remember that under the constitutional allocation of powers federal authorities are in charge of foreign relations and most domestic policymaking. Furthermore, the executive branch has access to more extensive sources of policy-relevant information than other branches of government, nongovernmental organizations, and the press.[1] Insofar as such information furnishes executive officials with exclusive intelligence, it can give them a decided advantage in their dealings with outsiders.

Of course, preeminence in policymaking is one thing; control over policymaking is quite another. The Federal Government as a whole has rarely, if ever, been able to make policy unilaterally in every area under its formal jurisdiction. And particular government leaders have time and again been compelled either to abandon cherished policy objectives, or to make haste slowly and, frequently, to settle in the end for less than what they wanted.

To begin with, a large part of what goes on a government's policy agenda—and in what order—is not simply up to its leaders. There are matters they are obliged to deal with under the laws of the Federal Republic and its treaty commitments. For instance, the executive branch is bound by West Germany's membership in the European Community to take all necessary measures for imple-

---

1. The Federal Government thus receives all sorts of privileged information through exclusive diplomatic and military channels, through inter-elite ties and intelligence agencies, and from expert consultants and advisory bodies. Periodic polls sponsored by the government furnish its leaders with a reading of the climate of public opinion for current policymaking, while the planning staffs in various ministries and the chancellor's office collect and process information for future policy actions.

menting EC decisions through domestic regulations. Then there will be developments emphasizing or deemphasizing particular issues and policy demands for government decision makers. An upcoming election, for example, may cause government leaders to put off the introduction of unpopular economic measures and make them especially sensitive to pressure from party and interest group elites. Or urgent problems may suddenly be thrust into the executive arena by unanticipated developments, such as the severity of the West German energy crisis and economic recession of the 1970's.

The range of items that the leaders of the Federal Government may choose to place on or leave off their their policy agenda, or to assign a different order of priority to, is thus limited. Here the personal preferences of key executive officials and their relationship with other policymakers, and the extent of policy consensus in the councils of the Federal Government are likely to be particularly important. Consider, for example, that the conservative government of Konrad Adenauer put much greater stess on internal and external security issues than the Social-Liberal Coalition headed by Willy Brandt, but far less on domestic reforms and friendly relations with Communist countries. And whereas under CDU Chancellor Ludwig Erhard explicit government planning programs were anathema, members of the Brandt government were intially seized by a virtual planning euphoria.

Procedures for processing the policy agenda in the executive arena have been practically as important as its contents in shaping the policy output of the Federal Government. Here we must note that although parliamentary party government has made for closer executive-legislative policy coordination than in the United States, pluralism *within* the Federal Government has been far more pronounced in West Germany. One reason is that all governments have been coalitions with factional cleavages within and between the ruling parties. Another is that the presistence of time-honored departmental prerogatives has accentuated the structural segmentation of the executive branch and complicated the coordination of functionally interrelated policymaking tasks.

Under so-called *Resort* principles, precise legal regulations de-

fine the special responsibilities of decentralized government departments and assign to about sixteen ministries exclusive original
jurisdiction over specific spheres of policy formulation. The Ministry of Economics has thus the authority to deal with some aspects
of foreign trade, but others come under the aegis of the Ministry
of Economic Cooperation, and the preparation of the government
budget is the business of the Ministry of Finance. Matters touching
on relations with East Germany are the concern of the Ministry
of Intra-German Relations, whereas diplomatic relations with
other Communist states are dealt with by the Foreign Ministry.

Overlapping partisan and bureaucratic politics may consequently delay, if not prevent decisive government action on pressing policy problems. The partisan dimension for policy conflicts
in the executive arena is defined by the shifting complexion of
political alignments and the degree of policy consensus in party
governments, the bureaucratic dimension by the range of policy
differences among civil servants in autonomous government departments. Both dimensions for potential disputes over ends and
means reflect the pluralist patterns of checks and balances in the
West German policymaking stratum, especially in the executive
arena. Personal and factional rivalries among elites inside and
outside the Federal Government are apt to become interlaced with
internal controversies over appropriate policy objectives, priorities, and procedures. At the same time, effective agenda management by the executive as a whole depends on the cohesiveness of
its top political officials—chancellor, ministers, state secretaries,
and key division chiefs—and on the loyal support of the regular
career civil servants in the bureaucratic substructure. Unresolved
policy disputes within the Federal Government are likely to weaken
its influence in the arenas of parliamentary and federal politics
and, consequently, its authority in domestic and foreign affairs.
Government leaders therefore consider effective arrangements
for the consensual resolution or, at least, the containment of such
conflicts a crucial prerequisite for the smooth operation of the
executive policymaking system.

The coordination of goverment policies calls first of all for
broad-gauged agreements among the executive and legislative

leaders of the ruling parties on what needs to be done and how. These understandings usually provide top government officials and their advisers with fairly general policy guidelines that allow for a good deal of flexibility in executive decision making. Specific policy options and action proposals are formulated by staff officials in appropriate ministries and submitted to the Federal cabinet by way of intra- and inter-departmental screening processes.

Coalition politics and organizational segmentation in the Federal Government have served to underscore the coordinating roles of the Federal chancellor and his chief assistants. The chancellor's office has grown over the years from a small secretariat into a staff of close to 500 employees. Its chief may be a federal minister with a seat in the Federal Diet as well as the cabinet, or a state secretary with civil service status; in any case he will be a political appointee who is close to the chancellor and who has been chosen by him to help him harmonize particularistic ministerial policies for which only the chancellor is ultimately responsible to the Federal Diet. This task usually calls for skill on the part of the chancellor and for circumspection on the part of the chief of the chancellor's office. The record of various incumbents has been rather mixed. Adenauer, for example, used his assistant Hans Globke well; Brandt's less diplomatic and more independent lieutenant Horst Ehmke antagonized the department heads and complicated rather than facilitated the chancellor's coordinating efforts. But even Adenauer, at the very height of his imperious chancellor democracy, was far more effective in coordinating the foreign than the domestic policy action of his government.

The Basic Law, as we noted in chapter 2, gives the chief of the Federal Government substantial control over executive policymaking. However, his powers are not nearly as vast as those of the American or French president. West German ministers, on the other hand, have enjoyed a good deal more latitude in running their departments and in shaping their particular policies than their counterparts in the United States and France. The chancellor's constitutional right to create and abolish ministries, to choose the members of his government and to determine its policies, has been sharply curbed by the practices of coalition politics. Moreover, under the procedural rules of the Federal Government, he cannot compel a department head to follow a specific course. Nor can he bypass the authority of a minister who will not cooperate; he can only request his resignation or ask the Federal president to dismiss him, and neither course may be politically feasible.

Coalition politics have provided the most obvious constraints on the chancellor's control over Federal ministers. The number and allocation of cabinet portfolios are usually crucial in the formation of governing coalitions; disputes on that score have sometimes required weeks of preliminary bargaining among party and interest group elites. Organized labor has to be accommodated with a trade unionist at the head of the Ministry of Labor, the farmers' organizations with one of their own in the post of Minister of Agriculture, and the business associations with acceptable ministers of economics and finance. Important party factions have to be represented, and a powerful party leader is unlikely to settle for anything less than a major cabinet post, such as minister of foreign affairs, defense, economics, or finance. This is not just a matter of prestige; government position may hold out the promise that the incumbent will be able to enhance his political reputation and advance his policy objectives by placing his personal imprimatur on particular government actions. In recent times, three out of five successful aspirants to the chancellorship—Erhard, Brandt, and Schmidt—promoted their claims to the top position in that manner.

Once a government is in place, the jurisdictional prerogatives of the ministers will further limit the chancellor's control over policy formation. Their partisan and personal interests now combine with the special policy concerns of their ministries to reduce the chancellor's freedom of choice and to complicate the development of cohesive executive policies. Much depends on whether ministers can strike a balance between their individual roles as department heads and their collective roles as members of the chancellor's cabinet. In the former capacity they represent the particularistic concern of their departments in relations with the chancellor, fellow ministers, legislators, and the public; in the latter they represent the common political objectives of a party government in their relations with subordinates in the federal bureaucracy and the interest group clients of their departments.

On the whole, Federal ministers have identified themselves more with their departmental than with their cabinet functions—and all the more so the longer they have stayed with one department. One reason is that elite and popular opinion has judged their performance in office on the strength of their ability to promote policy demands associated with their ministries. A closely related reason is that ministers have depended on the loyal services of their in-house bureaucracy and in return have felt obliged to look after its interests, especially in budgetary allocations. A third reason is that ministers have relied on staff briefings and position papers that present policy issues in terms of a restricted departmental focus rather than overall government objectives.

In effect, the combination of coalition politics and ministerial prerogatives has allowed the chancellor and his office only limited control over policymaking in the executive arena.[2] As we noted earlier, how much use the chief of government can make of his formal coordinating powers depends largely on his personal authority in a government of ruling party leaders. On the other hand, the autonomy of a department head and his influence over government policies will be all the greater the less he is politically beholden to the chancellor and the more the chancellor depends on his cooperation and that of the minister's supporters inside and outside the executive branch.

The policy actions of the Federal Government have always been the products of collegial decision making—less so in Adenauer's days and more so since then. The chancellor, unlike the American president, does not have the legal right to disregard or overrule his cabinet on major policy issues, but ministers need the support of the chancellor and a majority of their peers to obtain necessary cabinet approval for their policy proposals and for senior appointments in their departments. By the procedural rules of the Federal

2. See Renate Mayntz and Fritz W. Scharpf, *Policy-Making in the German Federal Bureaucracy* (New York: Elsevier, 1975); and Neville Johnson, *Government in the Federal Republic: The Executive at Work*, 2d ed. (Oxford: Pergamon, 1983), on this and other matters discussed in this section.

Government, the Federal cabinet must give its formal blessings to the government's budget and all other legislative measure and legal ordinances before they can be submitted to the Federal parliament. It is also the ultimate authority for settling policy disputes in the executive arena. A Federal minister will therefore not normally seek cabinet approval for a policy measure unless he knows he can get it, and he will try to resolve policy differences with the chancellor and other ministers before they reach the cabinet.

By enabling a chancellor to promote or block policy action by the Federal Government, these formal provisions tend to strengthen his authority as its chief executive; by compelling him to base his own policies on a ministerial consensus, they also tend to weaken it. Should most cabinet officers refuse to go along with the chancellor, he would have four legitimate recourses: he can (a) defer to their wishes, (b) request their resignation, (c) ask the federal president to dismiss them, or (d) press them to change their minds—if need be by threatening to ask the Federal Diet for a personal vote of confidence or to bring down the entire government with his own resignation.

An astute chancellor will see to it that such conflict situations do not arise, especially if he lacks the resources for mobilizing decisive outside support on his side. All of the above four contingencies would reflect on his performance as chief executive and might even cost him his job. Chancellor Erhard's inability to surmount conflicts with his ministers, for example, led to his involuntary retirement. Chancellor Adenauer, on the other hand, would avoid such confrontations by staging tactical policy retreats and agreeing to face-saving compromise solutions in the name of government harmony.

For the sake of his public image, a chancellor must at least appear to be in control of a united Federal Government—even if he is not in fact. The more fragile an alliance of powerful party leaders and the greater the divisive pressures from the outside, the more important it is that he be able to manage and contain internal policy controversies. He cannot allow partisan and bureaucratic conflicts to paralyze the policymaking functions of the Federal Government and he cannot permit any minister to saddle him with responsibilities for policies he does not endorse. Take the case of Karl Schiller, an unprecedented "superminister" who headed both the finance and economic ministries in Chancellor Brandt's first Social-Liberal Coalition cabinet. Schiller worked for some time in close collaboration with the chancellor and initially enjoyed strong elite support inside and outside a government that commanded only a bare majority of the Federal Diet and none in the Federal Council. However, when Schiller's policies led to bitter dispute with fellow ministers, Brandt evidently welcomed, if not encouraged, the resignation of a man who lacked an independent power base in the ruling Social Democratic party.

The pluralist constraints on joint policymaking in the Federal Government have emphasized the importance of harmonious associations among its top officials. A good working relationship between chancellor and ministers holds mutual advantages, and it is particularly essential for close collaboration between the principal majority and minority party leaders in coalition governments. CDU Chancellor Kurt Kiesinger thus worked in tandem with his SPD Deputy Chancellor and Foreign Minister Willy Brandt in the 1966–1969 Grand Coalition of Christian and Social Democrats. When Brandt became chancellor of the subsequent Social-Liberal Coalition, he teamed up with Walter Scheel, the leader of the FDP; the pattern was maintained by their immediate successors—SPD Chancellor Helmut Schmidt and FDP Deputy Chancellor and Foreign Minister Hans-Dietrich Genscher and then CDU Chancellor Helmut Kohl and Genscher. Along with other key governmental and legislative leaders of their respective parties, these men settled outstanding policy differences in the ruling coalitions and forged agreements outside rather than inside the formal sessions of the Federal cabinet. For instance, in 1974, cabinet approval of the federal budget was ensured after a series of informal meetings at Chancellor Schmidt's vacation home; and in the following year the Social-Liberal Coalition leaders resolved their differences on a new codetermination law in a similar fashion.

Policy disputes in the executive arena are most likely to become enmeshed in bureaucratic politics when they involve departments with competing pressure group clienteles. For example, officials of the ministries of agriculture and finance may lock horns over the size of tax benefits for the farmers and those of the ministries of economics and labor over the formulation of measures affecting social security benefits. Such interbureaucratic conflicts are apt to be all the more intense when they engage civil servants who have pursued most or all of their careers in a single department; these tend to be the most jealous guardians of their ministry's prerogatives and to identify themselves closely with the promotion of its particular policy interests.

The executive policymaking system is designed to prevent such bureaucratic controversies or, if that is not possible, to resolve them at the earliest possible stage. To begin with, low-ranking department officials are not likely to get very far with their policy proposals if their superiors believe that these proposals will run into trouble at higher department levels. Second, the heads of government departments are unlikely to consent to proposals that will provoke strong opposition from their ministerial colleagues or the chancellor. Third, institutionalized arrangements for resolving policy conflicts between departments call for interbureaucratic negotiations between senior officials that will produce a compromise solution at the subcabinet level. If differences persist, the state secretaries may enter the fray on behalf of their minister, and the chief of the chancellor's office may endeavor to act as an honest broker.

The Federal cabinet as such has consequently been a more deliberative than decision-making organ. It normally meets about once a week, mostly to listen to expositions of current policy problems by the chancellor and various ministers and to consider appropriate government responses. Perfunctory approval of a particular course of action or inaction usually follows from preliminary understandings among top political officials and senior civil servants. The cabinet's formal authority to settle policy disputes has been rarely exercised. Its members may agree to disagree if differences have not been resolved at an earlier stage; more likely, the chancellor will put off a cabinet decision, rather than let it come to a vote that might split or, at least, reveal cracks in his government.

THE LEGISLATIVE ARENA OF
THE FEDERAL DIET

For most West Germans the popularly elected lower house of the Federal parliament is the most conspicuous arena of national policymaking. Its public plenary and committee sessions are covered by the mass media and schoolchildren from all over the country are taken to watch "democracy at work' from the visitors' gallery of the chamber. But for all that, what the ordinary citizen reads, sees, and hears gives him a rather limited and not particularly impressive picture of the policymaking functions of the Diet.[3]

Nominally, the Diet has rather extensive constitutional powers in this respect since all laws and treaties of the Federal Republic require its approval. In actual fact, the chamber as a whole has, however, appeared to wield only very limited influence over authoritative policy choices and consequently has not been held in particularly high public esteem.

The initiation, formulation, and enactment of legislation has generally been controlled by the Federal Government and its legislative managers. Roughly eight out of ten of the bills passed by the Diet from 1949 to 1981 originated in the executive branch; the relatively few and unimportant bills introduced from the floor of the chamber required the consent of the Federal Government for passage. Most deputies have had to confine their legislative

3. As this section deals with the legislative functions of the Diet it does not discuss the elective and control functions set forth in chapter 2. The replacement of a chancellor through a "constructive vote of no-confidence" has been tried only twice. It failed in 1972 against SPD Chancellor Brandt, who then asked the chamber for a vote of confidence which he had arranged to loose so that he could get dissolution and a popular vote of confidence through new elections; it succeeded in 1982 against SPD Chancellor Schmidt, and the new CDU Chancellor Kohl then also arranged to loose a vote of confidence so he could establish his popular mandate through new elections. Plenary debates and question periods have provided especially opposition deputies with some, mostly indirect means of control over the government by bringing alleged shortcomings of its policies or members to the attention of the interested public. Special investigative committees have on a few occasions proven to be more effective means of such control, as in the recent public hearings on charges that leaders of the governing Christian and Free Democratic parties had received illegal payments from the Flick industrial concern.

efforts to shaping specific details in government bills, usually on behalf of particular partisan and pressure group interests.

One major reason for the predominance of executive authority in the legislative arena is that the directly elected representatives of the people labor under the same handicap as lawmakers in other advanced industrial countries. That is, the vast scope and complexity of policymaking inhibits the effectiveness of deputies, who lack the expertise, information, and supportive service available to executive leaders. Recent measures have somewhat improved that situation by providing the Diet and its component parties with more office space and a larger staff. In this respect West German deputies are now better off than members of other European legislatures, but still far less so than American congressmen. Nor do they wield as much of the critical power of the purse over governmental revenues and expenditures. The Diet not only has to share this legislative authority with the Federal Council of the state governments; it also may not increase or shift allocations in the Federal Government's proposed budget without the consent of the finance minister. Moreover, its fiscal powers have been further limited in recent years by governmental programs that have tended to structure legislative appropriations for scientific research and development and other key areas of national policy.

A second and related reason for executive predominance is that the constitutional authority of the Diet has been profoundly affected by the evolution of party government and party alignments in the Federal Republic. The authors of the Basic Law built on nineteenth-century principles of parliamentary government and sought to prevent excessive bureaucratic and legislative control over policymaking through a system of checks and balances between executive and legislature. What they did not anticipate was, first, that both would become controlled by the leaders of just one or two parties, and second, that party government would penetrate deeply into the executive bureaucracy and also reduce the autonomy of the direct representatives of the electorate.

In contrast to the United States, top officials of the West German Federal Government participate directly in legislative processes.

Government bills are shepherded through the Diet by the chiefs of appropriate departments and their principal lieutenants and government leaders can at any time intervene in policy disputes; they may not only ask to be heard but must be allowed to voice their views in plenary or committee sessions of the chamber. The chancellor, ministers, and parliamentary state secretaries may intercede as members of the executive branch or as members of the legislature; regular state secretaries and other key civil servants play less conspicuous roles as representatives of their political superiors in committee meetings of the lower house and in private conferences with Diet deputies.

Most plenary meetings of the Diet are pretty dull affairs, though they have occasionally been enlivened by demonstrative interruptions from the floor and touch-and-go votes in a narrowly divided house. The public media have therefore made all the more of exceptional dramatic clashes between proponents of ostensibly sharply conflicting policy positions.

A more meaningful measure of the legislators' role in policymaking is provided by the activities of the major organizational components of the Diet—its parliamentary parties and committees. The former are the setting for intraparty disputes in the legislative arena, the latter for interparty conflicts. They are connected through the specialized working or study groups (*Arbeitsgemeinschaften*) formed by the legislative committee members in each parliamentary party. Consequently, these deputies represent not only their party and its clients in the Diet committees, but also the cross-party policy interests of their particular committee and its constituencies in the caucus meetings of the parliamentary parties.

As we noted in chapter 6, the members of the parties in the Diet are tied to local constituencies and regional party organizations, to various ideological camps and vested interest organizations. The resulting pluralist patterns in the parliamentary parties resemble the patterns of executive pluralism in the Federal Goverment and require equivalent arrangements for internal conflict management and policy coordination. The major difference is that in the legislative arena such arrangements are not shaped nearly as much by formal rules; informal bargaining processes therefore play a correspondingly greater role in the resolution of policy disputes within the parliamentary parties.

The constitutional lawmakers do not simply dance to the tune of their legislative leaders; ruling party elites cannot ignore opposition in the parliamentary parties in pushing for a particular course of action. They lack the means to enforce their wishes and may have to go to a good deal of trouble to persuade reluctant deputies to buy a controversial measure. Chancellor Adenauer usually delegated this task to his legislative lieutenants; in more recent times both chancellors and ministers have made it a practice to argue their points personally in party caucuses.

Caucus meetings are subject to democratic procedures for arriving at a common policy position. When an issue gives rise to significant internal disagreements there may be extended deliberations, and if these fail to produce a concensus the party leaders will usually call for a vote. However the Basic Law allows deputies to disregard the outcome. In the SPD a high sense of party loyalty and discipline has normally led dissenters to adhere to majority decisions on votes in the Diet and its committees; Christian and Free Democrats have been somewhat more prone to disregard them, especially if their dissent is backed by powerful party or interest group factions or secured by a safe seat in the Diet.

Legislative committee meetings take up a large part of the deputies' time. The reason is that they are unwilling to approve skeletal laws that would give the Federal Government great leeway in interpretation and application and consider it their duty to submit bills to meticulous consideration in committee. In part this outlook is a legacy of German parliamentary traditions, which define highly explicit legislative codification as the principal means of popular control over the executive. In part, too, it is based on the deputies' belief that the input of pluralist interest demands in the Diet can be most adequately and efficiently processed through the committee system of miniparliaments. Moreover, committee assignments provide both majority and minority party members with opportunities to look after the needs of their pressure group clients and their local constituencies in specific policy outputs.

How much influence Diet committees wield over policymaking is a matter of considerable dispute among West German political observers. Some argue that the Diet "has disintegrated into a conglomerate of incoherent, highly specialized committees and working groups which are coordinated only by the leaders of the parliamentary parties, and whose horizons remain limited to narrowly defined areas of specialization."[4] In this view, the committees are totally dependent on guidance from the ministerial departments and are bureaucratic in their working patterns and in the perception of their tasks. Other observers maintain that "an elaborate committee structure with the most influential parliamentarians of all parties as chairmen of the important committees will assure the West German parliament of a degree of substantive influence in policy processes that is not found in the classical parliamentary systems."[5] In this view, the Diet, through its committees, is seen as closer in power to the American Congress than to legislatures in other representative democracies.

Judging by past experiences, it would appear that the influence exercised by Diet committees depends on their spheres of jurisdiction and on particular circumstances. Committees that deal with key areas of policymaking—such as the foreign affairs, defense, and budget—have tended to be most closely guided by cues from the executive branch; more highly specialized committees— such as the Agriculture Committee, the Committee for Urban Affairs and Home Construction, and the Committee for Labor and Social Affairs—are more autonomous and more amenable to interest group pressure. Consequently deputies who are primarily concerned with attending to the needs of particular constituencies are likely to prefer a seat on the latter type of committee, whereas those who are more interested in broader domestic and international issues opt for the former.

That circumstances may make a difference in the policy influence of Diet committees can be shown by two illustrations. During the Grand Coalition between the CDU/CSU and SPD in the late

4. Joachim Hirsch, "Scientific-Technical Progress and the Political System" in Klaus von Beyme, ed., *German Political Studies* Beverly Hills: Sage, 1974), 1:119.
5. Mayntz and Scharpf, *Policy-Making in the German Federal Bureaucracy*, p. 36.

1960s, the committees wielded an unprecedented degree of power and were often able to block or significantly change legislative proposals of the executive branch. Just because the government was based on an overwhelming parliamentary alignment between the two major competitive parties, it could not automatically rely on the support of a disciplined majority on specific issues. Policy differences that could not be settled in the executive arena were often resolved by compromise agreements in legislative committees. The second illustration is the situation when the opposition in the Diet commands sufficient votes in one or both houses of the Federal parliament to block key policy objectives of the Federal Government. The Social Democrats were in that position in the 1950s and early 1960s, when the CDU/CSU led the government; the Christian Democrats in the 1970s, when the SPD headed the Social-Liberal Coalition. In both instances the parliamentary opposition employed the leverage of its veto power in the legislative arena to extract substantial concessions from the government in committee meetings of the Diet.

THE FEDERAL ARENA

The governments of the ten constituent states of the Federal Republic play major roles in national policymaking. Their importance is all the more noteworthy in the light of recent efforts in other advanced industrial countries to curb the concentration of public authority through regional devolution. Territorial dispersion of decision-making sites is said to extend the opportunities for democratic participation and control. It is also said to promote political harmony by allowing for a more effective expression and accommmodation of sectional interests than in a centralized state. And it is held to increase the efficiency of the public administration and its responsiveness to popular needs and demands.

Informed observers are divided over how far any of these claims have been sustained in the Federal Republic, and whether for better or for worse. Some laud the principles and practices of West German federalism for enhancing democratic pluralism, as well as political stability and administrative efficiency in government.

Others maintain that they make it singularly difficult for the Federal Government to cope with pressing national policy problems, or that they serve to promote and legitimate the joint executive authority of federal and state leaders.

The patterns of conflict management in the federal arena are first of all conditioned by formal rules for integrating national and subnational institutions. As we noted in chapter 2 the Basic Law both fuses and divides the constitutional powers of federal and regional authorities and interposes state structures between central and local organs of government. And we observed in subsequent chapters how both are reflected in the electoral system and in the organization of political parties and pressure groups. The key agencies for countrywide policy coordination are intergovernmental committees, the Federal Council, and the top echelons of the major parties and interest associations. The principal mechanisms of the resolution of policy conflicts are negotiations among officials of the central and state governments, bargaining between federal and state party leaders, and adjudication by the Federal Constitutional Court.

Three developments have especially affected policymaking in the federal arena. The effective autonomy of the states has diminished over the years as the scope of federal regulations has increased. The progressive nationalization of public policy problems has furthermore eroded the legislative authority of the state parliaments and accentuated the role of the state governments in the formulation of policies for the entire country. And policy disputes in the federal arena have come to focus largely on issues related to differences in the political economy of the various states as sectional religious distinctions have become less important in West German politics.

The state governments are legally empowered to develop common policies on their own—that is, without the participation of federal organs—in two areas. One covers issues that fall under the exclusive jurisdiction of the states, principally control of the primary and secondary schools, the public radio and television media, law enforcement, and local government administration. The other concerns the few matters that remain subject to the policies of the state governments because federal authorities have not exercised their overlapping legislative powers.

In these spheres interstate negotiations resemble international negotiations among sovereign countries in that no state government can be compelled by the others to follow a particular course of action. State officials deal with each other in regular ministerial conferences and special joint commissions as the spokesmen for parliamentary state governments with similar, but not always identical interests. For example, diverse regional concerns and traditions have complicated efforts to coordinate local government operations, and sharp ideological differences among state government leaders have surfaced in disputes over the contents of a standardized school curriculum. Policy conflicts on such issues can be settled only by mutual agreement. Even then, there is no assurance that a settlement will be implemented in all the states. State officials may turn out to lack sufficient authority in their governments and parliaments to deliver what they agreed to. In any event, more often than not the mutual understandings will be kept in general terms and the more precise implementation will vary a good deal from state to state.

The state governments have been impelled to strive for more "self-coordination" under the pressure of expanding federal authority. Most often this takes the form of executive agreements on joint formulas for the solution of shared policy problems. For example, when in the early 1970s, the demand for higher education became greater than the available space in the most popular fields, the state governments established joint admission standards and selection procedures for the state universities. However, voluntary self-coordination has proven most difficult under the unanimity rule in interstate negotiations, and the nature of their common policy problems has largely compelled the state governments to rely increasingly on federal regulations and funding. Their disputes over policy contents and procedures have to a corresponding extent shifted more and more from the subnational to the federal level of decision making.

The federal policymaking system may be compared to a wagon wheel. The outer rim consists of the state parliaments and administrative agencies at the periphery. They are joined to the center by the spokes, the state governments. The Federal Council, at the hub, connects the state governments to the Federal Government and the Diet. As a permanent assembly of their delegates, the Council fulfills two primary functions. It stands apart from the national executive and popularly elected lower house as an instrument for the defense and promotion of the interests of the state governments and their particular clients. But it is also a part of the Federal parliament and, as such, serves to coordinate the formulation of national policies with their implementation by subnational organs of government.

In a strictly legal sense the Council is not, like the United States Senate, a coequal chamber of the national legislature. Although the upper house considers all bills passed by the Diet, it cannot block legislation that falls under the exclusive jurisdiction of federal authorities, most notably defense and foreign policy measures. Its approval is needed for constitutional amendments—which require a two-thirds majority vote—and for laws that come under the joint legislative powers of federal and state authorities.[6] But here the Federal Constitutional Court has ruled that legislation derived from a law already approved by the chamber does not require its consent. And though the Federal cabinet must submit all of its legislative proposals to the Council before they are formally introduced in the Diet, it does not have to accept changes recommended on a majority vote of the state governments.

However, these formal provisions convey only a very limited picture of the state governments' actual involvement in the formulation of federal policies. In 1985, one out of two bills required the approval of the Federal Council to become law, compared to one out of ten in 1949. And the state governments have lately performed an increasing number of so-called joint tasks with the Federal Government. A compromise formula for more "coopera-

6. When the consent of the Council is not essential, a bill that is defeated by a majority vote of its members must be passed by a majority of the deputies in the Diet to become law; if the bill is defeated by a two-thirds vote in the Council it can only become law if it is subsequently approved by a two-thirds vote in the Diet that includes at least a majority of all of that chamber's members.

tive federalism" has led to a proliferation of interministerial co-ordinating committees of executive officials from the central and state governments. These bureaucratic organs develop national programs for urban and regional economic development, for scientific research and educational projects, for coordinated federal and state budgets, and for federal financial assistance to the states. Such projects are in turn translated into broad-gauged legislative proposals of the federal and state governments which, in effect, leave the state diets with no other choice but to accept or reject them in their entirety. Consequently, the state diets will almost invariably give their approval without much ado—especially when they would otherwise forfeit federal matching grants. In late 1975, for example, a general higher education law that emerged from six years of hard bargaining between federal and state officials was quickly passed by both the federal and state parliaments.

In the Federal Council the state governments are in some ways in a stronger position relative to the Federal Government than are the members of the Diet. Unlike the lower house, the upper one cannot be dissolved in the event of a conflict with the national executive and the Federal Government is thus more amenable to compromise. The state governments can also deal with the Federal Government on a more equal basis than the deputies because their own civil servants provide them with a much larger and more knowledgeable staff of expert advisers. And although the Federal Government may not make the Diet privy to its deliberations and may deny it a good deal of policy-relevant information, formal rules as well as practical considerations require that the state governments are kept informed.

All legal ordinances of the Federal Government, and all of its administrative regulations that affect the states, must have the approval of the Federal Council (see figure 8.1). But beyond that, both the national executive and Diet need to take into account the fact that the effective implementation of most domestic policy decisions is the business of the state governments. Although the latter are bound by the Basic Law to execute federal regulations faithfully and uniformly, they must be allowed a good deal of leeway in the interpretation and application of such measures.

As a rule, every Federal Government will do its best to work in tandem with the state governments. The greater their cooperation, the less cost and effort has to go into coordinating activities of the small supervisory staff of the federal civil service. Moreover, the Federal Government has really not much choice but to rely on the voluntary compliance of each state government. What are its alternatives? Apart from withholding funds for specific revenue sharing projects, it can either bring a recalcitrant state government before the Constitutional Court—which may involve protracted and chancy proceedings—or it may seek majority support from the Federal Council for the application of the as yet untried measure of federal enforcement. These legal alternatives may serve the Federal Government as bargaining weapons, but they are rather blunt instruments.

The state governments, for their part, have a vast stake in the formulation of federal policies, for they are touched by virtually all of them. Federal legislation determines how much each state will get of the tax revenues that flow into the national treasury.[7] Federal measures designed to steer the national economy shape the resource base for state and local taxes and, therefore, what subnational governmental authorities can collect or must borrow to meet expenses. In this regard the size and shape of the federal budget and federal grants are particularly important, not only for the economic well-being of the state governments but for their political fortunes. Consider, too, that federal policies on regional economic development and domestic welfare legislation, on foreign trade and investments and the employment of foreign workers, and so forth, have a very decided effect on socioeconomic conditions in the various states. And note that state authorities rely on federal organs for information and procedural arrangements that will enable them to discharge their assigned tasks properly. The police functions of the states are one example. The

7. State and, even more, local governments have little tax income of their own in West Germany. At least 60 percent of all tax revenues goes into the national treasury; of this, about two-thirds is allocated to federal agencies, most of the rest to the state governments, while local governments receive by far the smallest share (see table 9.1).

uniform application of federal traffic regulations and internal security measures throughout the country calls for means of enforcement that all the state governments will consider technically feasible and adequately funded.

As in the United States Senate—though not to the same extent and in the same manner—the representatives of states with small populations wield a disproportionate degree of influence in the Federal Council (see table 8.1). Although the distribution of the citizenry among the states has shifted quite a bit, the allocation of seats in the chamber has not changed since the establishment of the Federal Republic. Remember that each state government controls at least three and at most five unit votes. Consequently, the government of the little city-state of Bremen can cast as many votes as that of the Saarland and that of Lower Saxony as many as the government of far more populous North Rhine-Westphalia. In effect, the bargaining powers of the small states is particularly great on issues that find the chamber narrowly divided.

Because the state governments play a greater and more direct part in national policymaking than in the United States, interstate party alignments are also more important in West Germany. At the same time party affiliation does not carry as much weight in the federal arena as in the legislative arena of the national Diet. Due to the growth of the party state and the predominance of just two major parties it has, however, assumed far greater importance than the framers of the constitution had expected.

Ever since the Council was established in 1949, the Christian and Social Democrats have waged a continuous battle for a decisive majority of the state votes. But neither the governing nor the opposition parties in the Diet have for any length of time been able to depend on favorable two-thirds majority in the other house. Parliamentary elections and changing coalitions in the states have repeatedly led to partisan realignments in the chamber. Moreover, party affiliation has sometimes proven less important than the promotion of particular sectional interests by state governments.

Party unity across state lines tends to be particularly strong when disputes in the federal arena are dominated by sharp partisan conflicts in the national parliament. This was most evident from

TABLE 8.1
The Political Economy of West German Federalism, 1983

| | PERCENTAGE OF FEDERAL COUNCIL SEATS | PERCENTAGE OF TOTAL POPULATION | PER CAPITA GDP IN 1,000 DM | SOURCES OF GDP | | | PERCENTAGE OF GDP EXPORTED | PERCENTAGE CONTRIBUTION TO NATIONAL TAXES |
				AGRICULTURE	INDUSTRY	SERVICES		
Federal Republic	100 = 41	100 = 59.8 mill.	28.2	2%	45%	53%	26%	100 = 379 bill. DM
Northern states								
Schleswig-Holstein	10%	4%	22.1	6%	37%	57%	19%	8%
Hamburg	7	3	48.0	0.5	35	65	11	9
Bremen	7	1	34.7	0.4	42	58	24	2
Lower Saxony	12	12	22.7	4	43	52	30	8
Central states								
North Rhine-Westphalia	12	28	25.4	1	47	52	27	29
Hesse	10	9	27.5	2	37	59	28	9
Rineland-Palatinate	10	6	24.2	3	50	47	36	4
Saarland	7	2	24.5	1	51	48	31	1
Southern states								
Baden-Württemberg	12	16	27.3	2	51	47	29	16
Bavaria	12	18	25.3	3	44	53	30	15

Sources: Calculated from data in *The Economist,* February 4, 1984; *Statistisches Jahrbuch für Bundesrepublik Deutschland, 1983,* p. 418; *Basic Statistics of the European Community,* 1983 ed., p. 59; *Fisdcher Weltalmanach, 1984,* p. 305.

1969 to 1982 when the Social-Liberal coalition government of the SPD and FDP commanded a majority of the votes in the popularly elected Diet and the opposition Christian Democrats came close to a two-thirds majority in the Federal Council. The constitutional powers of the chamber in effect greatly strengthened the position of the Christian Democrats in national policymaking.

At other times particular policy issues have been more likely to transcend party ties and produce shifting cross-party alignments that find the members of parties opposed to each other in the Federal Diet aligned on the same side in the Federal Council in interstate conflicts. This has been especially notable on issues related to differences in the political economy of the states (see table 8.1 above). For example, the heavily industrialized states do not share the problems of those where agriculture remains important. And consider that the rate of long-term unemployment has been much higher in North-Rhine Westphalia, a state with largely old and hard-pressed industries such as steel and coal mining, than in Baden-Württemberg, which has more profitable high technology industries. Note, above all, the persistence of intergovernmental conflicts over the distribution of national tax revenues among the states. Under the prevailing formula the four richest states subsidize public services and economic development projects in the other six. Their governments seek to recapture as much as possible for their own use. On the other hand, the states with large populations demand a more equitable per capita distribution, whereas the smaller and poorer states want both more than they contribute and more than they can claim on the basis of population.

The state governments, like the deputies of the Diet, take most of their policy cues from the Federal Government. Although they have the collective authority to introduce federal legislation through the Federal Council, they have seldom done so and then only on minor, noncontroversial matters. Policy conflicts in the federal arena are therefore usually prompted by actions of the national executive, either directly or by way of the Federal Diet. Correspondingly, the management of such disputes also rests principally with officials and legislative agents of the Federal Government. How they are dealt with depends on the nature of the issues and the alignment of political forces.

Differences over administrative procedures are normally resolved through interbureaucratic negotiations. These are conducted almost entirely out of the public view and far from partisan strife by federal and state civil servants. For the most part, they concern complex but mundane issues, or entirely nonpartisan issues, which the respective government leaders are content to leave their subordinates to settle inside and outside the committees of the Federal Council. Expected and actual electoral outcomes seldom impinge on such negotiations, and the rare deadlocks have been invariably due to the intrusion of more profound disputes on the content of federal policies or constitutional issues. Disputes between federal and state government leaders on such substantive issues have only rarely ended up in the Federal Constitutional Court. Usually they are decided in the Federal Council. And if the Federal Government lacks the votes to have its way, it is likely to modify its position. Moreover, the Federal Government will endeavor to formulate its policy proposals in such a manner that it will not have to stage a public retreat in the face of opposition in the Council. The demands of the controlling majority are accordingly frequently anticipated when a law or ordinance is drafted and often need not even be made explicit; an unspoken threat of rejection in the upper house can suffice. If need be, negotiations will continue while a bill is considered by the Diet, and in this stage, bargaining within and among parties will be particularly important. Should a bill be nonetheless defeated in the Council after passage in the lower house, a compromise solution may still emerge from secret deliberations in the joint conference committee of the two chambers. From 1949 to 1984 only one out of ten laws needed to go through this process—mostly in the 1970s when the Social-Liberal majority in the Diet was at loggerheads with the Christian Democratic majority in the Council—and 90 percent of these laws were ultimately approved in an amended form by both chambers.

THE SYSTEM IN OPERATION

We observed early in this chapter that major controversies in the policymaking stratum have been rare in the Federal Republic. And as we also noted, when disputes do arise they tend to be settled through behind-the-scenes negotiations among the elites rather than on the open stage of West German politics. Conspicuous conflicts in authoritative decision making arenas are accordingly atypical, but they illuminate interrelationships and processes that are obscure at other times. Let us therefore conclude this chapter by taking a look at six such cases. Each of them, in various ways, illustrates the close connection between formal structures and political dynamics in a pluralist context for policy conflicts and their management.

Antitrust Legislation

The Policy Problem. Soon after the establishment of the Federal Republic, the CDU-led coalition government of Chancellor Adenauer became embroiled in a major policy dispute over innovative antitrust legislation.[8] Business cartels that had flourished under earlier regimes and survived regulatory efforts by the occupation powers were blossoming again; the question at issue was what the authoritative decision makers could and would do about this development.

Initial Actions (1950–1953). The first round in the extended battle over cartel legislation was fought principally in the executive arena. It involved three sets of leading contestants: the allied high commissioners for Germany, the big-business elite, and the Adenauer government. The joint American-British-French High Commission (HICOC) exercised far-reaching collective authority over policymaking, since the Federal Republic had been granted only limited sovereignty by the three former occupation powers.

8. Case study based on Gerard Braunthal, "The Struggle for Cartel Legislation" in James B. Christoph and Bernard E. Brown, eds., *Cases in Comparative Politics,* rev. ed. (Boston: Little, Brown, 1969), pp. 187–206.

HICOC demanded speedy action on stringent antitrust legislation that would prevent any kind of cartel. West German industrial leaders, on the other hand, were just as adamantly opposed to such measures. The Adenauer government, in the middle, was thus confronted with strong countervailing pressures. The situation was further complicated by two additional factors. One was that economic growth through industrial exports had high priority on the government's policy agenda and that here the powers represented on the High Commission were also major competitors. The other problem was that the ruling parties and their supporters in the business community were internally divided on cartel control.

The CDU Minister of Economics, Ludwig Erhard, was a fervent proponent of maximal competition in a free enterprise system and wanted to outlaw trusts while maintaining a minimum of state control over the economy. The cartel division of his department prepared a government bill to this effect which Erhard presented to the Federal cabinet in March 1951, for its necessary approval. Prolonged deliberations at the top of the executive branch followed because the tripartite High Commission maintained that the proposed legislation did not go far enough whereas the business lobby held that it went too far. A year went by and, in March 1952, the cabinet was ready to approve the submission of a compromise bill to the Federal parliament. It provided for the prohibition of industrial cartels and for an enforcement agency, but dismissed HICOC demands for the outlawing of cartels in agriculture, banking, and transportation.

Even before this measure was formally introduced in the Federal Diet, it encountered strong opposition from the Federation of German Industries. The BDI maintained that it was willing to accept controls over industrial cartels, but not their total prohibition. This produced a deadlock between Erhard, who threatened to resign, and leading industrialists, who informed Chancellor Adenauer that they might withhold contributions to the Christian Democratic campaign in the coming 1953 election. Broader domestic and foreign policy considerations induced Adenauer to support Erhard's position, but with the end of the legislative period, the initial government bill died in the Economic Affairs Committee of the Federal Diet.

Bargaining and Negotiations in the Executive Arena (1954–1955). The second round in the battle over anticartel legislation featured a sparring match between Economic Minister Erhard and West German industrialists. Intervention by the High Commission ceased to be a significant factor, since the three Western powers gradually turned over their authority to the Federal Government and, in May 1955, granted full sovereignty to the Federal Republic. In domestic politics, the CDU/CSU now held a majority in both houses of the Federal Parliament and the SPD opposition was also in favor of outlawing industrial cartels. In February 1954, the Adenauer coalition cabinet approved a new Erhard bill to this effect and, on the face of it, speedy legislative passage seemed ensured. However, the government bill was not even to be submitted formally to parliament for another year; the industrialists were by no means ready to surrender, and Erhard delayed introduction in the hope of overcoming their opposition.

According to constitutional procedures, the proposed measure was initially sent from the cabinet to the Federal Council for preliminary consideration. While the upper house sat on it for three months, it became evident that the CDU/CSU's nominal parliamentary majority—and SPD support—did not ensure easy passage for the government bill. The heterogeneous Christian Democratic party and business elites were deeply split on the issue. Under pressure from industry leaders, representatives of CDU/CSU-dominated state governments in the Federal Council recommended changes to the cabinet that weakened some key provisions of the Erhard bill. The cabinet considered it advisable to accept a number of these suggestions and Erhard, in lengthy negotiations with BDI spokesmen, agreed to accept further emasculating amendments when the government bill reached the Federal Diet.

Conflict and Conflict Resolution in the Legislative Arena (1955–1957). The third and final round in the battle over anti-cartel legislation took place in the Federal Diet. Its fate there shows what can happen when a strong pressure group fails to obtain satisfaction in the executive arena and is able to exploit the division of the governing parties on policy issues in the lower house of parliament.

In March 1955, the government's regulatory bill was formally introduced in the Federal Diet with its first reading and entered the usual committee stage. Five committees were to deal with its contents for more than two years, but for the most part the legislative struggle between the proponents and opponents of effective regulations focused on the deliberations of the Economic Affairs Committee. Two bills, one more and one less restrictive, were introduced by deputies of the governing CDU/CSU, but neither received much support. The government's proposals, on the other hand, were endorsed by a single-issue majority coalition composed of left-wing Christian Democrats, most Free Democrats, and the opposition SPD.

In view of this alignment, the industry lobby sought to keep the government bill bottled up in the Economic Affairs Committee with the help of its accommodating CDU chairman. When that did not prove possible, the BDI sought in vain to get Chancellor Adenauer to withdraw his support. However, it was more successful in applying both direct pressure on individual CDU/CSU deputies and indirect pressure through their party organization. Though the BDI was unable to block the Federal Government's regulatory proposal altogether, it managed to win further exeptions through compromise solutions to bitter committee battles.

Policy Enactment and Its Effects. In the summer of 1957, the final committee version of a much watered-down government bill was passed without much further debate in its second and third reading by the Federal Diet. The Federal Council went along, the Federal president attached his signature, and in January 1958, a cartel control law at last went into effect—eight years after the first try. Many of the deputies who had voted for it declared themselves far from satisfied with a policy measure that was so much weaker than the original Erhard proposals. However, business leaders who had opposed restrictive legislation from the outset considered the emasculated law still too severe. But they found they could live with it. Its administrative implementation by the new regulatory cartel office demonstrated that the concessions won by business pressure groups safeguarded many of the old practices in restraint of trade. The industrial lobby made no attempt to repeal the law and was able to block efforts to strengthen it substantially.

Subsidies for the Railroads

The Policy Problem In 1953, the publicly owned federal railway system was in deep financial trouble and the CDU/CSU-dominated Federal Government of Chancellor Adenauer was legally bound to come to its rescue.[9] The plight of the railway system was essentially due to two factors. One was that it was obligated to maintain regular services on unprofitable lines, the other that it had to transport unwieldy cargoes at fixed low rates in the face of growing competition from private truckers. The problem for the government was to obtain ameliorative legislation that would provide the railway system with more income without reducing existing services and increasing charges.

Policy Formulation and Conflict in Executive Arena (1953–1954). The Adenauer government started from the position that closing down the unprofitable operations or raising the passenger and cargo rates of the railroads was out of the question. The only feasible alternatives appeared to be (a) massive government subsidies, (b) measures to improve the competitive position of the railroads in relation to private trucking, or (c) some combination of the two. In the summer of 1953, the government settled on the third option, but it realized that its legislative proposals would have to take into account potential opposition from trucking firms, from their suppliers and customers, and from commercial concerns that

9. Case study based on Gerard Braunthal, *The West German Legislative Process: A Case Study of Two Transportation Finance Bills* (Ithaca: Cornell University Press, 1972).

did their own trucking. It therefore sought a measure that would provide for new highway construction on behalf of these interests and, at the same time, provide subsidies from new taxes for the railroads and transfer a portion of long-haul trucking to the railroads' ownership.

Since the contemplated solution to the problem was first of all a revenue matter, the task of drafting a transportation finance law fell initially to appropriate officials in the Ministry of Finance. But as it also involved the concerns of other government departments, these civil servants were under instructions to consult officials from the Ministry of Transport and the autonomous Federal Railway Administration. Almost at once, interbureaucratic conflicts arose that eventually took in the ministries of justice, economics, and foreign affairs and cabinet-level political officials. At issue were such questions as whether and how much to increase taxes on motor vehicles, transportation, and motor fuel and whether to introduce tolls on the superhighways. The departments and their chiefs approached the problem from their particular perspectives and those of their respective interest group clients. For example, the Ministry of Finance sought to change the existing tax structure to increase revenues for the railways, whereas the Ministry of Economics held that such a change would harm industrial expansion by cutting into the profits of private automobile construction and trucking concerns.

By early 1954, interministerial negotiations had failed to resolve these differences. Opposition SPD deputies in the Federal Diet began to question the Federal Government's ability to cope with the problem, and embarrassed Christian Democrats pressed their government leaders to come up with an agreement. At the same time, major interest groups—notably the Federation of German Industries (BDI) and the German Federation of Trade Unions (DGB)—endeavored to influence the shape of the government bill, though with little effect. The intense governmental controversy was veiled in exceptional secrecy and the mandatory consultations with concerned interest organizations were kept to a minimum. Moreover, both of the major peak associations of business and labor were internally divided on the issue. In the BDI,

for example steel producers identified their interests with substantial aid to the railroads, whereas the manufacturers of motor
vehicles saw this aid as contrary to their interests. In the DGB a
similar conflict along functional lines set the Federation of Rail-
road Workers against the Federation of Public Service and Transport Workers.

*Policy Conflict and Conflict Resolution in the Legislative Arena (1954–
1955).* In March 1954, the Federal cabinet gave its reluctant approval to a proposal that still did not suit some of its members,
especially the Minister of Economics Ludwig Erhard. From there
the bill took its usual course to the Federal Council for preliminary
consideration. The pressure groups on both sides of the issue
persuaded the state governments to recommend a substantial
number of changes. On return of the bill, the cabinet accepted
about half of these and in June 1954, sent the amended government bill to the Federal Diet for its first reading. At that point the
disagreement in the Federal government and among CDU/CSU
deputies was underscored when a Christian Democrat took the
unusual step of introducing a rival proposal from the floor—one
that came closer to the wishes of the Economic Ministry. Even
more exceptional was that when the two proposals went to the
Economic Affairs Committee of the Diet, the Economic Ministry
went out of its way to indicate its opposition to the official government bill. This, in turn, prompted the Federal cabinet to recon-
sider and reaffirm its collective endorsement of the government's
measure. Nonetheless, legislative passage of the government
proposal was still not ensured. Contending alignments of bureaucratic, partisan, and pressure group interests fought over the contents during lengthy deliberations in the Committee for Finance
and Taxation. Deputies of the government's own party battled for
major changes and the votes of the opposition Social Democrats
were needed to defeat their amendments before the government
bill was reported out of committee for a second reading and vote
in the Diet.

The bill passed its second reading despite an intensive lobbying
campaign by its diehard opponents. Their efforts to mobilize pub-

lic opinion against the measure failed, probably because the bill was too complex and technical to command wider attention. But even after preliminary passage, there were last-minute efforts to change the bill through amendments from the floor when it came up for a vote on the third and final reading. All of them failed. The government's proposal took its last hurdle in the Diet easily, and then was approved by the Federal Council without significant amendment. With the signature of the federal president, the transportation finance law took effect in April 1955.

Although the final version of the law conformed essentially to the original draft of the Ministry of Finance, it also bore the marks of the conflicts, bargains, and compromises that accompanied its course from initiation to enactment. Of the thirty-one original clauses, only nine remained unchanged; four were altered in interdepartmental bargaining, two were amended by the Federal Council, and sixteen were changed in the Federal Diet. Throughout, the federal chancellor and his chief of staff in the chancellor's office acted as brokers in the resolution of bureaucratic, partisan, and pressure group disputes that led to the law's final passage.

Cost Sharing

The Policy Problem. The vast majority of West German employees are covered by mandatory medical insurance programs run by private companies but regulated by public authorities.[10] In May 1957—after five years of controversy and shortly before federal elections—the CDU/CSU-dominated Federal parliament enacted a health insurance reform law sponsored by the Adenauer government. It maintained a formula under which all of the funds for sick-leave payments and medical bills were provided by the insurance companies and employers; the latter, particularly, were required to pay larger amounts than before. In view of rising medical costs this requirement did not sit well with the business community, and its leaders demanded a new formula that would

10. Case study based on William Safran, *Veto-Group Politics: The Case of Health Insurance Reform in West Germany* (San Francisco: Chandler, 1967).

require direct contributions from the insured. After receiving assurances on this score from the Christian Democrats, the business elite gave large sums to the CDU/CSU electoral campaign and, after the landslide victory of Adenauer's party, pressed for a speedy return on its political investment.

Policy Response and Conflict in the Executive Arena (1957–1960). In October 1957, Chancellor Adenauer honored his party's policy commitments to the business community. In a policy statement to the newly elected Federal Diet, he announced that his government intended to introduce legislation that would make patients shoulder a portion of their medical costs. This requirement provoked at once strong public counterpressure from interest groups opposed to such cost-sharing, a strategy that interfered with the usual procedures for discreet negotiations between appropriate government departments and nongovernmental peak associations. The Federal Chamber of Physicians (BAK) objected in the name of the entire medical profession; it took the position that the proposed measure would lead insured persons to consult their doctors less frequently and held that this would be good neither for public health nor for the economic well-being of the doctors. The Federation German Trade Unions also opposed the measure, declaring that it was a scheme designed to benefit big business and the medical profession, and that it would deprive low-income workers of adequate medical care. The opposition Social Democrats endorsed this view, whereas members of the labor-wing of the Christian Democrats voiced more cautious reservations—at least in public.

During the following year, the Adenauer government did not let these objections deter it from its chosen course. Under the organization of jurisdictional authority in the executive branch, the task of translating the general policy aim of the political leadership into a specific government bill fell to the Ministry of Labor. Its officials had closer connections to the trade unions than those of other concerned departments—notably, the ministries of health, economics, and finance—and they were more sympathetic to the wishes of organized labor. Labor representatives sat on a special advisory committee of the Labor Ministry that had a major hand in working out a first draft. But whatever influence labor may have exerted was evidently undercut by countervailing pressure from the business elite during subsequent interdepartmental negotiations; in October 1958, a special cabinet committee presented the public with a list of "basic principles," which called for cost-sharing as a means to stem the growth of a welfare state mentality in the country. The Federation of German Employers' Associations expressed its wholehearted approval, whereas the German Trade Union Federation reiterated its adamant opposition. The medical profession was deeply divided on the issue; the Association of German Physicians endorsed cost-sharing, whereas the Federal Chamber of Physicians and the Federal Association of Medical Insurance Physicians rejected it.

The Federal Government was apparently taken aback by the strength and vehemence of the opposition to its plan. Although it published the text of a cost-sharing bill in December 1958, the cabinet did not formally approve it for another year. In the interval the Ministry of Labor engaged in lengthy negotiations with the critics of the government proposal, but these failed since the ministry was neither willing nor able to scrap previous agreements with other departments and pressure groups. The government reportedly considered dropping its plan altogether before the conflict spilled over into the legislative arena, but decided to go ahead when the Social Democratic opposition challenged it to take that risk.

Sustained Conflict (1959–1961). Ordinarily, the government's proposal would have been approved by the Federal parliament without much difficulty since the Christian Democrats controlled both houses. As it was, the prospects for passage became increasingly remote as the policy conflict moved into the legislative arena. In November 1959, the Federal cabinet sent the bill to the Federal Council for preliminary consideration; cost-sharing was rejected by a committee of that chamber, but was rescued by its supporters in plenary session. The Federal cabinet thereupon reaffirmed its endorsement of the bill in February 1960, and dispatched it to the Federal Diet.

In the meantime, the opponents had launched a concerted pressure group campaign that was designed to block the bill in the Diet. The trade union elite staged mass rallies and obtained commitments from Christian Democratic deputies that they would not support cost-sharing. The leaders of the medical organizations opposed to the concept mounted a simultaneous lobbying drive that reached a quite unprecedented scope for these professional groups; as a result, medical leaders who endorsed the proposal considered it necessary to meet with the chancellor and emphasize their support.

The first reading of a bill in the Diet is normally a routine affair. However, in this instance, the opposition SPD used the opportunity to stress the government's failure to adequately consider the objections of the trade unions and medical associations; furthermore, CDU deputies went out of their way to voice their reservations. Next, the bill went to the Diet Committee on Social Policy whose members, regardless of party, had particularly close associations with the trade unions. In the course of the committee's deliberations, spokesmen for some twenty-eight interest groups opposed to or in favor of cost-sharing argued their case; representatives of the Federal Government sought to steer the bill past the committee stage before it could be caught up in the 1961 election campaign for a new Diet. However, in the light of this forthcoming event, deputies from all parties were increasingly sensitive to mounting pressure group opposition on the outside. The leadership of the Federal Association of Insurance Physicians warned that their members would go on strike if the Diet should pass an unsatisfactory law and the DGB elite mobilized its mass membership against the government bill.

Conflict Resolution (1961). Although the Diet Committee on Social Policy decided to report out a cost-sharing bill for a second reading vote by the entire house, the government proposal was clearly in trouble by late 1960. Opinion polls suggested overwhelming public disapproval, and when spokesmen for the medical opposition sought out Chancellor Adenauer in December 1961, he was ready to stage a strategic retreat. Adenauer acknowledged that the critics had not been properly consulted and placed the blame on government bureaucrats and deputies of his own party; these, in turn, felt that the chancellor had let them down after they had worked hard to realize his announced objective. The chancellor then tried to negotiate a compromise, but in the end was persuaded by other leaders of his party that the best political course was to let the bill die in committee. In early February 1961, the Social Policy Committee of the Diet voted to give it no further consideration.

Emergency Powers

The Policy Problem. For close to a decade after its establishment, the independence of the Federal Republic was limited in a potentially crucial respect.[11] The United States, Britain, and France retained the legal right to declare a state of domestic emergency and to intervene with their military forces in the event "a serious disturbance of public security and order" should threaten the maintenance of a democratic regime or the safety of their troops in West Germany. They were pledged to renounce their prerogatives as soon as appropriate national legislation furnished West German authorities with equivalent emergency powers. In order to provide such legislation the Basic Law had to be amended as it did not provide for such comprehensive powers. And such an amendment required a two-thirds majority vote in both houses of the Federal parliament.

Initial Actions (1958–1961). The first efforts to effect the necessary constitutional changes came to grief in the legislative arena of the Diet because of irreconcilable differences between the gov-

11. Case study based on Gerard Braunthal, "Emergency Legislation in the Federal Republic of Germany" in Henry S. Commager et al., *Festschrift für Karl Loewenstein* (Tubingen: Mohr, 1971). See also R.J.C. Pierce, "Federal German Emergency Powers Legislation," *Parliamentary Affairs* (1969),12: 216–225; Carl C. Schwertzer, "Emergency Powers in the Federal Republic of Germany," *Western Political Quarterly* (1969), 12:112–121.

erning and opposition parties. Both sides agreed in principle that West German authorities should assume the emergency powers of the three Western allies, but they sharply disagreed on the content of appropriate measures. The conservative ruling coalition of Christian and Free Democrats led by Chancellor Adenauer maintained that the executive had to be able to act swiftly and decisively in times of crisis to protect the fragile constitutional order. However, the Federal Government needed the votes of the opposition Social Democrats and these were not prepared to go along unless several stringent conditions were met. Above all, they insisted that basic civil liberties had to be safeguarded and executive powers carefully circumscribed if emergency powers were to be employed to maintain and not subvert West German democracy. Social Democratic party and labor elites and their supporters pointed out that constitutional emergency powers had been employed by executive officials to undermine and ultimately destroy the democratic Weimar Republic. The leadership of the German Federation of Trade Unions particularly opposed any measure that would allow the Federal Government to curb the rights of organized labor—especially the right to stage a general strike.

The Adenauer government's drive for crisis powers got off to a bad start in 1958, when Interior Minister Gerhard Schröder declared that an emergency would be "the hour of the executive." His statement provoked a storm of controversy as members of the attentive political public took it to mean that parliament would be allowed only a minor role under the pending government proposal. Over the following year the staff of the Interior Ministry drafted a constitutional amendment under Schröder's supervision, which was revised in numerous consultations with officials of other federal ministries and CDU/CSU-controlled state governments. Social Democratic party and labor leaders, however, were not drawn into these secret intragovernmental deliberations and did not learn about the contents of the government proposal until it was approved by the Federal cabinet in 1960. They immediately announced that they could not support the text as it stood, because it made no distinction between internal and external emergencies and lacked adequate guarantees against a misuse of the Federal Armed Forces to quell domestic disturbances.

The government nevertheless sent its version to the Federal Council for preliminary consideration. There it encountered a host of objections from Social Democratic state governments. The cabinet chose to ignore them when the measure came back and dispatched it to the Federal Diet, where the proposed constitutional amendment died in committee at the end of the legislative period. With a federal election in the offing, both the governing and the opposition parties were unwilling to seek a compromise solution, and that finished the first try.

Elite Negotiations, Public Controversy, and Conflict Prolongation (1961– 1965). The 1961 election kept the conservative coalition in power and parliamentary party alignments essentially unchanged. However, with the election out of the way, political observers expected that a compromise would now be possible. Chancellor Adenauer named a new interior minister, Hermann Höcherl, who appeared more conciliatory than his predecessor and more willing to consult with the SPD and labor leaders and to accommodate their demands. After lengthy interelite neotiations, Höcherl obtained cabinet approval for a constitutional amendment that met many, but by no means all, of the objections to the ill-fated earlier version. In November 1962, the new government text was dispatched to the Federal Council, which recommended a number of changes. The cabinet accepted only half of these and then sent the proposal to the Federal Diet. There it remained in committee for more than two years while governing and opposition party leaders continued to bargain for a compromise solution.

By the time the legislative period drew to a close in mid-1965, the Federal Government evidently believed that no further interparty differences stood in the way of parliamentary approval before the impending Diet election. But then the SPD leadership suddenly announced that it could not give its consent to the constitutional amendment after all because it still considered some emergency provisions entirely unacceptable. In fact the SPD leaders had yielded to heavy pressure from the DGB elite which told them to withhold their assent if they wanted the electoral support of organized labor. Such pressure was all the more telling since a coalition of trade unionists, prestigious academicians, and Protestant theologians, assorted pacifists, and radical leftists had launched an unusual, fervent civic action drive against emergency powers among the political public. Ordinarily, such a campaign to block legislative action would not have been successful, but this time it coincided with the sentiments of many back-bench SPD deputies. Under these circumstances, the second government proposal could not obtain the necessary two-thirds majority in the Diet.

Elite Realignment and Conflict Resolution (1966–1968). The 1965 election showed a continuing gain in votes for the SPD, but the CDU/CSU was still the strongest party. Party leaders on both sides were now ready to work out an effective compromise in collaboration with the trade union elite. At a DGB congress, top Christian Democratic and Social Democratic leaders jointly called for an end to organized labor's opposition. A breakthrough in the long dispute came with the formation of a coalition government between the two major parties in late 1966. The members of the new cabinet quickly agreed on a new text drafted by Minister of Interior Paul Lücke and his staff. It provided that basic civil liberties, including the right to strike, would not be touched in any emergency. The compromise proposal was rapidly approved by the cabinet and the Federal Council and introduced in the Federal Diet by June 1966.

Nominally, the governing parties now had between them more than enough votes to amend the Basic Law. However, all was not yet smooth sailing. While the Diet's committees deliberated at length on the new version submitted by the executive branch, about a third of the SPD deputies joined in a dissident group that declared itself far from satisfied with the revised text. Most of the SPD leaders, however, were not willing to let demands for further major changes endanger the fragile government alliance with the CDU/CSU. As it was, the Christian Democratic leadership had trouble enough keeping conservatives in line who held that the party had already made far too many concessions to its Social Democratic partners on this and other issues. Tactical political considerations also induced the DGB elite to withdraw from the extraparliamentary opposition and accept the compromise aggreement as the best it could get under the circumstances.

As a last resort, the diehard opponents of any emergency powers mounted a massive, unprecedented campaign in 1967, to block parliamentary passage. Particularly for radical student leaders, the fight had become a battle against the entire "establishment." In order to ease this extraparliamentary pressure, Federal Diet committees invited several university professors to testify for and against the constitutional amendment in a series of exceptional public hearings. But the die had already been cast. In May 1968, emergency legislation was passed over the opposition of fifty-three deputies—one-tenth of the Diet's membership—and then approved by a unanimous vote of the state governments in the Federal Council.

The Basic Treaty with East Germany

The Policy Problem. When the SPD-FDP coalition government of Chancellor Willy Brandt came to power in 1969, better relations between East and West Germany was one of its declared policy objectives. This constituted a major departure from the previous policy of successive CDU/CSU-led governments, which had adamantly refused to accept the legality of another successor state to the former German Reich. But although German reunification "in peace and freedom" had remained official policy, quasi-official "intra-German" relations with the German Democratic Republic had grown in recent years. The Brandt government wanted to anchor these relations in firmer legal commitments by both sides as a part of its more general policy for improved relations with the European Communist countries. Accordingly, it undertook to negotiate a series of agreements with the GDR that culminated in the "Treaty on the Basis of Relations Between the Two German States" of 1972. To take effect, the so-called Basic Treaty had,

however, first to be ratified by the Federal Diet, and this involved
the Brandt Government in a major political and constitutional
policy dispute.

The Battle in the Legislative Arena (1973). Even before the Federal
Government formally submitted the Basic Treaty for parliamentary approval in spring 1973, the battle lines had taken shape. On
one side were the governing coalition parties, the SPD and FDP,
and on the other the opposition CDU/CSU, which controlled a
majority of the votes in the Federal Council. With only a few
exceptions, the Christian Democrats—and especially the Bavarian
Christian Social Union—were against the entire "eastern policy"
of the Social-Liberal Coalition. A year earlier their opposition to
treaties with Poland and the USSR had almost led to the overthrow
of the Brandt government in an evenly divided Diet; it had taken
an unprecedented special federal election to sustain the government's claim to popular support on the issue and provide it with
a firm parliamentary majority in the lower house.

In February 1973, the Federal cabinet submitted the treaty to
the Federal Council for the usual preliminary consideration by
that body. It was immediately rejected there on the vote of the
CDU/CSU-controlled state governments, but this did not mean
that the treaty could not be ratified. As the issue did not involve
the constitutional authority of the states, the council would not be
able to exercise an absolute veto, and the government had the
votes in the Federal Diet to override a suspensive veto with a simple
majority. Therefore, when the treaty came back to the Federal
cabinet, that body felt free to disregard the objections of the CDU/
CSU majority in the Council and quickly sent the measure to the
Diet for its first reading.

At this point in the proceedings, the question of the constitutionality of the treaty came to the fore and split the ranks of the
opposition Christian Democrats. A minority—consisting mostly
of deputies of the Bavarian Christian Social Union—maintained
that the agreement with East Germany violated the Basic Law,
which called on "the entire German people" to strive for the reunification of the two Germanies. Their demand that the CDU/CSU

parliamentary delegations should jointly exercise their legal right to place the matter before the Federal Constitutional Court was rejected by the CDU leaders. Unlike their Bavarian CSU colleagues, most of them held that such a move promised little success and would only enhance the legitimacy of the treaty if the court should endorse it.

After that episode, the legislative battle featured a good deal of heated rhetoric on the floor of the Diet, but Christian Democratic arguments against the agreement with the GDR failed to sway the general public; opinion polls indicated that it was supported by most of the voters. In committee stage, the treaty was processed as a piece of domestic legislation and considered by the Committee on Intra-German Affairs rather than the Foreign Affairs Committee. It was ratified by the Diet in May 1973, and then went to the Federal Council. The matter of a suspensive veto by that chamber was laid to rest when the Basic Treaty was passed with the votes of the states governed by Social and Free Democrats over the sole opposition of the Bavarian CSU government; the rest of the Christian Democrats preferred to abstain rather than renew the battle. On June 6, 1973, the treaty was signed by the Federal president some seven months after it had been initialed by the East and West German negotiators.

Judicial Review (1974). The Bavarian CSU undertook a last-ditch battle in the judicial arena by exercising the right of a state government to challenge Federal legislation in the Federal Constitutional Court. Before the treaty had been approved by the Federal Council, the court had refused to grant the Bavarian government an interim injunction that would have halted legislative process pending a judicial decision. However, it agreed to consider the constitutionality of the treaty after it became domestic law. The case went before one of the court's two chambers, where the Bavarian government held that the treaty conflicted with the Basic Law and the Federal Government argued that it did not. In late spring 1974, the judges rendered a unanimous verdict which sustained the latter position, but with a great caveat that held potentially important implications for future West German domestic and foreign policies touching on intra-German relations. The court cautioned executive and legislative public officials that they were at all times constitutionally obligated to do all they could to promote German reunification and to do nothing that would hinder it.

Legalizing Abortion

The Policy Problem. When the Social-Liberal government of Chancellor Willy Brandt came to power in 1969, a new abortion law stood high on its announced policy agenda for major social reforms. Under existing regulations, abortions were permitted only in cases of dire medical emergencies, and heavy penalties were provided for all persons involved in illegal abortions. Illicit operations were, nonetheless, frequent. By current estimates, every year some 200,000 women had abortions; women who had the necessary money went to countries where abortions were legal, and women who did not obtained them where they could—which often meant with medically unqualified abortionists. Opinion polls indicated that more West Germans favored than opposed a reform law. Prominent professional women became particularly active in a drive for the abolition or at least the drastic modification of prevailing restrictions. On the other hand, the Roman Catholic Church, its lay organizations, and leaders of the preponderantly Catholic Christian Democrats, demanded that the Brandt Government leave well enough alone.

The Search for a Compromise in the Executive Arena (1971–1972). The Brandt government was in quite a quandary on the issue. Although its members were on the whole in favor of abortion reform, they were by no means in agreement on the precise form it should take. Moreover, the SPD chancellor and ministers—one of them a prominent Catholic lay leader—were not at all keen for a conflict with the Catholic hierarchy, as they had only recently managed to soften its longstanding hostility toward their party. Then, too, any legislative reform proposal by the government had to allow for the fact that the Christian Democrats commanded close to a majority in the Diet and controlled the Federal Council. Furthermore, it had to take into account legal considerations dictated by the Basic Law.

The difficult task of drawing up appropriate legislation came under the jurisdiction of SPD Minister of Justice Gerhard Jahn, who favored a measure that would permit abortions only under special conditions. His proposed limitations were more liberal than those on the books, but they were still too narrow for other members of the government. Consequent disputes among the ruling party leaders transcended bureaucratic and partisan differences and involved personal convictions and religious ties. The Free Democrats were pretty well united in favor of minimal restrictions on abortions during the first three months of pregnancy. However, the Social Democrats in the government, parliament, and SPD organization were divided on the question. As a result, officials in the Justice ministry were working on the eleventh draft for a government bill when the special election of 1972 brought proceedings to a halt.

The search for a compromise in the executive arena became all the more difficult as the public conflict became more embittered before and, especially, during the 1972 election campaign. The proponents of an end to all restrictions on abortion waged a publicity campaign that was as much directed against the restrictive measure advocated by the minister of justice as against the old regulation. The adamant opponents of any reform—spearheaded by Catholic clerical and lay leaders—were no less active. For example, they gave wide publicity to an article by an official of the Vatican which likened a liberalized abortion law to Nazi euthanasia measures for the destruction of "useless lives." And one of the West German cardinals declared that a candidate for the Federal Diet who did not explicitly reject abortion reform did not deserve the support of devout Roman Catholic voters.

Actions in the Legislative Arena (1973–1974). The 1972 election gave the Social-Liberal Coalition a solid majority in the Federal Diet, while the CDU/CSU remained in control of the Federal Council. Abortion reform was put back on the policy agenda in the spring of 1973, although not by action of the Federal Government. Its failure to come up with a bill led deputies in the Diet to seize the initiative—a highly unusual step. Four alternative proposals were introduced from the floor of the lower house. One, sponsored by members of the SPD and FDP, provided for abortions during the first three months of pregnancy by agreement between patient and doctor; a second, sponsored by a smaller group of SPD and FDP deputies—including the minister of justice—was less liberal; a third proposal, introduced by a majority of the Christian Democratic opposition, was even more restrictive; and a fourth, sponsored by a group of particularly conservative CDU/CSU deputies, called for virtually no substantial changes in the existing rules.

The four bills went to the Diet's Select Committee for Reform of the Criminal Code. None of them obtained the support of a majority of its members after almost a year of public hearings and closed deliberations; all of them were reported back to the entire Diet for a second and third reading vote as a compromise in committee proved impossible. In April 1973, the most permissive proposal, providing for abortions during the first three months of pregnancy, passed by a close vote that evidently cut across party lines. Two weeks later the CDU/CSU majority of state governments in the Federal Council turned the bill down and called for a meeting of the inter-house Conference Committee to work out a compromise. That body was not convened because the Brandt government held that in this instance the consent of the Council was not required and believed that there were by now sufficient votes in the Diet to override a suspensive veto. And, indeed, the lower house passed the reform bill with the necessary majority in June 1973, and it was signed into law by the federal president. That, however, was not to be the end of the matter.

Judical Review (1974–1975). While the reform bill was still in committee, the conference of German Catholic Bishops had called for an appeal to the Federal Constitutional Court if the bill should pass. When it did, the CDU government of Baden-Württemberg got the court to issue an injunction that prevented the new law from taking effect until a constitutional complaint by the state government could be adjudicated. In late February 1975, the Constitutional Court rendered its authoritative verdict: A majority of the justices declared the law unconstitutional on the grounds that it violated the spirit of provisions in the Basic Law which guaranteed the sanctity of life. The Court held that more permissive abortion laws in other countries could not serve as a guide for West Germany in view of its Nazi legacy.

Mass opinion polls indicated that most West Germans disapproved of the court's decision and only about a third endorsed it. But that did not alter the fact that the reform law was dead and that the old regulation remained in force until a new one meeting the court's constitutional criteria was passed. These criteria were spelled out for the lawmakers in policy guidelines which the justices appended to their decision, and which subsequently were closely observed by the Federal Government in obtaining the passage of another, more restrictive, abortion reform bill.

9

Policy Consequences

The dynamic interrelationship between the sources and consequences of public policy has been a constant theme in our study of West German politics. Participating actors, as we have seen, do not just respond to environmental conditions; they also try to shape them, as best they can, in accordance with their personal preferences. The analysis of policy effect patterns can thus provide us with a reading of the long-range distribution of political power in terms of the lasting indentation it leaves on the topographical map of domestic and foreign affairs.

This is easier said than done when we deal with as complex a society as that of West Germany. It is usually hard to discern the full extent of policy consequences, and all the more so when they involve gradual, cumulative, and subtle developments in political relationships, social standards, and life-styles.

In theory, public policies in the Federal Republic can have practically infinite ramifications. We may thus attribute socioeconomic and cultural changes to particular policy measures, but it is usually very difficult, if not impossible, to establish a clear cause-and-effect linkage. Frequently there is simply not enough evidence to warrant such conclusions, or the evidence can all too easily lead to distorted or spurious conclusions.

A further problem is that policy fallout may have intangible effects. Take, for example, such elusive factors as "the investment mood" of the West German business community or the good will of public opinion abroad—particularly in the United States. Both may influence demands on and support for the policymakers, but their effects are not readily analyzed.

We shall therefore confine ourselves in the following sections to a narrower range of direct and manifest policy consequences. And if socioeconomic matters seem particularly important it is because they have been—and are likely to remain—in the forefront of domestic and international political issues.

PUBLIC FINANCE

The authority of elected officials to raise and spend money is a key policy instrument at every level of government in the Federal Republic. The allocation of the costs and benefits of public expenditures affects citizens and noncitizens, elites as well as nonelites, and it enters into most disputes among parties and pressure groups. Budgetary issues, therefore, attract a particularly high degree of public attention and obtain exceptionally prominent exposure through the mass media.

Taxation

Who pays what in general taxes is as much a perennial issue in West German as in American politics. There, too, taxpayers resent apparent inequities in the distribution of the burdens and complain that they have to pay too much for what they receive in public goods and services. And political leaders are no less sensitive to such sentiments, especially around election time. If they are out of office, they will do their best to exploit those sentiments to get in. Governing policymakers, on the other hand, are cautious about introducing tax measures that are likely to prove widely unpopular. Apart from these tactical, short-run factors, tax policies have been fairly constant since the establishment of the Federal Republic and have not been substantially affected by changes in ruling decision makers.

Here we should note that national tax policies have everywhere at least two, and sometimes three, objectives. One is to provide public authorities with funds to meet their current expenses, including debt payments on money borrowed for limited periods at fixed rates. A second is to influence economic developments and, more particularly, to shape the patterns of domestic production, savings, and consumption. In addition, tax policies may be deliberately designed to structure the distribution of wealth and income in a country. But even if not, they will invariably affect it.

Now let us see how these factors work out in West Germany. To begin with, we need to remember that the policymakers are not faced with the revenue problems of a country with a subsistence economy; they can tap a per capita income that is one of the highest among leading world powers. And we must also remember that overall economic policies in the Federal Republic have from the beginning set a course for sustained productive growth through a capitalist market economy operating under a pluralist democratic system.

For these reasons, we do best to compare West German tax policies with those in similarly constituted major industrial countries. To begin with, governmental tax revenues absorb about a third of the gross domestic product (GDP), which is more than in the United States and Japan but less than in Britain and France.[1] When we look at the sources of such revenues we find that in West Germany taxes on personal incomes provide a smaller share than in the United States, but a larger one than in Britain, France, and Japan. Indirect taxes on goods and services, on the other hand, form a much larger proportion of tax revenues than in the United States and Japan and about the same as in Britain and France. But note that though corporate profits make up a major portion of the West German national income, they constitute an exceptionally small percentages of tax revenues.

1. Gross domestic product (GDP) figures provide a rough monetary measure of the total output in goods and services. In 1982 the proportion of the GDP going into tax revenues was 37.0% for West Germany, 26.9% for Japan, 31.2% for the U.S., 40.0% for the U.K., 43.7% for France, and 50.3% for Sweden. See *The Economist*, December 3, 1983, p. 69.

These patterns are largely the outgrowth of a basic precept of West German economic policies. We might call it the fallout principle. It is based on the notion that everybody benefits from a high rate of private investment at home and abroad; that is, the higher the profits of West German business, the more they will boost national income and general affluence. Accordingly, if corporations and individuals earn more, they will also pay more income taxes and consume more taxed products and services. And public authorities, in turn, will have more money for general welfare expenditures.

Income tax regulations are consequently designed to encourage productive investments. As in the United States, capital gains from business ventures are taxed at a much lower rate than other incomes, and income splitting among family members provides further tax advantages on gains from investments. Moreover, in the Federal Republic taxes on corporate profits are paid either by the business enterprise or by the stockholders, but not by both as in the United States.

These provisions tend to favor the wealthy more than lower income groups. But the latter are also offered considerable tax inducements to put what money they can spare into direct or indirect investments. A series of laws passed between 1964 and 1971, for example, set forth increasingly favorable tax breaks for capital accumulation through savings deposits in banks, building and trust funds, and similar private investment institutions. Other legislation has given income tax advantages to employees participating in the profit-sharing arrangements that exist in quite a few West German business establishments, and to small investors who own so-called people's shares in such enterprises as the vast Volkswagen corporation. Of course, more extensive participation in investments involves not only a broader scattering of business profits, but a larger dispersion of losses and risks.

As we noted in chapter 3, West German income tax policies have neither sought nor produced a significant redistribution of wealth from the most to the least affluent. The decision makers have rather accented what they consider a fair allocation of income tax burdens. A good many West Germans are exempted from paying any income tax because they earn too little; in the mid-1980s roughly a fourth of all wage and salary employees paid no income tax. Higher incomes are subject to a graduated tax under which those who earn more are supposed to pay more.

Economic as well as political considerations have led West German lawmakers to rely more heavily on indirect consumption taxes than on direct income taxes when it comes to raising general revenues. Such taxes serve as policy instruments for influencing demand patterns in a supposedly free market economy. In the 1970s, for example, the Social-Liberal government of Chancellor Schmidt raised some consumer taxes steeply in order to put a lid on rising prices, while keeping other taxes low to stimulate production, increase employment, and promote foreign trade.

Indirect taxes also tend to be politically less sensitive than income taxes. West German taxpayers resent increases that reduce their disposable income at least as much as taxpayers in the United States do. And since top- and middle-income groups are key elements in the West German electorate and are particularly well represented in parties and pressure groups, their sentiments carry a good deal of weight with the decision makers. Indirect taxes, because they are less visible, can be increased more easily without significant political repercussions.

What distinguishes indirect taxes from income levies is, first of all, that they are not graduated on the basis of earnings, but are pegged to the prices of covered goods and services. Accordingly, when prices go up—as they have been doing in West Germany— indirect taxes will go up too. And if the tax rate is increased as well, they will rise even more. Second, indirect taxes on producers are usually passed onto the final purchaser and, therefore, bear most heavily on ordinary consumers. Third, they are more easily administered than income taxes. Most of them are automatically added to the sales price and do not require specific tax assessments, like income levies.

Indirect taxes affect a vast range of goods and services in the Federal Republic. They include levies on beverages and tobacco, sales taxes on clothing and household items, and property taxes included in the rents for offices, stores, and apartments. The most widespread and lucrative is the value added tax (VAT), which West Germany shares with other members of the European Community. It is called a turnover tax. That is, a new levy is added at every stage that increases the cost of goods and services on their way to the final consumer. A person who buys a car, for example, will thus foot the bill for the manufacturing taxes paid in the course of its production from imported iron to last component.

Apart from economic conditions, West German officials can be pretty certain that their tax measures will produce desired revenues. On the whole, the system contains fewer loopholes than the American and French and, therefore, fewer opportunities for tax dodges. Of course, it helps to have a good tax adviser, and that takes money. But outright tax evasion has been fairly rare. Appropriate regulations are tightly enforced by a large bureaucracy, and infractions carry stiff penalties.

Spending

Government spending, like taxation, reflects as well as affects the policy environment for West German politics. How much money is appropriated by the decision makers and for what purposes thus depends on prevailing socioeconomic and political circumstances. As instruments of public policy, however, budgetary expenditures are also designed to influence these conditions. On both counts, the authoritative allocation of public funds poses constant policy problems and can involve major distributive conflicts.

In the Federal Republic, as in the United States, public expenditures are only partly covered by tax income. Consequent deficits have to be covered by interest-bearing loans. And in West Germany, as in the United States, increasing government indebtedness is a major political issue. Especially local authorites, with only a small tax base of their own, have had to borrow more money to meet greater expenditures (see table 9.1). Many of the larger municipalities are consequently heavily in debt to banks and such other lending agencies as trust and pension funds. In West Germany, in contrast to the United States, the repayment of such obligations is normally guaranteed by the state or federal government; but

TABLE 9.1

*Distribution of Public Expenditures and Tax Income
by Level of Government, 1982*

	LEVEL OF GOVERNMENT		
	FEDERAL	STATE	LOCAL
Share of total government expenditures (622.2 bill. DM)	40%	36%	24%
Share of total government tax income (366.0 bill. DM)	50	36	14
Proportion of expenditures covered by own tax income	75	58	33

Source: Calculated from data in *Statistisches Jahrbuch für Bundesrepublik Deutschland, 1983*, pp. 416, 418.
Note: Tax payments to the European Community have been excluded.

these higher authorities also wield greater financial control over local governments than in the American federal system.

Although West German authorities have the power to tax people, they cannot compel them to supply free goods and services to the state. Even soldiers drafted into the armed forces must be paid something. Spending patterns are thus conditioned by (a) the budgetary priorities of the official decision makers, (b) the purchase price of the items they need or want, and (c) the amount of money that can be raised to pay for these items. Current price levels determine the cost of such things as military hardware, the construction and upkeep of public buildings, and supplies and equipment for government offices. Public officials, employees, and government advisers need to be adequately compensated for their services—at levels more or less commensurate with payments for equivalent work in the private sector. And if tax revenues are insufficient to meet such expenditures, money must be borrowed and repaid with interest on terms that compete favorably with those offered in the domestic and international bond market.

Keeping these factors in mind, let us now look at the patterns of budgetary allocations in the Federal Republic over time. As shown in tables 9.2 and 9.3, government expenditures in general and those of the Federal Government in particular grew enormously from the establishment of the Federal Republic onward.

TABLE 9.2

Changes in Federal, State, and Local Government
Expenditures, 1950–1981

	1950	1961	1972	1981
Total budgetary appropria-tions (in bill. DM)	28.1	95.3	251.3	770.6
Allocations				
General government services	17.7%	23.8%	25.2%	18.8%
Police and judiciary	4.0	3.9	4.1	3.0
Military	16.7	13.8	9.9	5.7
Transport and communications	4.5	7.2	8.3	4.0
Health and social welfare	30.6	27.2	25.9	53.03
Education, research and culture	7.4	9.5	15.8	11.99
Subsidies to economic enterprises	19.1	14.5	10.8	3.5
Total	100.0	100.0	100.0	100.0

Source: Calculated from data in the *Statistisches Jahrbuch für die Bundesrepublik Deutschland, 1975,* p. 398; *1983,* p. 412.

Where did the money go? Table 9.2 indicates that for the first ten years or so the incrase in expenditures was largely due to the rise in administrative services at all levels of government of the new West German state. But it was mostly a period of growth for the public administration in the constituent *Länder,* which was then primarily responsible for implementing government policies for socioeconomic recovery and political reconstruction. The Federal administration grew more in the following period of expanding domestic and foreign policy commitments, and this accounts largely for the great increase in the allocations for general services in the Federal budget at that time (see table 9.3).

Another major budget item, military expenditures, went at first almost entirely into substantial payments for allied forces stationed in the unarmed Federal Republic. This was the price West German policymakers had agreed to pay for the defense of their country and of West Berlin by other countries when the military government of foreign powers was replaced by a new German

TABLE 9.3

Changes in Federal Government Expenditures, 1950–1980

	1950	1961	1975	1980
Total budgetary appropria- tions (in bill. DM)	11.6	39.7	155.3	217.8
Allocations				
General government services	9.9%	14.9%	24.4%	29.8%
Police and judiciary	0.1	0.7	0.7	0.7
Military	36.7	32.6	20.5	18.7
Transport and communications	3.3	4.2	7.2	6.3
Health and social welfare	38.4	32.0	35.6	35.1
Education, research, and culture	0.4	4.2	5.5	5.4
Subsidies to economic enterprises	11.2	9.8	5.1	4.0
Total	100.0	100.0	100.0	100.0

Source: Calculated from data in *Statistisches Jahrbuch für die Bundesrepublik Deutschland, 1955*, p. 398; *1963*, p. 430; *1975*, p. 399; *1983*, p. 422; and *Finanzbericht, 1981*, pp. 160–161.

government in 1949. Since then military expenditures—including continued payments to allied NATO powers—have declined in relation to the total budget but have, in fact, increased. West Germany by now has a large military establishment of its own, as we shall see, and its policymakers have consistently treated substantial defense appropriations as essential items in the Federal budgets. The much smaller share allocated for direct subsidies to economic enterprises has also diminished with the expansion of the Federal budget. But figures on that score can be misleading since they do not cover indirect subsidies, such as tax advantages for industry and assistance payments to agriculture from funds funneled through the European Community.

The budgetary consequences of a major policy change in the late 1960s and early 1970s show up in the substantial proportionate increases for education, research, and other cultural activities. In this period the Federal Government and especially the state governments put large sums into the expansion of higher education. A similar priority is evident in the increased allocations for transport and communications. Health and social welfare expenditures were especially high in the early years of social dislocation after World War II and then declined somewhat. The subsequent increase of the proportion of expenditures in this category resulted from the expansion of national welfare programs in the late 1960s and early 1970s.

Such trends within a country over time are in some ways more reliable and informative than cross-country comparisons because they are based on identical or, at least, similar units of analysis. When we compare national budgetary expenditures in West Germany and the United States with those in France, Britain, and Japan, we need to remember that in the latter countries the central government foots almost all of the bill for public goods and services whereas in the former it does not.

In table 9.4 we find that general government services accounted in the early 1980s for a larger proportion of the national budget than in any of the other major Western democracies. The percentage for military expenditures was second only to that in the United States. Health and social welfare took up a smaller share than in the United States and Britain, but a larger one than in France and Japan. On the other hand, in both of these countries

TABLE 9.4

National Government Expenditures in Major Industrial Countries, 1981–1983 (in rounded percentages)

	G.F.R.	U.S.	U.K.	FRANCE	JAPAN
General government services	21.7	5.3	17.0	20.3	19.8
Military	19.1	25.8	18.0	16.1	6.7
Health and social welfare	34.4	44.7	37.6	21.6	30.3
Education and culture	5.5	4.8	2.8	23.1	12.6
Transport and communications	5.0	2.9	2.7	4.5	6.2
Subsidies to economic enterprises	3.2	2.8	6.2	8.0	7.7
Debt payments	11.1	13.7	15.7	6.4	16.7
Total	100.0	100.0	100.0	100.0	100.0

Source: *Statistisches Jahrbuch für die Bundesrepublik Deutschland, 1983,* p. 702.

the national government put more into education and culture than in the more decentralized federal systems of the United States and West Germany. Such figures reflect structural differences between countries, but they also indicate variations in the policy priorities of their leaders.

SOCIAL WELFARE

In the Federal Republic, as in other Western democracies, social welfare policies deal primarily with public arrangements for ensuring an adequate standard of living for all members of society. Appropriate income maintenance and health care programs have been extensive and, until lately, relatively uncontroversial in West Germany. There was widespread agreement that such programs were needed and that there were sufficient resources to pay for them. Since about the mid-1970s, however, the increasing load of benefit programs in difficult times for the West German economy has led to policy disputes that have pushed social welfare issues to the forefront in domestic politics.

The state's ultimate responsibility for the social welfare of its citizens has been a long-standing principle in Germany, sustained over various regimes. Now, as in the past, leading officials place the most importance on measures designed to prevent widespread social distress and divisive political repercussions. Appropriate corresponding social policies apply to both public and private institutions. The former are usually autonomous agencies of the state run by public officials. The latter are regulated by the state and usually supported by government subsidies; the social services provided by the major religious organizations are, for example, aided by tax exemptions and tax funds. Private as well as public social welfare expenditures are included in the so-called social budget of the Federal Government, an annual report on the allocation of all goods and services for the contemporary West German "welfare state." By this accounting the proportion of the gross domestic product (GDP) going into all kinds of social welfare benefits increased substantially during the 1970s and by the early

1980s took in about a third of a barely expanding economic output.

The apparent gap between the cost of social welfare programs and lagging revenues for supporting them has raised the question whether the country can still afford to honor benefit commitments made by social policymakers in more prosperous times. A politically feasible resolution of the deficit has, however, proven difficult. Higher taxes for social welfare benefits have been resisted by employers and employees who have to pay them. But cutting program expenditures substantially is no less unpopular as three-fourth or more is for social insurance payments to millions of West Germans.

The Federal Republic has one of the most comprehensive social security systems in the world. The roots reach back a century to the social insurance laws of Imperial Germany, which served as models for subsequent legislation in other countries. Government policies determine who is covered against what risks, who contributes and how much, and who is to receive what, when, and for how long.[2]

All of the components of the social security system are designed to be self-sustaining. That is, contributions to the various funds are supposed to exceed or, at least, match out payments and administrative expenses. Disbursements to those who are entitled to collect benefits are thus to be met through transfer payments from those who are obliged to pay social security taxes, rather than from general government revenues.

As in the United States and other countries, most social security contributions represent enforced savings through payroll deductions. In West Germany, practically all wage and salary earners are required by law to pay a sizable part of their earned income toward unemployment, health, maternity, work injury and disablement, and retirement and survivors insurance. In addition, both private and public employers must make a proportionate "fringe benefit"

2. Federal regulations to that effect are implemented by the Social Security Administration and other public agencies; disputes over claims are adjudicated by the Federal social courts.

contribution. Self-employed individuals, including farmers, pay the entire premium for their social insurance.

All told, working people may have to pay up to a fifth of their earned income for mandatory social insurance. The size of contributions is much higher than in the United States, but the range of benefits is also more extensive. In West Germany, too, incomes above a level set by law and so-called unearned personal incomes from sales, investments, rents, and savings are not subject to social security taxes. Consequently, the more an employed individual gets from such exempted sources, the smaller will be the bite which these taxes take out of total income and the less onerous are across-the-board increases in the rate of personal contributions. Moreover, since benefit payments are based on entitlement, the more an individual has previously earned under the social security system, the more he or she will receive on becoming eligible for disbursements. The same holds for the qualified dependents and survivors of the insured. In effect, these measures place a proportionately greater burden on the lower than the higher income groups and provide them with smaller financial pay-offs.

The mounting load of benefit payments has weighted most heavily on the health, old age, and unemployment insurance funds. The social policy problems arising from increasing demands for legally guaranteed medical insurance benefits are long-standing; we saw this in the dispute over the cost-sharing of medical bills discussed in chapter 8. But they have become more pressing in recent times with a sharp rise in the price of health care and the rate of unemployment. Perhaps even more troublesome for policymakers are the political issues posed by greater expenditures for old age security pensions and for unemployment benefits.

Public pensions and health care insurance for the elderly relieve their families, private charities, and the state of expenses for their material welfare. Here West German social security payments have rested on the principle that retired people should share in the economic gains of the working population. As a result, insurance benefits for the elderly are now more generous than ever before, but their costs are also greater and promise to mount with an aging population.

Practically all West German adults are covered by old age security insurance for themselves and their spouses. Under current legislation women may begin to draw their full pension when they are sixty, and men when they are sixty-five, but most of the elderly retire early with a partial lifetime pension. The average age of retirement was 59 in the early 1980s and only five out of every hundred persons over 64 were still employed,—about half as many as in the mid-1960s. Moreover, old age security payments have gone up substantially over the past two decades as a result of legislation that pegged these payments to rising wages. In short, the number of retired people as well as the size of their pensions has increased.

The Federal Republic has by now a dependent population of some 13 million pensioners who are supported by the mandatory insurance contributions of about twice that many working people. If current trends in retirement and employment hold, the number of pensioners will continue to rise whereas the number of contributors will decline. This means that West German policymakers will sooner or later be faced with a public pension crunch unless they can find ways to avoid it.

A solution that accords with demands for social harmony and popular concensus in West German politics may be hard to come by. The increasingly costly terms of the intergenerational contract for old age security bequeathed to young West Germans by elderly, retired, or deceased policymakers suggests to some observers an emerging new social conflict. On one side are said to be the beneficiaries of old age insurance—and that includes not only the elderly who already constitute about a fifth of the electorate, but all sorts of public and private agencies that have vested interests of their own in the maintenance of old age incomes and services. On the other side are said to be the young who will have to contribute to that insurance for many years before they can collect whatever share may then be due to them—if they live that long. Neither side, it seems, would readily accept cost-saving changes in the terms of the intergenerational contract that would in effect reduce promised benefits without commensurate reductions in obligatory contributions.

In view of the drain on the public pension funds it may seem odd that West German policymakers, unlike American ones, have actually encouraged working people to retire early. Their intent, at least in recent years, has been to open up jobs for the unemployed and thus reduce the outflow of mandatory payments from the unemployment insurance fund.

The present arrangements for unemployment compensation were fashioned in the golden years of full employment and sustained growth in national and personal incomes. There were usually more jobs available than people to fill them, unemployment was on the average less than one percent, and far more money flowed into the insurance fund than was taken out. Most benefit payments then went to West Germans who were temporarily shopping around for suitable new positions.

These conditions favored legislation that now provides the unemployed with more generous income-maintenance payments than in other major Western countries. All insured persons are entitled to collect up to two-thirds of their last previous earnings for almost a year—as long as they are willing to take commensurate jobs. Short-term joblessness is thus not likely to cause financial hardship for the insured and low rates of unemployment will not burden the insurance fund.

The system was, however, not designed for extended periods of mass unemployment, such as the present one. In the mid-1980s one out of ten persons who were willing and able to work had no job and one out of five of the officially registered unemployed had been out of work for more than a year. The prospect of continued and, possibly, even higher rates of long-term mass unemployment has led West German policymakers to mandate repeated increases in the required contributions to the insurance fund. The Federal Government is not only committed by law to make up shortages in the fund by dipping into general tax revenues; it also has to finance less generous, unemployment assistance for West Germans who have exhausted their benefits or have little or no insurance coverage to start with. The latter category has in particular included an exceptionally large number of young people who are just entering the labor market.

The recent efforts of the Schmidt and as well as the Kohl government to husband the resources of the unemployment insurance funds aroused the opposition of organized labor; according to the trade unions these moves took more out of the pay of the employed and, at the same time, denied adequate compensation to an increasing number of unemployed. The business community, on the other hand, supported measures to conserve the resources of the unemployment insurance fund; it did not want more general tax funds committed to unemployment compensation payments. By current indications long-term unemployment is likely to cause more and sharper policy disputes over financial assistance for the jobless.

Unemployment assistance and other forms of public assistance, unlike social insurance, are based on need rather than entitlement and come out of budgetary appropriations from general tax revenues. Policies on that score have not been as controversial in the Federal Republic as in the United States. That may be in part because they take in social benefits that are not considered welfare services by Americans. Social benefits that come under general public assistance in the social budget of the federal government consist largely of services and indirect aid to middle- as well as low-income groups. For example, public funds and tax benefits provided subsidies for public housing, health care services, labor exchanges, recreational facilities, and vocational training centers. They also supported private welfare agencies, hospitals, nursing homes, and rehabilitation centers. And both low- and middle-income groups received family allowances for dependent children in the form of tax rebates.

Relatively few people, though an increasing number in recent years, have been poor enough to qualify for so-called social assistance for the truly needy. It seems, moreover, that a good many West Germans who might be eligible have been too proud, or too poorly informed about the availability to seek such help. Under the federal social assistance law they must either have no other sources of income—such as savings and insurance benefits—or, as is more often the case, require supplementary aid to maintain a "decent" standard of living. For instance, chronically ill and physically handicapped people and destitute widows and orphans may receive cash payments, goods, and services on the basis of rather strict means tests.

Most better-off West Germans suscribe to the social policy principle that such public assistance should constitute neither charity nor a subsidy for freeloaders supported by the taxpayers. It is rather supposed to enable persons who are economically underprivileged and socially disadvantaged, through no fault of their own, to surmount their difficulties. Of course, West Germans have found it all the easier to endorse such notions as long as the cost has been fairly small and the relief payments have gone more to their fellow citizens than to impoverished foreigners in the Federal Republic.

Compared to the large outlays for social insurance benefits, the public expenditures for social assistance have remained quite small, though they have increased quite a bit in recent years. In 1983 they still added up to no more than about 4 percent of the entire social budget. But these relief payments are particularly susceptible to economic conditions that cause a drop in government income and narrow the range of preferential policy decisions on the allocation of limited financial resources. When confronted with a forced choice between increasing general tax levies or cutting down on "nonessential" expenditures West German governments, like those in other countries, have of late sought to reduce the cost of social programs. In 1984 the government of Chancellor Kohl thus asked state and local governments in the Federal Republic for proposals to contain public expenditures for social assistance to the needy. If there should be no marked improvement in economic conditions, the chances are that the austerity budgets of West German policymakers will reduce outlays for relief payments well ahead of defense expenditures, debt payments, and tax benefits for powerful pressure groups.

ECONOMIC CONCENTRATION

Fiscal and other policy measures for economic growth through private enterprise have, in effect, furthered the consolidation of large-scale business establishments. As we observed in chapter 3, the prominence of big business in contemporary public affairs is in large part the product of authoritative decisions taken in the early postwar years of economic reconstruction. Legislation intended to stem the trend toward ever larger corporate mergers has not been particularly effective.

Favorable public policies have enabled just six major banks to control most of the financing and much of the managing of corporate enterprises in the Federal Republic. About three-fourths of all business capital and investments flows today through the banks which, under prevailing law, may also own substantial voting stock in corporations as well as wield proxy votes for other stockholders. By far the largest of the banks remain the privately owned and managed Deutsche Bank and Dresdner Bank; a 1967 law that was to curb their preeminence and produce more competition failed to halt the elimination of smaller financial institutions. In manufacturing the hundred largest enterprises now account for a quarter of the productive output of West German industry. Neither the cartel law of 1957 nor subsequent antitrust legislation appears to have had much of an impact in this respect.

Remember, too, that West German agricultural policies—in consonance with those of the European Community—have deliberately promoted the consolidations of farm holdings. Consequently, large proprietors—often members of the old German nobility—have been the principal beneficiaries of subsidies for agricultural development. Moreover, substantial profits from land sales for suburban growth, along with special tax breaks, have helped them (a) to buy out small, marginal farmers, (b) to invest in expensive modern equipment needed for large-scale agricultural production, and (c) to hold on to valuable land for speculative purposes. Here we should not overlook the effectiveness of land ownership as a hedge against inflation. For all these reasons, left-wing Social Democrats have demanded higher taxes on income from land property and closer government controls over real estate speculations, but so far their demands have not been met.

You may also recall that economic consolidation in the private mass media had led to the rapid decline of independent newspapers and periodicals. Even in the case of the favored few who have been aided by overt and covert government subsidies, such aid has frequently not been large enough to offset the gap between rising publishing costs and revenues. Legislation designed to limit the size of publishing empires has failed to save independent publications from extinction.

Economic concentration in the retail trade accounts for much of the marked decline in self-employed persons. Small shopkeepers have found it increasingly difficult to compete with large supermarket and department store chains that have extended their operations from the inner cities to suburban shopping centers. Current legislation, similar to American "blue laws," provide small shopkeepers with some protection; all stores throughout the Federal Republic are required to close early in the evening and to remain shut on Sundays and holidays. But though this may help the owners of "mom and pop" stores, it also restricts the opportunities of other West Germans for employment and overtime pay in sales and services. Moreover, such legislation makes it most difficult for low-income working people to shop around for bargains before the stores close and prevents a fuller utilization of consumer service facilities.

ECONOMIC DEMOCRACY

Earlier, in chapter 7, we took note of the rather unusual policy principle in West Germany that legal arrangements for collective bargaining between employers and employees should be guided by the notion that they are basically "social partners," rather than adversaries, in the production of goods and services for the public. This principle has been given specific expression by West German policymakers in so-called codetermination legislation designed to give both organized and unorganized workers a say in the operation of the enterprises where they work.

Economic democracy through codetermination is supposed to supplement collective bargaining for labor contracts. It takes essentially two forms under the federal legislation enacted in 1951, 1971, and 1976. Both incorporate the principle of representation—rather than direct participation—which prevails in other areas of the highly organized society of the Federal Republic.

In every productive and service enterprise with more than five employees, including government departments, the employees elect shop stewards to a works or personnel council. Foreign workers can vote along with West Germans for these representative spokesmen who may, but need not be trade union members. Their chief responsibility is usually to deal with employers and management on the conditions of work in a particular shop, plant, or office. For example, the works council may ask for better safety features or for a reduction in the noise level in a factory. Its consent is required on such matters as changes in working shifts and hours, annual leave arrangements, rest periods and paydays.

The Codetermination Act of 1951 stipulates that employers and works councils "shall work together in a spirit of mutual trust. . . for the good of the enterprise and its employees, and with due regard to the interest of the community." But although the law may set forth goals and procedures, it takes more than that to give substance to this grassroots form of economic democracy. It can only work if both sides want it to work and if the employee councils do not become the battleground for industrial conflicts, as they did in the Weimar Republic. Particularly in the large public and private enterprises that employ most of the present work force, harmonious relations require mutual trust and shared responsibilities not only between the representatives of management and labor, but between the shop stewards and their clients. The council members are the men and women in the middle; management expects them to be reasonable in their demands and the workers expect them to take care of their grievances. This may not present much of a problem on such matters as the length of coffee breaks and adequate toilet facilities. But when it comes to dismissals not covered by union contracts and to production quotas set by some distant corporate headquarters or public authority, the effectiveness of the employee councils is likely to depend on their determination to have their way and the willingness of management to give way.

The councils are not empowered to negotiate labor contracts, though they have the authority to see to it that the terms are observed by employers. What is more important is that they lack the legal power to block managerial decisions in public and private employment that are supposedly justified by economic conditions, but that may also have a substantial effect on employees. For instance, when cuts in the budget of a government agency require staff reductions, its personnel council cannot prevent the discharge of workers who are not protected by civil service regulations. In privately owned business establishments, employers or management must consult the works council on decisions that are said to be warranted by circumstances in a competitive market economy. But then they do not need its consent to reduce or increase the labor force, capital investments, and production quotas, to introduce technological and organizational changes, or to merge the enterprise or even close it down entirely. In effect, key decisions affecting employment and working conditions in a public or private enterprise are thus made by the owners or their managerial representatives and are not controlled by the employee council.

This brings us to the second and more novel form of economic democracy in West Germany. The enterprises that turn out most of the goods and services in the Federal Republic are owned by private corporations. These are run by supervisory boards of directors who appoint the top management and consider—though not necessarily decide—corporate policies on such important matters as production and investment programs. The board members may control a majority of shares of the voting stock as owners or through proxies for small shareholders and large institutional investors. However, they are not required to own or control any stock in the company under West German corporate law and thus legislation could be passed to place employee representatives on the supervisory boards.

The Codetermination Act of 1951 provided that in the iron, coal, and steel industry five out of eleven company directors were to be elected by the employees and five by the stockholders; the board chairman is an eleventh "neutral" member, chosen by both sides and empowered to break a tie vote. Though the law had been passed under the auspices of the conservative Adenauer govern ment, many of the business leaders felt that it had caved in to pressure from the Trade Union Federation and professed to be deeply troubled about the consequences for "free enterprise capitalism."

In the two decades that followed such concerns appeared unwarranted to West German and foreign observers. Limited codetermination at the top evidently did not deprive management of control over company affairs, but seemed, in fact, to contribute to unusually harmonious relations between organized capital and labor in the affected industries. However, when in the 1970s the leaders of the Trade Union Federations pressed the SPD-FDP Federal government for equal employee representation on all company boards, the business elite refused to go along. The labor elite was forced to settle for less to obtain the passage of a much watered-down extension law with the votes of the opposition as well as government parties in both houses of the Federal parliament. The still dissatisfied peak employers' organization then asked the Constitutional Court to throw out the new legislation, which enraged the trade union leadership but failed to kill the law since the Court declared it constitutional.

The Codetermination Act of 1976 maintains equal representation for capital and labor, along with a "neutral" chairman, on the boards of coal, iron, and steel companies. In all other companies with more than 2,000 employees one-half of the members of the supervisory board are to be elected representatives of the employees. One of these, however, must be a member of top management chosen by the salaried white-collar staff from a slate nominated by senior company officers.[3] Moreover, the board chairman must be a representative of the shareholders and can cast the decisive vote in case of a deadlock among its twenty members. In short, capital and management retain control over policymaking in these companies.

How far and how effectively these changes have extended economic democracy through codetermination remains to be seen. Up to now the consequences appear to be not nearly as significant

3. Three of the other nine employee representatives are chosen by the entire staff from a trade union slate and six are nominated and elected by the company's blue- and white-collar workers from their midst.

as labor leaders had hoped and employers had feared. Most West Germans generally favor codetermination, according to opinion polls, but even trade union members evidently attach relatively little importance to the board room representation won by their leaders. A great deal will no doubt depend on economic developments and consequent stakes in labor-management negotiations. If codetermination should serve to maintain a sense of consensual policymaking in hard-pressed economic enterprises, it may well prove a most effective way to reconcile labor to more consolidation and modernization in West German industry. If codetermination founders in the face of industrial conflicts and sustained mass unemployment, it is likely to be seen as an experiment that was doomed to fail in hard times.

EUROPEAN COMMUNITY

When the Federal Republic became a founding member of the European Economic Community by the Treaty of Rome of 1957, there was a good deal of speculation among interested West Germans over the likely consequences. At one extreme were those who hoped or feared that the EEC headquarters in Brussels would before long become the seat of a supranational European government. At the opposite end were those who predicted either that irreconcilable national interests would soon lead to the disintegration of the Community, or that it would have no significant effect on domestic and foreign affairs.

As we know by now, none of the expectations was confirmed by subsequent events. The promise of a European political union contained in the Rome Treaty has not been realized, but the European Community has also not come to grief. Its membership and the scope of its policy-coordinating functions have expanded over the years and West German leaders have played major roles in promoting these developments.

According to opinion surveys, elite as well as popular support for the Community has consistently been much higher in the Federal Republic than in other member countries. For West German policymakers of every political persuasion there is no turning back, but there are strong reasons of pushing onward. We need not go into the details since we have already considered most of them. But to see what is at stake, it may be helpful to recall a few key points. One is that interlocking trade and monetary ties to fellow members of the European Community have become major factors for the development of the export-dependent West German economy. A second is that the problems posed by the foreign workers in the Federal Republic are affected by the fact that migrants from other EC states—notably the poorer ones in Southern Europe—are not subject to the same restrictions as those from other countries. A third point is that common EC taxes, custom duties, and economic regulations have a significant bearing on employment and income levels in the Federal Republic. And, finally, remember that intra-German relations with the Communist Democratic Republic are very much conditioned by special trade arrangements that exempt East German products from the common custom duties leveled by the Community.

West German bonds with the EC have been forged primarily along two lines. One has been essentially technocratic and has featured functionally specialized, interbureaucratic relations with the European Commission in Brussels and government agencies in other EC countries. The other has been a more general international dimension involving diplomatic negotiations among government leaders of the member states.

The technocratic ties developed most rapidly during the Community's great leap forward in the 1960s. In this period the EC's Commission, staffed by so-called Eurocrats, became its principal organ for joint economic policy planning and administrative coordination. A particularly important development was that the Commission acquired the authority to maintain a common pricing system for agricultural products through EC subsidy payments and marketing regulations. For West Germany this development had three major consequences. 1) Its government, and more particularly the Federal Ministry of Agriculture, lost direct control over many policy decisions in this sphere. 2) The Federal Republic assumed the largest share of the financial burden for farm price supports that benefitted not so much its own as French agricultural

proprietors. 3) Since West Germany depends heavily on agricultural imports, these measures for the protection of producers in
the Community have kept consumer prices at artificially high levels. West German leaders reluctantly acceded to French demands
on this score; they considered the costs for their country steep,
but necessary for continuing European integration.

Of late, West German ties to the EC have been affected by a
pronounced leveling-off in the movement toward integration.
There has been a less intensive forward movement along technocratic lines and more of a sideways development on the diplomatic
dimension. The Commission and its Eurocrats are not as much
involved in establishing common policies as in the 1960s and the
locus of joint decision making has shifted more to the meetings
of government leaders. And here—with the gradual expansion of
the Community from six to twelve member countries—policy
agreements must now accommodate a wider range of interests. A
further shift to the political side was supposed to follow from the
direct election of the European parliament by the voters rather
than, as before, the national legislatures of the member countries.
But this was seen in all of them as a rather empty gesture toward
greater popular participation in Community affairs. Even in West
Germany, an unusually large number of voters did not bother to
cast a ballot in the 1984 election of a practically powerless European parliament. Of much greater political significance for European integration, in the view of West German policymakers, is
the recent inclusion of Spain and Portugal in the Community.

But for West German, as for other European leaders, the principal purpose of the Community remains economic collaboration
rather than political integration. Economic interdependence
among the member countries has grown to a point where for all
of them internal EC trade now constitutes more or less half of
their total trade. At the same time, however, the policymakers in
these countries are still primarily accountable to their own people.
And that can lead to bitter conflicts, if not paralysis, in Community
decision making when domestic political considerations are at
odds with the common purpose. In these times of high unemployment and intense international economic competition, do-

mestic pressures for nationally oriented, protectionist measures in EC countries—notably France, Britain, and Greece—tend to conflict with West German desires for closer European collaboration in trade, scientific research and development, and currency stabilization.

The Federal Republic is likely to remain for the forseeable future the foremost industrial, commercial, and financial power in the European Community. It contributes the lion's share to EC budget funds, which not only go into transfer payments to French farmers, but support regional development programs in Greece and Italy and a host of other projects dear to other member countries.

In light of the exceptionally strong commitment to European integration in the Federal Republic, West German leaders may be expected to continue their efforts to draw other EC countries into more intimate mutual assistance arrangements for coping with common economic problems. By present indications their chances for success are rather poor, at least for the near future. They seem likely to win even less cooperation than in 1978, when West German leaders who wished for a European Monetary Union had to settle for a far more limited European currency exchange arrangement that did not include Britain.

ARMAMENT AND THE
WESTERN ALLIANCE

On February 27, 1955, the West German Diet voted for the inclusion of the Federal Republic in the North Atlantic Treaty Organization and for a substantial military contribution to the Western alliance against the Soviet bloc. Under a series of agreements with the United States, Britain, and France that ended the last vestiges of foreign control, the heretofore unarmed country was to acquire a "defense force" of some half a million men for its external security.

The policy decision came after years of intense domestic and international controversy on the issue, and observers at home and abroad expected West German armament to have far-reaching political consequences. The proponents held that it would help to maintain peace in Europe and democracy in the Federal Republic; opponents feared that it might lead to the revival of aggressive and autocratic German militarism. Some three decades later, disputes on this issue were conspicuous by their absence. An armed West Germany on the side of the Western alliance was viewed neither as a threat to world peace nor as a danger to the democratic order of the Federal Republic.

Changes in the policy environment no doubt contributed to this development. However, a good deal was due to the way West German leaders implemented the armament policy. Pressed by the American government to make haste, they chose to proceed with deliberate speed to ensure firm civilian control over the new defense establishment. Here Social Democratic leaders—who had at first opposed the decision to join NATO and arm—collaborated closely with the Adenauer government. Both major parties wanted to make certain that a military elite would not, as in the past, become an independent and dominant element in German politics.

Accordingly, a good deal of bipartisan effort was devoted to shaping a Federal Defense Force (Bundeswehr) of "citizens in uniform" that would be subject to elected officials and support the constitutional order. A civilian screening committee carefully selected the initial cadre of senior officers to ensure its loyalty to the regime. Administrative and command functions in the Ministry of Defense were divided among military men and civil servants. All service branches were put under a civilian state secretary accountable to the defense minister, rather than to a general staff as under former regimes. The administration of military justice was placed almost entirely in the hands of the regular judiciary. To prevent the covert expansion and secret armament of the military establishment, its itemized annual budget and personnel strength were to be submitted to the Federal Diet for scrutiny. The Diet's Defense Committee was authorized to investigate the conduct of military affairs by the Federal Government whenever it saw fit. The office of a special parliamentary plenipotentiary for military affairs was set up to see to it that regulations affecting the armed forces were properly executed and the constitutional rights of soldiers adequately protected.

Not all of these arrangements turned out to be workable once the military buildup got under way. The design for a democratic citizens' army was considerably modified in the name of military efficiency. The supervisory powers of the Diet's Defense Committee proved not as effective, and those of its military plenipotentiary less important, than the reformers had hoped. However, on the whole, the innovations took root—not least because political leaders in the executive branch vigorously asserted their authority over the new military elite. Some initial friction on that score diminished as a new generation of professional soldiers that was more in tune with current trends replaced the veterans.

The present Federal Defense Force bears very little resemblance to past German military establishments and appears to be well integrated into the society and polity of the Federal Republic. The political influence of the military is not only much lower than in former times, but evidently a great deal smaller than in the United States. About half of the some 450,000 men in the army, navy, and air force are short-term conscripts recruited from all walks of life; the rest are regulars.[4] By all accounts relations between officers and enlisted men are generally good, based on mutual respect, and fairly informal. Sharp differences that once divided the ranks no longer prevail; the proportion of workers' sons among the officers is now not only greater than at any other time, but is appreciably larger than among university students. Most commissioned and noncommissioned career officers, particularly the

4. By current estimates the Federal Republic could bring its forces up to 2 million men within a few days of mobilization. Conscripts are presently required to serve fifteen months on active duty and must then join the stand-by reserve. Conscientious objectors to military service are assigned to some sort of alternative service—say, as hospital orderlies—which now lasts twenty months. Permanent residents of West Berlin cannot be conscripted for any form of service in the Federal Republic. According to official figures more than 10,000 young West Germans per year have sought to escape conscription by this route in recent times; those who manage to establish legal residence in the city must, however, remain beyond the age of conscription—currently twenty-eight—to avoid being called up on returning to the Federal Republic proper.

younger ones, have little use for traditional German military concepts of duty, ideals, and ethics. They see themselves as public employees with specific job assignments in organizations that require hierarchy and discipline for efficient operation. With rapid advances in military technology, the professional soldiers of West Germany have increasingly become specialists and managers cooperating closely with equivalent experts in other sectors of the society as well as in interallied military bodies.

Although armament has not given rise to a new military-industrial complex, it has produced an arms production and export industry. By all indications the Federal Republic has honored its treaty commitments not to manufacture or acquire atomic, biological, and chemical warfare weapons, or any other kind of "offensive" weapons. It has evidently not made use of its "nuclear capability" and, along with Japan, remains in this respect a significant exception among the major countries of the world. The production and export of so-called defensive conventional weapons, however, has come to be of some importance for the economy—though not nearly as much as in the United States, Britain, and France. By some accounts it may become more important should unemployment continue to increase in other branches of West German industry. But for the moment, at least, the Federal Republic—like Japan—seems for political reasons in no position to compete with its major allies and the Soviet Union for massive arms sales to Third World countries.

In international politics West German armament is no longer a negotiable issue for allied countries. Other NATO members have come to rely on a substantial West German military contribution to their own defense. American insistence that West German policymakers honor their commitment to the installation of new U.S. nuclear missiles in the Federal Republic in the 1980s overruled objections from the Soviet Union and West German dissidents. And though some leaders of the Social Democratic and Green parties have, on occasion, suggested that the Federal Republic might some day withdraw some or even all of its forces from the Western alliance, for the foreseeable future it appears most unlikely that any West German government will fail to honor treaty obligations to the common defense of Western Europe.

Under these commitments West German troops have become the mainstay of NATO's "conventional" military forces in Europe. All of the active combat units of the Federal Defense Force are under direct NATO command, and their fighting efficiency is rated rather highly by Western military experts. Questions concerning the disposition, training, logistics, and equipment of these forces must be settled in agreement with other NATO countries. However, under the terms of the Basic Law of the Federal Republic, West German forces could probably not be employed outside NATO territory like those of other member countries. They could thus not serve as peace-keeping forces in the Middle East or come to the aid of some beleaguered government in Asia, Africa, or South America.

HIGHER EDUCATION: A CASE OF UNANTICIPATED CONSEQUENCES

In the mid-1960s, West German policymakers came under growing public pressure to open up the highly restrictive system of free higher education to far more students. At that time, the proportion of university students and graduates in the population was appreciably lower than in other advanced industrial countries and opportunities for upward mobility into high status and income white-collar positions were correspondingly more limited. Although government revenues had greatly increased with rising national affluence, the share of government expenditures for higher education had not. There was a severe teacher shortage, and educational experts pointed with alarm to a lack of all sorts of university-trained specialists. The Federal Republic was said to face a "cultural catastrophe" if drastic action was not taken to remedy the situation quickly.

The policymakers responded to demands for action with a massive program for the expansion of higher education. The state governments established many new universities, and the Federal government took a major hand after the Social and Free Democrats came to power in 1969. By 1970, the Ministry for Education and Science had worked out a national master plan in collaboration with the state ministries of education and sundry quasigovernmental advisory bodies. The Federal parliament approved vast new appropriations for student aid and university construction. Federal matching grants, in turn, induced the states to step up their own outlays for higher education. Altogether, these outlays accounted for much of the increase in public funding for education and research from 9 percent of per capita governmental expenditures in 1961 to more than 15 percent in 1971.

As it happened, the answer to one policy problem produced new problems that had not been anticipated by West German decision makers. By 1974, the principal planners were forced to conclude that they had tried to do too much in too short a time and had failed to take full account of possible consequences and unfavorable economic developments. The release of previously pent-up demands for a free higher education swamped the universities and university-preparatory schools. On top of that, an unexpected economic downturn led to a reduction in government funds for higher education and in the demand for university graduates in the job market.

In 1974, three times as many students attended institutions of higher learning than in 1960. For 1975, the master plan of 1970 had projected an enrollment of 665,000, but the actual number turned out to be 842,000. The substantial increase in teaching personnel and facilities proved to be more costly than expected and the absorptive capacity of the most popular university departments proved unequal to the demand load. Moreover, the educational planners had failed to anticipate that the expansion of the universities would have a significant effect at lower levels of the educational system. The number of students in the university-preparatory schools jumped from 850,000 in 1961 to 1.7 million in 1975. The proportion that graduated increased from four of ten in 1971 to six out of ten in 1975—that is, from 11 percent to 15 percent of their age group—while the proportion wanting to go on to the university remained fairly constant at nine out of ten.

Consequently there were about 155,000 secondary students seeking a higher education in 1975, compared with 87,000 only four years earlier.

The policymakers were confronted not only with the inability of the most popular university, departments to take care of the mounting student body, but with a potentially serious political problem. As the number of university graduates increased, more and more would be unable to find the sort of jobs they had been trained for and thought themselves entitled to. Under these circumstances there loomed a threat that an underemployed, if not unemployed academic proletariat of disaffected status seekers might before long cause trouble for the present regime, as it had for that of the Weimar Republic.

In the light of these conditions and their possible outgrowth, West German policymakers decided to abandon the traditional principle of open admission to institutions of higher learning and to apply tighter performance criteria. Whereas in the past any graduate of a university-preparatory school was able to matriculate, a centralized national computer system now selects those with the highest grades for whatever spaces are available in disciplines of their choice. In addition, measures have been instituted to limit the number of years a student can stay at a university at the taxpayers' expense without passing required examinations. In short, who can study what, where, and for how long has become less a matter of personal preference and material resources and more a matter of academic achievement and state control.

The lessons of this case can be applied to other policy processes in West Germany and elsewhere. Policy formulation and attendant political conflicts focus on a future state of affairs, and decision makers need to consider what consequences are likely to follow from their actions. Eventually, the question becomes: Will the policy outputs of executive and legislative bodies sell? Satisfied policy consumers are likely to ask for more of the same, whereas dissatisfied ones are likely to seek different policy products and, perhaps, policymakers.

Of course, leading West German officials will, and usually do, claim to know all the answers. But, more often than not, they are by no means all that sure. Selecting one policy over another is usually a gamble. Authoritative decision makers will proceed on the basis of what they expect to happen; but they can never be entirely certain that the outcomes sought will be realized in fact, no matter how carefully a measure has been planned and crafted.

As in the above instance, a policy move may unleash unforeseen demands that give rise to new political issues and disputes. We have observed such policy feedbacks throughout this book. Recall, for example, that government regulations for rapid economic growth in the early years of the Federal Republic gave rise to new policy problems, such as urban congestion, industrial pollution, and the social tensions created by the mass influx of foreign workers. Or consider that energy programs providing for a massive shift from native coal to foreign gas and oil supplies failed to allow for a sudden, steep increase in the cost of these imports. As a result, policy decisions taken in the 1960s came to haunt leading West German officials in the 1970s and 1980s.

Looking backward and forward, we find that one factor is clearly basic to any consideration of policy outcomes and their actual or potential effects on West German politics. As has been emphasized repeatedly, the performance of particular public officials and agencies is judged by the affected elites and nonelites in terms of the perceived costs and benefits. But beyond that, the operation of the entire regime is ultimately evaluated by West Germans on the strength of its evident ability or failure to promote their personal well-being and that of their children.

Thus, the authoritative leaders must at all times be able to adapt their policies to changing conditions without appearing to yield simply to the force of circumstances. Above all, they must be prepared to diffuse highly charged political issues. If these should blow up, it will do little good to plead ignorance of their being loaded. In this regard, the future may well reveal explosive charges that are presently concealed in the domestic and foreign environment.

10

The Quest for Security

During our tour through West German politics we have repeatedly
addressed two major questions. One is comparative: how heavy is
the German accent? what distinguishes policy-relevant attitudes
and processes in the Federal Republic from those in other advanced industrial societies with democratic regimes? The other
question concerns the future development of West German politics: will there be significant changes or will present patterns
continue?

West German politics, of course, are not just like politics in any
other country. They have distinctive features and are shaped by
unique conditions. Indeed, we underscored these in preceding
chapters. But we should not exaggerate their significance. To a
considerable extent the attitudes and processes we observed in the
Federal Republic differ more by degree than in kind from those
in the United States and other advanced industrial societies with
capitalist socioeconomic systems and liberal democratic regimes.
The notion that West German politics are largely formed by factors
attributable to the cultural peculiarities of a singularly German
"national character" is anachronistic.

Our question concerning future developments in West German
politics is less easily and quickly answered. Political forecasts are
not prophecies; they are at best educated guesses based on im-

perfect information. Developments, especially long-range ones, are usually not as evident to contemporary observers as to later historians. To focus merely on prominent persons and dramatic current events such as national elections and international summit meetings can all too easily obscure our view of the road ahead for West German politics. Our concluding considerations will there-fore avoid conjecture about particular individuals and groups, about precisely who is likely to do what to whom and when. At the same time, we must remember that the further we seek to peer into the future, the more we are limited to broad speculations about conceivable, but by no means certain, developments.

It is safe to say that the politics of tomorrow in the Federal Republic will be different from those of today. But exactly how different we cannot really tell. The clues we have are too few and too ambiguous to let us predict the nature, direction, and mag-nitude of coming changes. We have noted some signs that point to an unspectacular evolution of policy-relevant attitudes and pro-cesses and others suggesting that we should not rule out major transformations. In any event, the dynamics of the international policy environment are bound to introduce new elements whose effect cannot be readily anticipated when we project present do-mestic patterns.

In short, when we contemplate what may happen over the next decade or so we can do no more than consider possible develop-ments. For that our preceding analysis allows us to identify some pending issues that are likely to have a particularly important bearing on political continuity and change in West Germany. These issues all pertain to a basic theme in West German politics: the quest for security.

For close to forty years West German policymakers have sus-cribed to three security principles for the Federal Republic. The first is that the established political order must be preserved, the second that its economic underpinnings must be protected, and the third that the people of West Germany should end up neither dead nor red in the event of a military conflict in Central Europe. In pursuing these principles West German leaders have felt ex-ceptionally constrained by factors more or less beyond their control—most notably the legacy of the Nazi regime, unpredictable international economic developments, and uncertain relations between the two superpowers. The quest for security under these conditions has found expression in cautious and conservative policies in domestic as well as foreign affairs. By current indications, this pattern is not likely to change a great deal in the foreseeable future.

SAFEGUARDING THE REGIME

The liberal democratic polity that was established four years after the fall of the Nazi regime as a temporary arrangement pending the reunification of Germany is no longer a fragile structure. The constitutional provisions of its Basic Law are today not seriously in question as legitimate guidelines for politics in a pluralist society. The possibility of significant alterations in the formal framework for party government in a federal state seems to have all but disappeared. The necessary political will and agreement to make such changes have evidently not existed for some time; the proposals of a constitutional reform commission in the 1970s are already practically forgotten. The authoritative role of West Germany's Constitutional Court in upholding the present political order has become correspondingly ever more important.

But though politics in the Federal Republic appear to be exceptionally prosaic, a good many West German opinion leaders remain uneasy about potential threats to the established regime. They worry over the supposed delegitimization of public authority and the possibility of disruptive domestic conflicts, whereas foreign observers look for some enlivening colors—environmental green or radical red—in what seems to them the rather dull gray of a highly stable political system. The problem, perhaps, is not that the democratic regime is in fact threatened by powerful foes, but that the persistence of strong fears for its survival could make it difficult for West German policymakers to effect political adjustments to changing circumstances.

Contemporary West German leaders, like most of their countrymen, tend to place a high value on harmonious relations in state and society. They are likely to consider sharp party and interest groups conflicts destabilization and to favor enduring arrangements for cooperation and accommodation between the elites. In the context of current West German politics these preferences can amount to a truly conservative outlook that embraces the institutionalized status quo and makes a dogma of the need for stability to safeguard the regime. In this view prevailing arrangements for political recruitment and participation—and for making and implementing government policies—are the best possible for the Federal Republic; where changes are unavoidable they should be introduced very gradually so as to maintain the necessary stability of the political system.

All this might be well and good if there were not considerable domestic pressures for speedy changes in the established political order. Leaders who dogmatically identify the preservation of a regime with the maintenance of political stability usually find it troublesome to cope with such pressures. As we have seen, there is a good deal of disatisfaction in the Federal Republic with the operation of the party system and with the limitations which the conventions of representative democracy place on popular participation in policymaking. Discontent is particularly rife among the politically most interested and active young adults who constitute the pool for the incoming generation of new West German leaders. Under these circumstances a decisive question for future West German political developments is whether the prevailing libertarian conception of an overarching Rechtstaat—a liberal democratic state under law—can be reconciled with conservative demands for domestic peace, stability, and order on the one hand, and populist demands for greater democracy and more responsive government on the other.

As we noted in chapter 2, constitutional principles call for as much personal freedom as possible and for as much collective internal security as necessary. The Basic Law contains an extensive catalogue of fundamental civic rights, including general guarantees for freedom of speech, association, personal privacy, and equality of opportunity under law. However, it also requires executive, legislative, and judicial authorities to take all necessary steps for safeguarding both the constitutional order and the public welfare.

What sort of balance should be struck between the two sets of provisions has long been a sticky political issue. Recall, for example, the intense controversy in the late 1960s over emergency regulations for contingent crisis situations. By current indications, difference over the "legitimate" scope of internal security regulations will prove no less problematical in the future and may prove even more so.

The scope of the state's internal security tasks can be broadly defined to include practically all aspects of West German political, economic, and social relations. Authoritative constraints on individual freedoms in the name of the collective interest may thus take in not only regulations for the protection of life, property, public health, and safety, but for the preservation of esteemed cultural values as well. In a narrower and currently more immediate sense, internal security measures focus on the permissible limits of political opposition and dissent.

By some accounts there is a clear and present danger that aspiring Communist and radical socialist "counterelites' will abuse their civil liberties to undermine the constitutional order from below—ostensibly to achieve more participatory democracy, but in fact to create a leftist dictatorship. According to other accounts West German democracy is threatened by the gradual erosion of civil liberties through autocratic measures from above—ostensibly for the good of all, but in fact to maintain the power of the ruling few. The former view stresses the pressing need for effective internal security controls *by* public officials, the latter the urgent necessity for more adequate popular control *over* public officials.

The alarming pictures projected from the more extreme positions on both sides of the internal security-civil liberties issue may strike us as rather stark and overdrawn. To be sure, Communist subversion and espionage—especially from East Germany—and the sporadic terrorist acts of small anarchist groups do pose internal security problems. And public authorities have no doubt imposed constraints on the civil liberties of not only leftist, but rightist dissidents; such curbs might indeed become more extensive and restrictive if violent opposition to the present regime should increase substantially.

But as matters stand now, at least, West Germans are not likely to lose their liberties to either a "capitalist" or "socialist" police state in the foreseeable future. But does that mean that the liberal democratic regime will persist? Complacent analysts see little reason for concern: The Federal Republic is believed to have a basically strong and effective form of government with a comparatively high capacity for handling difficult policy problems. In this view, one should not attach too much importance to domestic political disputes and criticism because, at bottom, West Germans of all ages overwhelmingly support their present regime.

More dubious observers see greater cause for concern. In their view the established political fabric is coming under serious strain and West German public opinion is potentially very unstable. Those who think it necessary to maintain present patterns of government and policy at all costs fear that incoming leaders might make major changes. Those who are more troubled by what they see as an ossification of democratic structures believe that the regime may become more authoritarian because West German are ill-prepared to deal with stressful conditions in a democratic fashion.

Conceivably the answer to the question lies somewhere between these views. The complacent analysts could be underestimating the potentially disruptive, if not destructive impact of bitter conflicts over domestic and foreign policy issues. The more anxious observers, on the other hand, could be underestimating both the strength of West Germans attachment to their liberal democratic regime and the flexibility of political actors and institutions in the Federal Republic. Time will tell.

ECONOMIC SECURITY

West German policymakers, like those in other European countries, are today trying to cope with mass unemployment and other problems involving the collective economic security of the population. They are, however, particularly prone to stress the political need for economic security because they tend to consider liberal democracy in West Germany much more dependent on general prosperity than it is in older Western democracies. Ever since the establishment of the Federal Republic its leaders have held that a thriving capitalist economy was a necessary condition for the "democratic and social" state called for by the constitution.

In the Federal Republic as well as abroad much of the credit for the postwar expansion of the West German economy into the strongest in Europe has gone to the so-called German Model for harmonious industrial relations in a market economy. Essentially the model constituted an understanding among top party, business, and labor leaders and key government officials that it was mutually advantageous to collaborate closely for economic growth, full employment, and price stability. On the whole this economic policy concensus held up pretty well until about the mid-1970s. More recently it has been seriously strained, if not broken, due to less favorable conditions for concerted action and joint economic crisis management.

West Germany's trade-dependent economy is going through a politically unsettling phase of adjustment to reduced domestic and foreign demand for its traditional products. Economic growth has been sluggish and barely adequate to keep the jobless below a tenth of the labor force. The prospect for sufficient growth to reduce long-term unemployment, particularly among young people, are considered poor by knowledgable analysts. Industries that had earlier sparked and largely sustained the postwar growth of the economy—steel, machine-building, automobiles, and electrical products—have been particularly hard pressed by foreign, especially Japanese, competition in domestic as well as international markets.

The conventional explanation for this situation is familiar. Much of the traditional West German economic strength came from now rapidly aging smoke stack industries that are not equal to the challenge of foreign competitors using either cheaper labor or technologically more efficient production methods. What is less evident is that the organization of economic activity in the Federal Republic may, in effect, be putting obstacles in the way of greater flexibility and innovation in the production of goods and services. Formal-legal arrangements appear to sustain cumbersome management structures for vast enterprises, costly consumer services, and hierarchical labor organizations with inadequate plant-level concerns.

According to opinion polls, a vast majority of West Germans considers mass unemployment the most important problem for the Federal Republic today. And all but a small minority of extreme environmentalists belive that more economic growth is needed to alleviate the problem. But how much growth and in what form are questions to which there are now no generally acceptable political solutions. By present indications the common quest for economic security is taking West Germans and their leaders along a road to more divisive social and foreign policy disputes.

There is little disagreement over the need to modernize manufacturing and services, but growing disagreement over how this can be achieved. Whose ox must be gored in a process of selective surgery for removing decaying enterprises? What should be the role of the state in restructuring West German industry to enhance its competitive position in the market for advanced high technology products? And what policies are desirable and feasible for promoting trade with Eastern as well as Western Europe, with the Soviet Union as well as the United States?

Political authorities in the Federal Republic are not as deeply and directly involved in national economic management and planning as those in other capitalist democracies, notably France, Japan, and Sweden. The pressures for modernization are unlikely to change this very much if, as now seems likely, West German governments continue to adhere to the "free enterprise" principle that the public benefits of minimal interference with market forces by the state outweigh the costs. Accordingly they can be expected to go slow on more protectionist measures for ailing as well as developing industries and to promote the flow of private investments and government funds into promising new ventures.

In domestic politics the quest for economic security through growth and modernization appears to involve particularly three points of friction. One is an issue which worries most West Germans almost as much as unemployment and much more than military security problems. That is the destructive impact of industrial growth on their natural environment, an issue that has been dramatized by smog emergencies, polluted waters, and dying forests—and politicized by the environmentalist and anti-nuclear movements behind the Green party. Thus far, at least, the authorities have been singularly unsuccessful in reconciling popular support for growth with popular fears of its ecological effects.

Regional disparities in economic development are emerging as another major source of friction between West German parties and interest groups. North-Rhine Westphalia and other northern states of the Federal Republic have been particularly hard hit by the decline of traditional industries, bankruptcies, and long-term unemployment. The southern states of Bavaria and Baden-Württemberg, on the other hand, are the beneficiaries of modernization in advanced technology and sophisticated service industries. Whereas the steel and mining centers of the Ruhr valley and the old ports of Hamburg and Bremem have fallen on hard times, places like Munich and Stuttgart have come to flourish as centers for research and development in electronics and automated precision instruments. As it happens, the northern regions have mostly been under Social Democratic rule while the southern ones have been governed by conservative Christian Democrats.

A third point of domestic friction in the quest for economic security could turn out to be the most serious source of greater political polarization and conflict. Business and government leaders pushing for the speedy restructuring of the economy consider it unavoidable that this entails technological unemployment and painful social readjustments for excess workers who are compelled to retrain, relocate, or retire early. This view is at odds with that of labor and party leaders who wish to modernize more slowly in order to ensure long-term job security for the employed and adequate incomes for the redundant jobless and premature pensioners. That means they want at least to retain, if not expand, protective labor contracts and costly social programs that hinder economic growth according to the more impatient modernizers.

For the time being most West Germans evidently prefer to go

slow on modernization rather than risk more technological unemployment. More than two-thirds of them took that position in
a 1984 international opinion survey; less than one out of five
considered it essential to modernize as quickly as possible even if
that meant more unemployment, a view that was supported by
twice as many or more of the Americans, British, and French in
the survey.

In foreign relations the quest for economic security focuses first
and foremost on the European Community. West Germans are
likely to remain pretty much in agreement that the benefits of
membership on the whole exceed the drawbacks and to continue
backing efforts by their leaders for tighter European economic
integration, though without much enthusiasm. The Community,
provides the Federal Republic not only with a relatively safe market
for most of its manufactured products, but with economic advantages of scale in high technology research and development projects with other member countries. However, the Community also
imposes costs and constraints on West German growth policies
and global economic relations that might some day prove more
onerous than they do now. Even then their quest for economic
security is likely to leave West Germans little choice but to pay
what it takes to maintain close cooperation among the leading
industrial powers of Western Europe.

The future of West German economic relations with Communist
Europe is more obscure. Trade with the Soviet Union and its East
European allies grew substantially in the 1970s. But according to
official West German figures it still amounts only to about 7 percent of the Fedral Republic's total foreign trade—and that includes
"intra-German" trade with the German Democratic Republic.
West German policymakers tend to characterize such transactions
as modest by-products of the improvement in political relations
with the Communist states in the 1970s and to play down their
significance for the economic security of the Federal Republic.
However, this seems to hold true more for intra-German trade
and financial transactions than for economic relations with the
rest of Communist Europe, especially the Soviet Union.

Such relations may not appear to amount to much in quantitative terms of trade, but lagging industrial growth, energy costs, and mass unemployment have decidedly increased their qualitative importance for the West German economy. The Federal Republic as well as its Communist trading partners seem to have acquired strong economic reasons for maintaining extensive trade and financial relations. The Soviet Union and the rest of Eastern Europe have become important customers for the products of West Germany's ailing industries; for example, they now absorb a fourth of its steel exports and provide the largest market for its machine tools. In exchange the Federal Republic receives above all natural gas supplies from the Soviet Union that are eventually supposed to meet about a third of its energy needs.

These developments worry observers who fear that the Federal Republic may become too dependent on trade with the Soviet Bloc for its economic security. Eastern European countries needing import credits have already accumulated a huge debt with West German banks and there is concern in the West that more of the same could give the Soviet Union substantial financial leverage in its future dealings with the Federal Republic. Moreover, it is often overlooked that the sale of West German advanced technology to the Soviet Bloc has been aided by the lack of serious American and Japanese competition. A relaxation of the current US embargo on strategic technology transfers to the Communist countries, or a tightening of West German restrictions, might therefore have serious consequences for West German producers who now rely on easy access to these markets.

In the last analysis West German's economic fortunes are bound to remain closely tied to those of the United States. For the Federal Republic, as for other major European countries and Japan, the American connection is the still most important bilateral economic relationship. The United States is its single most important trade and investment partner and there is little reason to expect this to change. To put it bluntly, American policymakers can call the economic tune and the West Germans will have dance to it, like to or not.

On this note let us return to the underlying theme of this section: how dependent is the survival of the present West German political system on the economic well-being of the country and a supportive economic concensus among the elites? By current indications, as we have seen, the conditions for such agreement are likely to be less favorable than in years past. But they also appear no longer as necessary to sustain the regime. The present political order seems to have achieved sufficient strength to survive the buffeting winds of a severe economic crisis and attendant political turmoil as well if not better than older liberal democracies.

NEITHER RED NOR DEAD

The need for American protection to ward off the threat of a Soviet invasion has been a basic principle of West German foreign policy since the establishment of the Federal Republic. And for more than thirty years West German defense policies have been shaped by the North Atlantic Treaty Organization's scheme for deterring an attack. This calls for credible military arrangements between the Federal Republic and its NATO allies that provide for the employment of so-called conventional as well as nuclear weapons. The Federal Republic stands committed to provide most of the conventionally armed forces needed for its defense and the United States to furnish almost all of the nuclear ones.

The details of NATO plans for meeting a Soviet attack from East Germany are shrouded in secrecy, but nonetheless subject to a good deal of public discussion and analysis. Along with the widely observed deployment and maneuvers of West German and allied forces in the Federal Republic, published accounts suggest that NATO plans call either for a "defense-in-depth" that involves fighting the invaders on West German soil, or for a "forward strategy" that would take the war into East Germany, or, perhaps, some combination of these strategies. The underlying notion, it appears, is that a workable NATO deterrent scheme will dissuade the Soviet leadership from launching or just threatening an attack. However, in view of the ongoing arms race between the superpowers, there are considerable fears in West Germany that current defense arrangements could produce a devastating nuclear conflict in Central Europe.

Various public opinion surveys provide some indication of the strength as well as ambivalence of these sentiments. The polls show, for instance, that most West Germans today attach less importance to strengthening the military power of their country than do most people in the United States, Britain, and France—the three NATO countries with nuclear deterrents of their own. They also indicate that though the fear of a Soviet attack has significantly diminished in the Federal Republic, this development has not been matched by a correspondingly greater sense of military security. New anxieties about uncertain trends in the global confrontation between the United States and the Soviet Union have evidently led ordinary West Germans to attach more importance than in the past to the need for defending their country's interests against the wishes of not just one, but both superpowers—though still not as much importance as people in France and Britain. Such indications of changing public sentiments on military security issues lend strength to the arguments of critics of current alliance arrangements who want West German defense policies to be less closely tied to American military power.

Soviet and East German leaders can be expected to play on West German fears in order to turn the quest for military security in a more neutralist direction. Concerned observers in other NATO countries, notably France, warn that West German policymakers might thus somehow be induced to follow a course of disengagement from the Western alliance. Some consider the West Germans especially susceptible to Soviet nuclear blackmail, others worry that West Germany could succumb to the lure of Soviet proposals for reunification through neutralization. The successful mobilization of substantial mass support by the West German peace movement of recent years has accordingly been viewed abroad as signifying eroding attachments to NATO. If neutralism is taken to mean quitting the alliance altogether then there are not many genuine neutralists in the peace movement. Its members do not represent a new form of German nationalism in pacifist guise. But the movement is also more than just a flash-in-pan reaction to the deployment of new American nuclear missiles in the Federal Republic. What makes the West German peace movement of more than passing importance is that it reflects, at least to some degree, the more widespread and, apparently, enduring dread of a nuclear holocaust.

It is in this sense that the so-called German Question has surfaced again in European politics. It is, however, no longer really a question of whether the two Germanies can somehow, someday be brought together in a democratic state or some sort of united Europe, as the various official West German versions still have it. The question now is rather whether the people of both Germanies can avoid mutual destruction by a scaling down of the risks posed by the protective nuclear forces of their respective allies. And that makes it not just a German, but a European question for the two superpowers to answer.

Both West and East German leaders may try very cautiously to reduce the common threat and to insulate intra-German relations and regional arms control from other issues between the superpowers. But these are really more interested in keeping their own alliance system intact and unraveling that of the opponent than in letting their respective German partners pursue more independent and converging quests for security. It is highly doubtful that Soviet leaders will run the risk of weakening their military control over other East European countries (notably Poland) by granting greater autonomy to the German Democratic Republic, strategically the most important of them all. And it is unlikely that American leaders, no more than British and French ones, will agree to any changes in Central Europe that might significantly reduce the Federal Republic's strategic role in the NATO alliance. In short, it seems that for the foreseeable future Germans in the East and the West are destined to search for military security without finding it.

Suggestions for Further Reading

This bibliography, limited for the most part to relatively recent studies in English, is designed for readers who wish to delve more deeply into topics surveyed in this book.

For new titles, see *The American Political Science Review, International Affairs* (London), *International Political Science Abstracts, West European Politics, Revue d'Allemagne, Neue Politische Literatur, Politische Vierteljahreshefte*. For current events, see the German weeklies, *Die Zeit* and *Der Spiegel, The German Tribune* (a weekly translation of article from the German press), and reports issued periodically in German by Inter Nationes (Bonn-Bad Godesberg).

GENERAL STUDIES ON GOVERNMENT AND POLITICS

Child, David and Jeffrey Johnson. *West Germany: Politics and Society*. London: Groom Helm, 1981.

Ellwein, Thomas. *Das Regierungssystem der Bundesrepublik Deutschland* (5. Auflage). Cologne-Opladen: Westdeutscher Verlag, 1983.

Markovitz, Andrei, ed. *The Political Economy of West Germany: Modell Deutschland*. New York: Praeger, 1982.

Paterson, William E. and Gordon Smith, eds. *The West German Model: Perspectives on a Stable State*. London: Frank Cass, 1981.

Schweitzer, C. C. et al., eds. *Politics and Government in the Federal Republic of Germany: Basic Documents*. Leamington Spa: Berg Publishers, 1984.

CONTEMPORARY SOCIETY, ECONOMY, AND CULTURE

Burdick, Charles, Hans-Adolf Jacobsen, and Winifried Kudszus, eds. *Contemporary Germany*. Boulder and London: Westview Press, 1984.

Claessens, Dieter et al. eds. *Sozialkunde der Bundesrepublik Deutschland*. Düsseldorf-Cologne: Diederich. 1981.

Craig, Gordon. *The Germans*. New York: Putnam, 1981.

Noelle-Neumann, Elisabeth, ed. *The Germans; Public Opinion Polls 1967–1980*. Westport, Conn.: Greenwood Press, 1981.

THE COLLECTIVE PAST

Bracher, Karl D. *The German Dictatorship: The Origins, Structure, and Effects of National Socialism*. New York: Praeger, 1970.

Burkett, Tony. "Germany 1948–1978: Evolution of the Bonn Republic." *Parliamentary Affairs* (1979), 32:177–191.

Calleo, David. *The German Problem Reconsidered: Germany and the World Order, 1870 to the Present*. Cambridge: Cambridge University Press, 1978.

Craig, Gordon. *Germany 1870–1945*. New York: Oxford University Press, 1978.

Grosser, Alfred. *Germany in Our Time*. New York: Praeger, 1971.

Herz, John H., ed. *From Dictatorship to Democracy: Coping with the Legacies of Authoritarianism*. Westport, Conn.: Greenwood Press, 1982.

Schoenbaum, David. *Hitler's Social Revolution*. New York: Anchor, 1967.

POLITICIZATION AND PARTICIPATION

Baker, Kendall L., Russell Dalton, and Kai Hildebrandt. *Germany Transformed*. Cambridge, Mass.: Harvard University Press, 1981.

Conradt, David. "Changing German Political Culture." In G. Almond and S. Verba, eds., *The Civic Culture Revisited*, pp. 212–272. Boston: Little, Brown, 1980.

Greiffenhagen, Martin und Sylvia Griffenhagen. *Ein Schwieriges Vaterland: Zur politischen Kultur Deutschlands*. Munich: List, 1979.

Kreile, Martin. *Legitimitationsprobleme der Bundesrepublik*. Munich: C.H. Beck'sche Verlagsbuchhandlung, 1977.

Schweigler, Gebhard L. *National Consciousness in Divided Germany*. Beverly Hills, Calif.: Sage Publications, 1975.

Weidenfeld, Werner, ed. *Die Identität der Deutschen*. Munich: Carl Hause, 1983.

POLITICAL PARTIES AND ELECTIONS

Braunthal, Gerard. *The West German Social Democrats, 1969–1982: Profile of a Party in Power*. Boulder, Colo.: Westview Press, 1983.

Carl-Sime, Carol. "Bavaria, the CSU and the West German Party System," *West European Politics* (1979), 2:89–107.

Doring, Herbert and Gordon Smith, eds. *Party Government and Political Culture in Western Germany.* New York: St. Martin's Press, 1982.

Dyson, Kenneth H. F. *Party, State, and Bureaucracy in Western Germany.* Beverly Hills/London: Sage Publications, 1977.

Edinger, Lewis J. and Paul Luebke. "Grass Roots Electoral Politics in the German Federal Republic." *Comparative Politics* (1971), 3:463–98.

Kaase, Mac and Hans-Dieter Klingemann, eds. *Wahlen und politisches System: Analysen aus Anlass der Bundestagswahl 1980.* Cologne-Opladen: Westdeutscher Verlag, 1983.

Norpoth, Helmut. "Choosing a Coalition Partner: Mass Preferences and Elite Decisions in West Germany." *Comparative Political Studies* (1980), 12:424–440.

Pridham, Geoffrey. *Christian Democracy in Western Germany.* New York and London: St. Martin's Press, 1977.

Raschke, Joachim, ed. *Bürger und Parteien.* Cologne-Opladen: Westdeutscher Verlag, 1982.

Rothacher, Albrecht. "The Green Party in German Politics." *West European Politics* (1984), 7:109–116.

Smith, Gordon. *Democracy in Western Germany: Parties and Politics in the Federal Republic.* London: Heinemann, 1979.

PRESSURE GROUP POLITICS

Andrlik, Erich. "The Farmer and the State: Agricultural Interests in West German Politics." *West European Politics* (1981) 4:104–119.

Brand, K.W., D. Busser, and D. Rucht. *Aufbruch in eine andere Gesellschaft: Neue soziale Bewegungen in der Bundesrepublik.* Frankfurt/New York: Campus, 1983.

Helm, Jutta. "Citizen Lobbies in West Germany." In Peter H. Menkl, ed., *Western European Party Systems: Trends and Prospects,* pp. 576–596. New York: Free Press, 1979.

Markowitz, Andre S. and S. Allen. "Power and Dissent: The Trade Unions in the Federal Republic of Germany Reexamined." *West European Politics* (1980), 3:68–86.

Nelkin, Dorothy and Michael Pollack. *The Atom Besieged: Extraparliamentary Dissent in France and Germany.* Cambridge, Mass.: MIT Press, 1981.

Offe, Claus. "The Attribution of Public Status to Interest Groups: Observations on the German Case." In Suzanne Berger, ed., *Organizing Interests in Western Europe,* pp. 123–158. Cambridge: Cambridge University Press, 1981.

Weber, Jürgen. *Die Interessengruppen im politischen System der Bundesrepublik.* Stuttgart: Kohlhammer, 1977.

Willey, Richard J. "Trade Unions and Political Parties in the Federal Republic of Germany." *Industrial and Labor Relations Review* (1974), 28: 38–59.

POLICY PROCESSES

Blair, Phillip M. *Federalism and Judicial Review in West Germany.* Oxford: Clarendon Press, 1981.

Dyson, Kenneth. "The Politics of Economic Management in West Germany." *West European Politics* (1981), 4:35–55.

Dyson, Kenneth. "West Germany: The Search for a Rationalist Concensus." In J. Richardson, ed., *Policy Styles in Western Europe*, pp. 17–46. London: Allen and Unwin, 1982.

Fried, Robert C. "Party and Policy in West German Cities." *American Political Science Review* (1976), 70:11–24.

Haftendorn, Helga et al. *Verwaltete Aussenpolitik.* Cologne: Wissenchaft und Politik, 1978.

Johnson, Neville. *Government in the Federal Republic: The Executive at Work*, rev. ed. Oxford: Pergamon, 1983.

Knott, Jack H. *Managing the German Economy: Budget Politics in a Federal State.* Lexington, Mass.: Heath, 1981.

Kommers, Donald P. *Judicial Politics in West Germany.* Beverly Hills, Calif.: Sage Publications, 1975.

Loewenberg, Gerhard. *Parliament in the German Political System.* Ithaca, N.Y.: Cornell University Press, 1966.

Massing, Orwin. "The Federal Constitutional Court as an Instrument of Social Control." In Klaus von Beyme, ed., *German Political Studies*, vol. 1. Beverly Hills, Calif.: Sage Publications, 1974.

Mayntz, Renate. "Environmental Policy Conflicts: The Case of the German Federal Republic," *Policy Analysis* (1976), 2:577–588.

Mayntz, Renate. "Executive Leadership in Germany: Dispersion of Power or Kanslerdemokratie?" In Richard Rose and Ezra Suleiman, eds., *Presidents and Prime Ministers*, pp. 139–170. Washington D.C.: American Enterprise Institute, 1980.

Mayntz, Renate and Fritz W. Scharff. *Policy-Making in the German Federal Bureaucracy.* Amsterdam: Elsevier, 1975.

Schmidt, Manfred G. *CDU and SPD an der Regierung: Ein Vergleich ihrer Politik in der Ländern.* Frankfurt: Campus, 1980.

Schmidt, Manfred G. "The Politics of Domestic Reform in the Federal Republic of Germany." *Politics and Society* (1979), 8:165–200.

Story, Jonathan. "The Federal Republic—A Conservative Revisionist." *West European Politics* (1981), 4:56–86.

von Beyme, Klaus. "The Politics of Limited Pluralism: The Case of West Germany." *Government and Opposition* (1978) 13:265–287.

Index